MYTHS ABOUT SUSTAINABLE CONSUMPTION: DISPELLED

Edited by Oksana Mont

Routledge
Taylor & Francis Group
LONDON AND NEW YORK

Designed cover image: FangXiaNuo via Getty Images

First published 2026
by Routledge
4 Park Square, Milton Park, Abingdon, Oxon OX14 4RN

and by Routledge
605 Third Avenue, New York, NY 10158

Routledge is an imprint of the Taylor & Francis Group, an informa business

The Open Access version for the book was funded by Mistra "Sustainable Consumption – from niche to mainstream".

For Product Safety Concerns and Information please contact our EU representative GPSR@taylorandfrancis.com. Taylor & Francis Verlag GmbH, Kaufingerstraße 24, 80331 München, Germany.

British Library Cataloguing-in-Publication Data
A catalogue record for this book is available from the British Library

ISBN: 978-1-041-01218-4 (hbk)
ISBN: 978-1-041-01217-7 (pbk)
ISBN: 978-1-003-61371-8 (ebk)

DOI: 10.4324/9781003613718

Typeset in Sabon
by Apex CoVantage, LLC

MYTHS ABOUT SUSTAINABLE CONSUMPTION: DISPELLED

Why, despite decades of warnings and solutions, does unsustainable consumption still persist? What keeps societies locked into business as usual even when the consequences are clear? This book contends that part of the answer lies in the myths we adhere to – powerful narratives that normalise the status quo, limit imagination and delay the transition to sustainability.

Gathering leading scholars from various disciplines, this book examines 12 of the most widespread myths about sustainable consumption – from the belief that information provision, small individual actions or technological fixes will deliver sustainability to the faith in economic growth as the goal of societal development and the idea that consumer demand drives sustainability. Each chapter explores the origin of a specific myth, details its environmental and social impacts and presents evidence-based counterarguments. Chapters also move beyond critique by offering practical strategies, policy and business implications and inspiring real-world examples, illustrating how alternative pathways can be implemented in practice. Collectively, the chapters reveal how myths endure through cultural resonance, institutional embedding, daily practices and political interests, while also providing a clear and applicable framework for diagnosing myths, debating them and designing alternatives. The book underscores recurring barriers to change but highlights leverage points and opportunities for transformation.

This volume will benefit researchers, students, policymakers, business leaders and engaged citizens seeking to understand why simplistic solutions fall short and how sufficiency, justice and systemic change can foster more sustainable ways of living within planetary boundaries. It ultimately empowers readers to rethink taken-for-granted assumptions and help accelerate sustainability transformations.

Oksana Mont is a professor of sustainable consumption governance at the International Institute for Industrial Environmental Economics, Lund University, Sweden, and a Wallenberg scholar.

CONTENTS

FIGURES

TABLES

ABOUT THE EDITOR

Oksana Mont is a professor of sustainable consumption governance at the International Institute for Industrial Environmental Economics, Lund University, and a Wallenberg scholar. She conducts trans-disciplinary and international research on sustainable and post-growth business models, sustainable consumption and lifestyles and sustainable consumption policy. She is an (co)-editor of several books: *Understanding the Urban Sharing Economy. Sustainability and Institutionalisation* (2025); *Research Agenda for Sustainable Consumption Governance* (2019) and *Sustainability and the Political Economy of Welfare* (2016). Her current topical domains are post-growth business, sufficiency-oriented business models and sustainability transformations.

CONTRIBUTORS

Ella Baybikova is a managing partner at Logic Moon, where she develops projects for the European Commission and other governmental bodies in mental well-being, sustainability and digital innovation. Formerly the head of research and strategy at the Eurasian Development Bank, she contributed to development initiatives across Central Asia. An MBA graduate and a certified yoga teacher (RYT-500), her work bridges economic and mindfulness-based approaches to explore how consumption, happiness and well-being interconnect.

Lea Becker is a research associate and a PhD candidate at the Research Institute for Sustainability, Germany, and is a part of the 'Transformation of Consumption and Provisioning' research group. As a political scientist, her research focuses on the nexus of democracy and sustainability and how they enable and support each other. She is currently pursuing a PhD in strategic climate litigation.

Paula Berendt is an academic advisor to the director at the Research Institute for Sustainability in Germany. Her research interests lie in the fields of social ecology, feminist economics and social-ecological transformation, currently focusing on questions of sustainable consumption and social justice.

Hervé Corvellec is a professor of business administration at the Department of Service Studies, Lund University, Sweden. He research focuses on infrastructures: railroad development, risk in public transportation, wind power siting, and the governance, planning, and organisation of waste management and the circular economy. He has also worked in business ethics, gender studies and diversity management.

Marianne Ekdahl is a science journalist focusing on environmental policy, social science and economics and formerly a junior researcher at the International Institute of Industrial Environmental Economics, Lund University. Her career has spanned EU policymaking, editorial journalism and public affairs and communications in European and Nordic R&D and policy organisations.

Patrick Elf is an associate professor of sustainable business at the Centre for Enterprise, Environment and Development Research (CEEDR), Middlesex University, and a co-investigator at the ESRC-funded Centre for the Understanding of Sustainable Prosperity (CUSP), the University of Surrey. Patrick's research investigates avenues for organisational change, sustainable business models and the mechanisms facilitating behaviour change approaches towards adopting more sustainable lifestyles. He is particularly interested in sustainable and transformative consumption, the circular economy, alternative organising and questions of post-growth and degrowth.

Göran Finnveden is a professor of environmental strategic analysis at the Department of Sustainable Development, Environmental Science and Engineering, KTH Royal Institute of Technology, Sweden. He is also the director of the research program Mistra Sustainable Consumption. His research includes sustainable consumption, environmental impacts of digitalisation and the development and use of environmental systems analysis methods.

Doris Fuchs is the scientific co-director at the Research Institute for Sustainability, a professor of sustainable development at the University of Münster and a member of the governing board of the University's Centre for Interdisciplinary Sustainability Research (ZIN). Her research includes questions on the relationship between democracy and sustainability, sustainable consumption and transnational sustainability governance.

Josefine Henman is a PhD candidate at the International Institute for Industrial Environmental Economics, Lund University, Sweden. Her research focuses on sufficiency, post-growth transformations and the role of business in a post-growth economy.

Amy Isham is a senior lecturer in psychology at Swansea University, where she founded and leads the Sustainable Wellbeing Research Group, and a research fellow at the Centre for the Understanding of Sustainable Prosperity (CUSP). Amy's work explores the relationship between human well-being and engagement in ecologically sustainable lifestyles. She has particular interests in consumer culture, self-transcendent states and behaviour change.

Emma Johnson is a researcher from the International Institute for Industrial Environmental Economics at Lund University. Her research focuses on sustainable pathways for production and consumption through examining the implementation of circular business models and their environmental impacts.

Mikael Klintman is a professor of sociology at Lund University. He investigates how social arrangements, cultural framings and knowledge practices steer environmental action and sustainability transitions, paying particular attention to how societies can anticipate and counter knowledge resistance and enduring myths about what counts as 'natural' or 'artificial' in production, products and everyday routines. He is the author of several books, including *Framing: The Social Art of Influence* (2025) and *Knowledge Resistance: How We Avoid Insight of Others* (2019), and contributes to policy and media debates on sustainable consumption and societal change.

Markus Larsson is a researcher at the Department of Sustainable Development, Environmental Science and Engineering, KTH Royal Institute of Technology, Sweden, and at the research program Mistra Sustainable Consumption. He works across disciplines such as economics, natural sciences and social sciences, with a focus on policy instruments, macroeconomic effects, and sustainable consumption.

Matthias Lehner is a senior lecturer in sustainable consumption at the International Institute for Industrial Environmental Economics, Lund University. His research concerns questions of consumption in numerous ways, as well as the systemic factors that shape it. Most recently, his research interests focus on the interrelations between digitalisation, time-use, consumption patterns and systemic questions of growth dependency.

Mikael Malmaeus is an associate professor of environmental analysis at IVL Swedish Environmental Research Institute. He works interdisciplinary with economics, natural sciences and social sciences, with a focus on economic instruments, macroeconomic future scenarios and post-growth economics. Ongoing research relates to fair climate transformations and sustainable consumption corridors.

Andrius Plepys is a senior researcher of sustainable consumption and production and circular economy transitions at the International Institute of Industrial Environmental Economics, Lund University, Sweden. His work focuses on the environmental impacts of industrial systems, eco-innovation and policy strategies for sustainable production and consumption. He has contributed to several European sustainability research networks and advises on the development of circular economy indicators and policies for sustainable development.

Jessika Luth Richter is an associate senior lecturer at the International Institute for Industrial Environmental Economics, Lund University, Sweden. Her research focuses on policies and initiatives enabling sustainable consumption through a circular and post-growth economy, including right to repair, extended producer responsibility (EPR), ecodesign and post-growth business practices.

Åsa Svenfelt is a senior associate professor of urban and regional studies at Linköping University. She conducts research on long-term planning for sustainable and just transitions and inclusive futures, focusing on sustainable consumption and post-growth planning approaches. The research is mainly within the multidisciplinary field of futures studies, encompassing theoretical approaches and methods for engaging in, exploring and envisioning alternative futures. Svenfelt led the Mistra Sustainable Consumption research program, phase one.

Maria Wolrath Söderberg is an associate professor of rhetoric at Södertörn University. She studies how people reason in relation to climate mitigation and transformation; how is the inertia in climate change maintained discursively and what drives and influences people who make changes.

ACKNOWLEDGEMENTS

Most chapters in this volume (with the exception of Chapter 2) were developed within the Swedish research programme *Mistra Sustainable Consumption* and also benefited from support provided by the European Union's Horizon 2020 research and innovation programme through the *EU 1.5° Lifestyles project*. The authors gratefully acknowledge the contributions of both programmes in enabling the writing of these chapters and in funding the editorial work that brought this book to completion. To further disseminate its insights and discussions, a MOOC with a similar title has been produced within the *Mistra Sustainable Consumption* programme.

Chapter 12

Funding for this work benefited from the European Union's Horizon 2020 research and innovation programme in the context of the *EU 1.5° Lifestyles* project. The sole responsibility for the content of this article lies with the authors. We would like to thank the *EU 1.5° Lifestyles* consortium and its advisory board for their expertise, ideas and contributions to the project.

ABBREVIATIONS

AI	Artificial Intelligence
BEA	Bureau of Economic Analysis
BNPL	Buy Now, Pay Later
CO_2	Carbon Dioxide
CSR	Corporate Social Responsibility
EC	European Commission
EEA	European Environment Agency
EPR	Extended Producer Responsibility
ERC	European Research Council
ETC CE	European Topic Centre on Circular Economy and Resource Use
EU	European Union
EV	Electric Vehicle
GDP	Gross Domestic Product
GHG	Greenhouse Gas(es)
GNI	Gross National Income
GPI	Genuine Progress Indicator
G7	Group of Seven
HDI	Human Development Index
HPI	Happy Planet Index
ICE	Internal Combustion Engine
ICT	Information and Communication Technology
IEA	International Energy Agency
IPAT	Impact = Population × Affluence × Technology
IPCC	Intergovernmental Panel on Climate Change
ITU	International Telecommunication Union
MIPS	Material Input per Service unit

MOOC	Massive Open Online Course
OECD	Organisation for Economic Co-operation and Development
PIRG	Public Interest Research Group
PSS	Product–Service System
QR code	Quick Response code
RECAP	Economy-Wide Rebound Effects Project
SDG(s)	Sustainable Development Goal(s)
SEPA	Swedish Environmental Protection Agency
SME	Small and Medium-Sized Enterprise
SUV	Sport Utility Vehicle
UN	United Nations
UNDP	United Nations Development Programme
UNFCCC	United Nations Framework Convention on Climate Change
UNU/ UNITAR	United Nations University/United Nations Institute for Training and Research
WCED	World Commission on Environment and Development
WEAll	Wellbeing Economy Alliance
WEGo	Wellbeing Economy Governments

Introduction

1

MYTHS WE LIVE BY

How do they sustain unsustainable consumption

Oksana Mont

1.1 Introduction

Sustainable consumption has been a part of the global agenda for over 30 years, yet it remains one of the most difficult sustainability goals to achieve. The Intergovernmental Panel on Climate Change (2022) warns that without major changes in how societies consume and produce, the 1.5°C target will become impossible to reach. Consumption is a key cause of greenhouse gas emissions, resource extraction and biodiversity loss, but it also shapes everyday routines, aspirations, and ideas of what it means to live well. Essentially, it is not just about what we purchase but also about how societies are organised around daily life. Improving the efficiency of individual products alone is not enough; the entire system of structures and institutions, including policies, business models, norms and cultural narratives that foster and sustain unsustainable consumption, must change (Mont et al., 2022). This is why progress has been so challenging to achieve. Instead of transformative change, responses have focused on promises of green growth, eco-innovation and consumer awareness campaigns, which have failed to deliver the necessary shift. A major reason for this lack of progress lies in the persistence of powerful myths that permeate policies, markets and everyday life, reinforcing unsustainable systems and stalling transformation. Examining these myths is therefore essential.

When we discuss myths in this book, we do not mean fairy tales, legends or ancient fables. Instead, we see myths as cultural stories, widely shared narratives and ideological frameworks that influence how people interpret and act in the world. They are powerful because they become deeply embedded in everyday life, making them appear indisputable. Myths rarely emerge as

DOI: 10.4324/9781003613718-2

outright fabrications; rather, they draw credibility from real experiences and values. They often build on kernels of truth, but these fragments are exaggerated, amplified or distorted in ways that conceal limitations and contradictions. For example, technology clearly plays a role in sustainability transitions, yet the myth that 'technology will save us' obscures the structural, cultural and behavioural changes needed alongside technological advances. Likewise, choice is a fundamental part of democratic societies, but the myth that 'more choice always equals more freedom' hides the paralysing effects of choice overload and the environmental consequences of endless consumer options. Similarly, services can reduce material intensity, productivity gains may create the potential for shorter working hours, and sufficiency can involve difficult trade-offs. The problem lies in how such fragments are selectively framed and exaggerated. In myths, a sliver of truth is elevated into the whole story, shielding the narrative from critique and giving it a veneer of reasonableness. Myths comfort individuals by telling them their role is insignificant, reassure businesses that incremental innovation is sufficient, and give policymakers excuses to delay ambitious regulation (Mont et al., 2013). By sustaining these illusions, myths keep societies locked into unsustainable systems of provision. Dispelling them is vital if we are to imagine and implement other ways of organising consumption that respect planetary limits while promoting human well-being.

This book treats myths as analytical objects and practical obstacles. By analysing myths, we expose how they emerge and are maintained and circulated across policy, business, media and everyday life. By confronting them, we challenge their hold on collective imagination and create openings for alternative narratives to guide sustainable transformation. To understand this dual role, it is helpful to situate myths in a longer lineage of thought. Myths have always been central to how people interpret reality, justify authority and negotiate collective values. Understanding their historical evolution is important because, although their forms have changed, their power to shape societies and legitimise dominant practices has remained.

1.2 Myths in history

From earliest times, myths have helped human societies make sense of the world. Long before scientific reasoning, people depended on stories to explain celestial movements, the rhythms of nature, disease and death. These narratives were not mere entertainment but offered guidance on how the world functioned and how people ought to live within it. In ancient cultures, myths linked natural events to the actions of gods and spirits, making the unfamiliar recognisable and the chaotic understandable. Thinkers such as Plutarch (1st–2nd c. CE) considered how myths preserved collective memory and conveyed meaning in both public and private life. In the classical philosophical tradition, myths were used not only to explain but also to teach. Plato's *Republic* (ca. 375 BCE/2002) features mythic stories such as the Allegory of the Cave and Myth of Er, conveying metaphysical and ethical insights beyond logical explanation. Later, the Stoics and Neoplatonists continued this symbolic use of myths, treating them as means to convey deeper truths about the universe, the divine, and the virtues necessary for leading a good life.

Christian writers, by contrast, often regarded myths as false or dangerous because of their connection to pagan beliefs. Thinkers such as Augustine of Hippo dismissed Greco-Roman myths as deceptive stories that misled believers about the nature of God and morality (O'Donnell, 2005). Myths provided competing explanations of the world, morality and the divine and were thus seen as misleading and harmful to the soul. Still, they did not vanish. Medieval theologians such as Thomas Aquinas reinterpreted mythological motifs as allegories compatible with Christian teaching (Aquinas, 1274/1947), while Renaissance humanists like Petrarch and later artists revived them as symbolic themes in literature and painting (Panofsky, 1960). By the early modern period, philosophers such as Francis Bacon used myth as a metaphor to reflect on human mistakes and wisdom. For centuries, they remained valuable tools for moral reflection. It was only with Enlightenment thinkers that myths came under systematic criticism. In the rationalist climate of the 18th century, they came to be seen as products of ignorance and irrationality that obstructed scientific progress. Both Voltaire (1764) and David Hume and H. E. Root (1757/1957) dismissed myths as incompatible with the ideals of modernity.

From the late 18th century onwards, Romantic philosophers began to defend myths as vital expressions of imagination, culture and emotional truth. Johann Gottfried Herder (1798/2006) and later Friedrich Nietzsche (1872/1999) argued that myths offered insights into human experience that reason alone could not capture. This intellectual shift laid the groundwork for a 20th-century revaluation of myth, where scholars began to reinterpret myths as essential symbolic and cultural resources. For instance, Eliade (1963/2025) regarded myths as sacred models that orient human life and provide meaning in times of chaos, while Cassirer et al. (1925/2020) conceptualised myth as a symbolic form that enables people to navigate uncertainty and crisis. From this perspective, myths are evolving stories continually reworked by societies during periods of upheaval and transformation, when other forms of meaning-making prove inadequate.

This orienting role did not disappear in the modern era but became increasingly entangled with ideology and political communication. Myths were no longer rooted in sacred cosmologies but served more worldly purposes: shaping public perception, justifying authority and reinforcing worldviews of the elites. Roland Barthes (1957/2009) analysed how myths are embedded in everyday images and signs, showing how advertising and lifestyle narratives present consumerism, nationalism or technological progress as inevitable while concealing the power relations that sustain them. Murray Edelman (1988) similarly demonstrated how democratic politics relies on constructing myths to reassure the public, divert attention from inequalities and uphold existing power structures.

These modern functions of myth are also evident in environmental discourse. Narratives of crisis, hope and responsibility shape how societies interpret and respond to ecological challenges. Stories of technological salvation, green consumerism and sustainable growth reassure audiences while setting boundaries on what is imagined as possible, often steering responses towards incremental adjustments rather than fundamental change. Bruno Latour (1991) pointed out how the modern myth of separating nature from society creates an illusion of progress, sustaining technocratic approaches and obscuring the necessity of confronting the economic paradigms and lifestyles driving environmental problems. Later, Naomi Oreskes and Erik M. Conway (2011) documented how fossil fuel interests constructed myths of scientific uncertainty to delay climate action, using debate as a pretext to delay action while safeguarding the economic interests of the fossil fuel industry. This history shows that in modern times, myths have become strategic instruments of persuasion, fostering division and reinforcing the priorities of those in power.

1.3 How myths emerge and gain initial traction

In sustainable consumption, myths are also shaped and promoted by powerful actors with vested interests in resisting sustainable trajectories. They take the form of promises that sustainability can be achieved through ethical shopping, voluntary restraint or market-led innovation. Such narratives are politically loaded stories that guide collective action into maintaining the status quo. For example, business models built on growth, advertising and obsolescence depend on the constant reproduction of such myths. The promotion of 'green' product lines enables fast fashion brands to appear responsible while continuing to expand overproduction. Fossil fuel companies successfully popularised the notion of the 'carbon footprint', shifting responsibility onto consumers while expanding fossil fuel extraction (Oreskes & Conway, 2011). To understand how such myths take hold, it is crucial to examine the mechanisms through which they emerge or are purposefully constructed.

The concept of framing explains how these myths are created. Frames are ways of presenting issues that emphasise certain aspects while hiding others, making some interpretations seem obvious and others less visible (Hajer, 1995). Frames are not neutral but influence how problems are understood and what solutions are seen as reasonable (Lakoff, 2010). Myths operate through such framing processes. As Barthes (1957/2009) argued, myths are not lies but cultural stories that turn history into 'nature'. In the case of sustainable consumption, myths are often framed to protect unsustainable practices. For example, novelty is framed as naturally better than repair, justifying planned obsolescence and making the constant buying of new products seem sensible and mainstream. Consumption is also framed as a way to find emotional relief; for instance, the myth of 'retail therapy' suggests shopping is an effective way to deal with stress or unhappiness. These framings make myths sound convincing because they appeal to widely held values such as freedom, progress and prosperity, gradually becoming part of what Bourdieu and Wacquant (1992) called 'common sense'. The aspirations themselves are worth pursuing, but myths distort them by limiting their scope. For example, prosperity is equated with rising GDP, freedom with consumer choice and progress with ongoing technological innovation. In this way, broader interpretations of these ideals are hidden, making alternative paths less imaginable.

These mechanisms help explain how myths emerge and gain initial traction; later chapters and the conclusion return to how they persist over time.

1.4 How do we dispel the myths?

If myths are so resilient, is there any point in challenging them? The answer is yes. Myths are not merely stories but powerful lenses that shape how problems are understood and which solutions appear plausible. Radical change is easily dismissed as irrational, utopian or naïve when myths dominate. Sustainability myths are therefore not neutral; they act as ideological barriers to action. Dispelling them does not mean blaming individuals for 'believing the wrong things'. Myths persist not because people are ignorant but because they are embedded in institutions, markets and infrastructures and reinforced by cultural norms. At the same time, myth-busting is not sufficient on its own. As Boström (2020) observes, transformative learning requires both external critique and self-reflection, making myth deconstruction not only an intellectual exercise but also a way to shift collective consciousness. Structural change demands more than intellectual clarity; it requires mobilisation, leadership and institutional redesign, but critical reflection remains a necessary starting point.

This book is an attempt to clear the ground for new thinking. Our purpose is not to replace one set of myths with another, but to make room for uncomfortable truths. By interrogating 12 of the most persistent misconceptions about sustainable consumption – from the illusion of consumer sovereignty to the seduction of digital services – we seek to provide readers with the tools to think more critically, act more deliberately and imagine more radically.

To achieve this, we draw on insights from economics, sociology, psychology, policy studies and sustainability science. As Fine (1997) observed, different disciplines interpret consumption through distinct lenses: economists associate it with utility, sociologists with stratification, businesses with profit and psychologists with identity and emotional fulfilment. Each perspective provides valuable insights, but they are often examined in isolation, producing fragmented understandings and partial solutions. This book integrates these perspectives into a more holistic account of sustainable consumption, while also incorporating reflexivity, that is, an awareness of how knowledge is shaped by historical and ideological contexts (Bourdieu & Wacquant, 1992). Reflexivity is crucial in sustainability debates because it allows us to question the assumptions embedded in dominant narratives and to rethink the roles of individuals, businesses and governments in driving change.

Dispelling myths does not mean providing ready-made solutions. Rather, it involves clearing conceptual ground by exposing contradictions and showing that these stories are not immutable truths. Doing so does not in itself deliver change, but it creates conditions that make change possible. History demonstrates that when dominant myths lose their grip, societies are able to imagine and implement alternatives that previously seemed out of reach. This book seeks to encourage such reflection: to question what appears self-evident, to examine the narratives that tie us to unsustainable consumption and to consider new stories that could support life within planetary boundaries.

In this spirit, we focus on the specific set of myths examined in this book. How did we choose these? The starting point was a report prepared for the Nordic Council of Ministers in 2013 (Mont et al., 2013), which first identified myths that limit policymaking on sustainable consumption in Nordic countries. Since then, these myths have been discussed in many presentations, academic conferences and stakeholder workshops. Their importance was revisited in a dedicated seminar with societal partners of the Mistra Sustainable Consumption programme in 2022. By then, a decade after the 2013 report, many original myths still persisted, despite years of research, debate and policy initiatives on sustainable consumption. At the same time, new myths had also appeared. For this book, we therefore selected 12 myths that we believe are both the most common and the most urgent to dispel. These myths are:

1. There's no point in me sacrificing myself when no one else cares – The 'Little me' myth.
2. The Infophilia – Information alone will change consumer behaviour.
3. Shopping is the perfect therapy – consumption offers lasting happiness.
4. The more, the merrier – the road to freedom and well-being is paved with endless choices.
5. In tech we trust – the environmental crisis can be engineered away and sustainable consumption attained.
6. Services will save us – sustainability without sacrifice through access, sharing and digitalisation.
7. It's not worth repairing: the myth of neophilia.

8. Sufficiency means the end of modern life, comfort and joy – people will never choose less.
9. Without economic growth, sustainable consumption is impossible.
10. Economic progress will naturally lead to more free time.
11. Transition to sustainable consumption is primarily driven by consumer demand.
12. Strong sustainable consumption governance means sacrificing freedom and well-being.

Read individually, each myth highlights a specific misunderstanding that holds back sustainable consumption. Taken together, they form a system of stories that keeps change incremental and insufficient, maintaining trajectories close to the unsustainable status quo

1.5 Chapter synopses

The book is organised into 14 chapters, with an introduction, 12 chapters that debunk 12 myths and a concluding chapter. The 12 chapters each focus on a specific myth about sustainable consumption and how it can be dispelled. They are organised into three parts, each focusing on myths operating at a particular societal level. The first four myths are situated at the *individual level*, where responsibility for sustainability is framed as a matter of personal action and choice. The next four shift attention to the *organisational level*, where businesses and institutions are in focus. The final four turn to the *societal level*, where myths shape the larger economic and political frameworks that guide collective action. Each myth chapter is divided into sections exploring the origins, consequences and arguments for dispelling the myth, concluding with implications and recommendations for policymakers, businesses and consumers. These chapters show how myths not only restrict what individuals believe they can do but also shape the ways companies and governments address sustainability challenges.

Introduction

Introduction *Myths we live by: how they sustain unsustainable consumption* by Oksana Mont provides an overview of the book's focus: the myths surrounding sustainable consumption and their role in impeding progress towards stronger and more effective sustainability practices.

Part I: Individual-level myths

The first part of the book explores four myths that speak directly to how individuals understand their role in sustainability.

Myth 1: 'There's no point in me sacrificing myself when no one else cares' by Maria Wolrath Söderberg addresses the widespread belief that individual actions are too small to matter. The 'Little me' myth provides a socially accepted excuse for inaction. It draws on feelings of powerlessness in the face of global challenges, but also on highly individualised cultures where collective agency is downplayed. By examining how this reasoning functions rhetorically, the chapter shows how appeals to futility reinforce inertia and shift responsibility away from citizens.

Myth 2: 'Infophilia – Information alone will change consumer behaviour' by Mikael Klintman takes on the conviction that simply providing more information will lead to sustainable behaviour. This belief, rooted in rational choice models, has supported decades of policy measures such as ecolabels and awareness campaigns. However, despite these efforts, unsustainable practices continue. The chapter demonstrates that decisions are influenced as much by norms, habits and emotions as by knowledge, and argues that policies based solely on information overlook the importance of structural change.

Myth 3: 'Shopping is the perfect therapy – consumption offers lasting happiness' by Oksana Mont and Ella Baybikova questions the cultural link between consumption and well-being. The idea that retail therapy provides comfort and relief is deeply rooted in advertising and post-war consumerism. However, as the chapter shows, shopping only offers temporary satisfaction and often leads to stress, debt and environmental harm. Drawing on psychology, the authors emphasise more sustainable paths to well-being, including intrinsic values, social connection and lifestyles based on sufficiency.

Myth 4: 'The more, the merrier – the road to freedom and well-being is paved with endless choices' by Oksana Mont, Patrick Elf and Amy Isham challenges the idea that more options always improve freedom. Based on research on 'choice overload', the chapter explains how too many consumer options can cause paralysis, dissatisfaction and overconsumption. Instead of linking freedom with unlimited choice, the authors argue that setting limits can promote both sustainability and well-being.

Together, these four chapters reveal how myths at the individual level exaggerate personal freedom and responsibility, while hiding the structural conditions that make sustainable living difficult. They reveal how appeals to futility, information, therapy and choice influence everyday practices and collective imaginaries, often leaving people feeling responsible yet powerless. By challenging these myths, the book promotes new understandings of agency that connect individual actions with supportive infrastructures and collective solutions.

Part II: Organisational-level myths

The second part of the book shifts focus from individuals to how companies and organisations respond to sustainability. Here, myths suggest that business innovation and new models of provision will make consumption sustainable, yet they often reinforce unsustainable trajectories. These four chapters show how faith in technology, services, novelty and affluence directs attention away from absolute reductions in resource use and deeper transformations in business practice.

Myth 5: 'In tech we trust – the environmental crisis can be engineered away and sustainable consumption attained' by Oksana Mont, Marianne Ekdahl and Andrius Plepys examines the belief that technological innovation and green consumerism alone are sufficient to achieve sustainability. The chapter demonstrates how techno-optimism reassures policymakers, businesses and consumers that superficial changes suffice, while delaying structural reforms. From aviation to electric vehicles, evidence shows that efficiency gains are quickly offset by rebound effects and that technology brings its own ecological and social costs.

Myth 6: 'Services will save us – sustainability without sacrifice through access, sharing and digitalisation' by Emma Johnson and Oksana Mont challenges the idea that services inherently reduce material impacts. The chapter shows that all service models, whether traditional, product–service systems, sharing platforms, or digital services, are resource-intensive. Tourism, health and entertainment sectors leave large footprints; product–service systems often increase usage and lead to rebound effects; sharing schemes can generate rather than reduce demand; and digitalisation relies on energy, minerals and infrastructure. The promise of effortless dematerialisation through services turns out to be misleading unless supported by strong governance and sufficiency principles.

Myth 7: 'It's not worth repairing: the myth of neophilia' by Jessika Luth Richter and Hervé Corvellec explores the widespread attraction to novelty and the marginalisation of repair. Marketing, design strategies and growth imperatives promote newness as progress, while repair is framed as outdated or uneconomical. The chapter highlights how repair can instead strengthen local economies, preserve knowledge and extend product lifespans. Examples from repair cafés, refurbished electronics and businesses designing for durability illustrate the cultural and economic potential of revaluing repair.

Myth 8: 'Sufficiency means the end of modern life, comfort and joy – people will never choose less' by Josefine Henman and Oksana Mont contests the assumption that sufficiency is about deprivation. The chapter argues that sufficiency offers a fairer and more sustainable future by redefining prosperity as living well within ecological limits. It presents sufficiency not as a niche lifestyle but as an organising principle for societies and companies, highlighting its potential to enhance well-being, ensure justice and support resilience.

These chapters illustrate how organisational myths shield businesses from confronting the limits of growth and material use. By placing faith in technology, services, novelty and affluence, companies sustain narratives that appear progressive but often maintain unsustainable models of provision. Dispelling these myths allows companies to experiment with sufficiency-oriented business models, revalue repair and accept responsibility for reducing consumption levels rather than shifting the burden onto consumers.

Part III: Societal-level myths

The final section of the book shifts to the *societal and policy level*, where myths influence entire economies and governance structures. These narratives depict growth, time, consumer demand and personal freedom as inviolable pillars of modern life. However, upon critical examination, they expose themselves as barriers to creating societies that can flourish within planetary boundaries.

Myth 9: 'Without economic growth, sustainable consumption is impossible' by Markus Larsson, Mikael Malmaeus and Göran Finnveden challenges the deeply held belief that growth is essential for sustainability. Using evidence of limited decoupling between GDP and environmental impacts, the authors demonstrate that insisting on growth not only fails to address ecological crises but also hinders the exploration of post-growth alternatives. They contend that prosperity and well-being can be sustained without continuous expansion and advocate for shifting policies and research towards futures that prioritise equity and sustainability over GDP growth.

Myth 10: 'Economic progress will naturally lead to more free time' by Matthias Lehner critiques the assumption that productivity gains automatically translate into more leisure. Tracing predictions from Keynes to the rise of automation, the chapter shows how deregulated labour markets, cultural ideals of overwork and weak collective bargaining have instead normalised long working hours. The consequences include inequality, reduced civic engagement and declining well-being. Rather than waiting for progress to deliver leisure, the chapter argues that societies must adopt deliberate policies for work-time reduction if they are to reclaim time for sustainable living.

Myth 11: 'Transition to sustainable consumption is primarily driven by consumer demand' by Oksana Mont and Åsa Svenfelt examines the framing of consumers as the main drivers of sustainability transitions. Based on economic theories of consumer sovereignty and popularised through 'vote with your wallet' campaigns, this myth shifts responsibility away from governments and businesses. The chapter demonstrates how infrastructures, provisioning systems and corporate strategies influence what is possible to consume and how individuals are often more willing to support ambitious policies than policymakers assume. It advocates for enabling structures and stronger regulation, highlighting that consumer agency should be understood in relation to broader systems.

Myth 12: 'Strong sustainable consumption governance means sacrificing freedom and well-being' by Lea Melissa Becker, Paula Berendt and Doris Fuchs examines the belief that ambitious governance inevitably restricts freedom and diminishes quality of life. This myth sustains weak governance focused on efficiency and technology while sidelining sufficiency. The chapter demonstrates instead that strong governance can enhance well-being by safeguarding opportunities for all to live good lives within ecological limits. Reframing freedom in qualitative rather than purely quantitative terms highlights how policies grounded in sufficiency, fairness and collaboration can strengthen resilience and trust in societies.

The four chapters reveal how myths at the societal level uphold the dominance of growth, justify overwork, shift responsibility away from powerful actors and portray ambitious policies as threats rather than opportunities. By dispelling these myths, the book opens up possibilities for economic models, policy frameworks and cultural imaginaries that prioritise sufficiency, equity and sustainable welfare as the basis for thriving societies.

Pathways beyond myths

In the concluding chapter, '*From myths to transformation*' by Oksana Mont synthesises insights from across the book to demonstrate how myths about sustainable consumption persist and hinder systemic change. Five mechanisms explain their persistence: cultural reinforcement, anchoring in practices, institutional embedding, psychological appeal and political function. A cross-chapter analysis identifies five recurring barriers – technological optimism, growth dependency, shifting responsibility onto individuals, consumption as identity and therapy and short-termism – which support each other and restrict sufficiency and structural transformation. The chapter outlines pathways for change and highlights new myths for future research, emphasising the need to diagnose, debate and develop alternatives for sustainable living.

1.6 For whom is this book?

This book is written for readers concerned with sustainability but who are weary of simplistic answers. It speaks to students, policymakers, businesses, activists and citizens alike – those who sense that something is amiss in the dominant narratives and are ready to ask deeper questions. It is especially for those who have encountered these myths in public discourse, policy frameworks or corporate strategy meetings and who wish to move beyond them. Whether you are seeking intellectual clarity, practical insights or a spark of hope, this book offers perspectives to unlearn the myths that constrain us and to imagine new ways of living within planetary boundaries.

References

Aquinas, St. T. (1947). *Summa Theologica* (Fathers of the English Dominican Province, Trans.). Benziger Bros. edition. https://www.documentacatholicaomnia.eu/03d/1225-1274,_Thomas_Aquinas,_Summa_Theologiae_%5B1%5D,_EN.pdf

Bacon, F. (1609). *Bacon's essays and the wisdom of the ancients* (B. Montagu, Ed., Vols. 1–13). Boston Little Brown and Company. https://web.seducoahuila.gob.mx/biblioweb/upload/Bacons%20Essays%20and%20Wisdom%20of%20the%20Ancients.pdf

Barthes, R. (1957/2009). *Mythologies*. Hill and Wang. (Original work published 1957)

Boström, M. (2020). The social life of mass and excess consumption: Transformative learning for sustainable consumption. *Sustainability: Science, Practice and Policy*, *16*(1), 168–182.

Bourdieu, P., & Wacquant, L. J. D. (1992). *An invitation to reflexive sociology*. University of Chicago Press.

Cassirer, E., Lofts, S. G., & Gordon, P. E. (1925/2020). *The philosophy of symbolic forms, volume 2: mythical thinking*. Routledge. (Original work published 1925)

Edelman, M. (1988). *Constructing the political spectacle*. University of Chicago Press.

Eliade, M. (2025). *Myth and reality*. Harper & Row Publishers. (Original work published 1963)

Fine, B. (1997). *Consumption matters: The production and experience of consumption*. Routledge.

Hajer, M. A. (1995). *The politics of environmental discourse: Ecological modernisation and the policy process*. Clarendon Press.

Herder, J. G. (2006). *Selected Writings on Aesthetics*. Princeton University Press. (Original work published 1798)

Hume, D., & Root, H. E. (1957). *A Natural History of Religion, David Hume*. Stanford University Press. (Original work published 1757)

Intergovernmental Panel on Climate Change (IPCC). (2022). *Climate change 2022: Mitigation of climate change. Contribution of working group III to the sixth assessment report*. Cambridge University Press.

Lakoff, G. (2010). Why it matters how we frame the environment. *Environmental Communication*, *4*(1), 70–81.

Latour, B. (1991). *We have never been modern*. Harvard University Press.

Mont, O., Heiskanen, E., Power, K., & Kuusi, H. (2013). *Improving Nordic policymaking by dispelling myths on sustainable consumption*. Nordic Council of Ministers.

Mont, O., Lehner, M., & Dalhammar, C. (2022). Sustainable consumption through policy intervention – A review of research themes. *Frontiers in Sustainability*, *3*, 921477. https://doi.org/10.3389/frsus.2022.921477

Nietzsche, F. (1999). *The birth of tragedy: Out of the spirit of music*. Penguin UK. (Original work published 1872)

O'Donnell, J. J. (2005). *Augustine: A new biography*. Ecco. http://archive.org/details/augustine00jame_qqt

Oreskes, N., & Conway, E. M. (2011). *Merchants of doubt: How a handful of scientists obscured the truth on issues from tobacco smoke to global warming*. Bloomsbury.

Panofsky, E. (1960). *Renaissance and renascences in western art*. Routledge & CRC Press.

Plato. (ca. 375 BCE/2002). *The republic* (IDPH ed.). https://www.sciencetheearth.com/uploads/2/4/6/5/24658156/plato_-_the_republic.pdf
Plutarch. (1st–2nd c. CE/1922). *Moralia* (Vols. V–VI, F. C. Babbitt, Trans.). Harvard University Press.
Voltaire. (1764). *The philosophical dictionary*. Printed for Wynne and Scholey.

PART I
Individual level

2

MYTH 1

There's no point in me sacrificing myself when no one else cares

Maria Wolrath Söderberg

2.1 The myth

We compare ourselves to others. We create meaning by orienting ourselves in relation to each other; not to anybody, however, but to those close to us or to the group we want to belong to.

This is how we form norms, our collective morality, from which we consider and justify our actions.

But we also use comparisons with others as arguments to avoid. Avoid acting, avoid cognitive dissonance or free ourselves from responsibility.

One of the most common ways to justify our passivity in the transition or to motivate climate-damaging consumption is by pointing to others who are worse or to our own smallness. My research partner, Nina Wormbs, and I saw this in a study where people talked about how they reasoned when they did things that harmed the climate, even though they knew they should not (Wolrath Söderberg & Wormbs, 2022). We called it the '*Little me*' argument. We have all encountered (or even used) that argument, haven't we?

Comparison is a very basic human cognitive capacity. Our propensity to orient ourselves so strongly towards others has probably taken our species far, but it surely also has problematic dimensions. Those problematic dimensions are what I refer to when I address the 'Little me' as a myth.

By myth, I mean a recurring or preferred pattern of reasoning, carried by metaphors, narratives, analogies, models or other structuring figures, which is also suggestive. It often has a factual side, but the mythical dimension occurs when the pattern of reasoning activates entire networks of assumptions, emotions, values and social contexts that build or maintain comfortable worldviews or desired conclusions.

DOI: 10.4324/9781003613718-4

Calling something a myth in this regard is not the same as saying that it is entirely false, but rather to point at a meaning making, a discourse, that is more or less suggestive or misleading, at least unless it is also challenged by competing perspectives.

The 'Little me' myth perpetuates unsustainable consumption. 'Why should I forgo my trip, a new jacket, renovating my kitchen, when my share is negligible and when no one else cares'. In this chapter, the perspective is rhetorical. We take a closer look at some of the thinking structures and types of arguments that the myth makes possible and how they appear convincing. Rhetoric plays a crucial role in sustainability debates, as it shapes public perception of responsibility, action and legitimacy. However, rhetoric plays an equally important role in our thinking, our internal deliberation, because our patterns of reasoning are shaped by what is considered reasonable and valid in the collectives to which we want to belong. Understanding how arguments like the 'Little me' gain persuasive power allows us to deconstruct them and foster new narratives that better support sustainable consumption.

2.2 Origins

It is, of course, not possible to establish a distinct birth of the 'little-me' reasoning. It has probably been with humanity for a long time. One can speculate on how it has been fuelled by the emergence of large social systems, industrialisation, globalisation and other developments that have increased the distance between the individual and the levels where more general decisions are made, thus weakening the individual's experienced agency. But it is paradoxical, because the same development has at the same time meant increased freedom of choice and thus more agency, at least of a certain kind, and at least in well-off countries. This development, on the other hand, has made possible and maybe promoted an increasing individualism, something that may have interacted with the emergence of the perspective of the human being as autonomous and as a consumer rather than as a citizen or part of a collective. Consumer culture and media representations perpetuate the myth by glorifying large corporations and governments as the primary actors in solving global problems, while individuals are portrayed as powerless bystanders. This leads to a focus on technological solutions rather than personal responsibility. Moreover, the increasing complexity of global supply chains and consumer behaviours has fostered a culture where individual choices seem trivial compared to the actions of big players, such as countries or industries.

The 'Little me' myth is often reinforced by political leaders, industries, and even some environmental organisations that prioritise systemic solutions over individual action. The narrative is frequently heard in debates that suggest 'it's not the individual's responsibility' but rather that of governments and corporations. This rhetoric can divert attention away from the significant role individuals play in driving demand for sustainable products and services.

On the other hand, from the individual's perspective, the 'Little me' myth seems like a reasonable response to the overwhelming scale of global environmental issues, such as climate change and biodiversity loss, which seem insurmountable when viewed from the individual's perspective.

The 'Little me' argument is, however, not equally applicable in all spheres of life, but has been given special power in regard to sustainability and climate. This becomes clear if you compare it to other contexts. No one would say to their child, who has just turned 18 and been given the right to vote, 'Don't vote. You are only one of many millions anyway, so it does not matter'. It is also hardly socially acceptable to say, 'I'm pouring the leftover motor oil into the bay. You see how much water there is, it makes so little difference'. But in relation to greenhouse gas emissions, the argument is both common and accepted. Why is that? Well, it's a wonderfully convenient argument that frees us from responsibility.

It is actually an infernal argument, because it confirms itself. If I reduce myself, I actually lose influence. But as with all arguments, it only works if it is accepted socially. This, of course, also means an opportunity for change. If we make it socially unacceptable by exposing it and questioning it, it loses its power.

2.3 Consequences

The 'Little me' argument is actually a member of a whole family of reasoning patterns based on relativisation. It is often used to displace or replace responsibility or to negotiate the size of a reprehensible act. Relativisation is deeply rooted in everyday reasoning. According to it, individuals compare their actions to larger contexts, thus diminishing their perceived significance. A study explains how people rationalise their climate-damaging behaviours by contextualising them within a broader societal framework, which makes their choices seem less problematic (Wolrath Söderberg & Wormbs, 2022).

Here are a few variants.

2.3.1 'I am only one'[1]

In this variant, it is a matter of amounts or proportions. 'I am only one of billions who buy Shein goods', or 'My emissions are just a tiny micro part of all emissions', negotiates *the size* of the responsibility.

Minimization, as Benoit and Drew calls it (1997), makes my action insignificant. 'Me sacrificing my vacation to Thailand would be a drop in the ocean' goes even further and implies that my actions are downright negligible and thus negates that there even is a responsibility. An even stronger focus on the action than on the person further distances oneself from liability 'My little piece of meat on the table is negligible'.

2.3.2 'Others are worse'

The '*Little me*' is, however, often put in a more explicit relation to others.

'What does my small action matter when others completely screw it up' emphasises the hopelessness of one's own situation, against the background of other people's morals. Often the 'Little me' poses oneself against 'everybody', 'people' or 'others'.

But it can be even more powerful as an argument when one poses oneself against others who should take a bigger responsibility due to their role. Like politicians, researchers or people with power or money (Attari et al., 2019). A minister of environment whose husband painted their boat with poisonous colour or a researcher going by air to the UN Climate Change Conference in Bélem are particularly appealing objects for comparison. 'If not even they, why should I?' The sense of hypocrisy adds extra spice to the argument. Or why not compare with celebrities or influencers, like Taylor Swift, who could be seen as morally obligated to take extra responsibility due to their impact?

Such an object of comparison can be combined with bitterness and resentment. It not only replaces one's own responsibility but also places the blame on someone else and even makes oneself the victim. This analysis might sound sarcastic. But I will not throw the first stone. We are probably all guilty of this to some extent, and there is something to the argument, even if it is a poor excuse for our passivity.

Sweden, where our studies were performed, can be seen as an illustrative example, relevant to many affluent countries. We, Swedes, are quite skilled at finding those who are worse, even though a majority of us are among the world's 25% highest emitters (Nilsson Lewis & Nelson, 2023). Our average resource use per capita would require four planets if all people on Earth lived like we Swedes do (Global Footprint Network). Yet, the 'Little me' arguments are very common in Sweden, both among individuals and in public debate. However, there is reason to believe that the same is true of many other well-off countries with high emissions.

The consumption, as well as the wealth needed for it, is, however, unevenly distributed in Sweden, as in many countries. But it is not just poor people or people with low emissions (which happens to coincide, as emitting greenhouse gases comes at a cost) who use the '*others are worse*' argument. I have lived for a long time in a quite affluent area, where people driving SUVs pointed at those with two cars. Those in turn pointed at people with houses in Spain, who pointed at those with yachts or helicopters, who pointed at Elon Musk, 'At least we don't send up space rockets'. Comparison with extreme emitters is very convenient and persuasive. Not least because there is reason for criticism. The extremely rich account for a disproportionately large share of emissions (Barros & Wilk, 2021), but again, that is not the same as freeing the rest of us, who also have too high emissions, if not that high.

I would say that people regularly underestimate their own emissions and overestimate what is 'normal'. In a study, we saw many testimonies about how shocked people were when they tried their emissions in a climate calculator (Wormbs & Wolrath Söderberg, 2021). This underestimation is connected to the fact that we also underestimate others' willingness to contribute to the climate transition (Andre et al., 2024). We state ourselves as willing, but since others are less willing, there's not much point in us doing anything, right?

2.3.3 'But my action is justified!'

Another variant of the 'Little me' argument has to do with the *motives*. 'I have a good purpose with my journey'. The thinking structure is that my emissions, unlike those of others, are justified. They can also be justified by my efforts in other heartwarming areas, 'I work with antibiotic resistance', or, as we have seen in another study, by exceptionalism – 'my professional role is so important' (Eriksson et al., 2022). Akin to the motive is the direction 'I am shopping less than last year' and the potentially worse choice 'I could have chosen a vacation in Australia, but we only went to Italy'. This is also a form of negotiation about the size of the 'crime', but the comparison is with oneself rather than with others.

Other forms of the 'Little me' are more connected to the private self, like 'I'm worth it – I have been ill', which *calls for empathy* and invokes exception. Another example points to the self-image 'I live such a sustainable life already, with all recycling'. A third refers to *one's love for nature* as a mitigating circumstance. Love for nature might be seen as a common Swedish self-image, which might at least partly explain the enlarged version of the 'Little me', namely *Little Sweden*.

2.3.4 'Little Sweden'

'Sweden's emissions are only one promille of the global emissions' is a parallel to the minimisation argument used to excuse individuals' climate-harmful behaviour. Even if we count consumption-based and include all emissions, it really is a small number, just over 16 promille. This is, of course, compelling. But only when omitting that we Swedes are about 13 promille of the globe's population, and we have been high emitters for decades. We thus emit more than our share. Regarding the dramatic pace with which the collected emissions have to decrease, this is alarming (UN Net Zero Coalition).

The only reasonable way of counting and comparing is per capita. It is a strange idea that a country's size or even the size of its population should determine its level of responsibility. The United States has large emissions. How should we look at the small states there, Oklahoma? Should we focus only on the big states and disregard the small? Bahrain's emissions per capita are about three times as high as Sweden's, but should they really have to care? It is such a small country. That kind of reasoning becomes very questionable in regard to the fact that a large portion of the world's high and extreme emitters live in small states. A kindred argument, of the '*others are worse*' type, is 'Why should we sacrifice ourselves when other countries are worse?' This argument is common in political contexts, as well as at the dinner table. Often, the country that is worse in terms of emissions is China, but India is up and coming in the discussions.

China has actually now, for the first time, caught up with us Swedes (consumption-based emissions). And it is, of course, worrying when such a huge country's emissions are rising. But it is rather arrogant to blame others for wanting to live as we do. Furthermore, when the argument comes together with the claim that instead of reducing our emissions, we should persuade China to do it, a fundamental misunderstanding of how persuasion works is made visible. If you do not live as you preach, you are giving away your most powerful argument. No one takes a hypocrite seriously.

India is emerging as a scapegoat in the Swedish public debate, and so is Nigeria, 'with all their bonfires'. Nigeria has less than one-tenth of our emissions per capita, and India has about a fifth (Our World in Data). Woe and horror if they want to live like us.

2.4 Dispelling the myth

It is true that I am small and that Sweden is small. Many countries are small. We can thus make a limited impact. That is the factual base of the 'Little me' claim. But the suggestive side of the argument – that we can go with the status quo, free of guilt – is mythical.

What makes the 'Little me' discourse appear logical is underlying beliefs about who is a climate villain, and about what is normal and just. But those beliefs might respond poorly to reality.

2.4.1 Sustainability self-deception: why our green self-image does not match reality

It is probably safe to say that most Swedes love nature. We grew up with the *Keep Sweden Clean campaign*, the *Right of Access to Public Places* and excursions in preschool with the troll *Skogsmulle,* who was supposed to teach us to be careful about nature. We profess a climate-friendly lifestyle. Most Swedes would never dream of throwing a beer can in a lake. Many believe that they live sustainably. They recycle their garbage and choose organic coffee.

However, this self-perception does not match reality. When it comes to invisible emissions, if you count all the greenhouse gases that we generate through our consumption and travelling, we are on average eight times higher than we need to be by 2045. After having declined somewhat, during a decade, Swedish consumption-based emissions are right now increasing (Swedish EPA, 2025a). Historically, the Swedes have 22 times higher emissions per capita than the global average (Alestig et al., 2024). Now, our emissions per year are about the global average. The comparison looks better than a few years ago due to a combination of reduced emissions from the production of what we consume (not from consuming less) and from the fact that other countries have increased their emissions. We are still on the global leader board regarding the use of energy (Our World in Data, 2025) and resources (Circle Economy & RISE, 2022), albeit in good company of some other affluent countries. This picture does not harmonise well with our self-image. Nor is it the image that is conveyed in the public debate. Many believe that Sweden has low emissions. Based on that assumption, it is reasonable, at least if the reference is to other countries, rather than to the levels, we have to go down to, to think that we have done our part.

2.4.2 Redefining normal: how prosperity distorts our sense of responsibility

We tend to see our own lifestyle as normal. We compare ourselves to our neighbours and groups we hang out with, and base our idea of what is normal on them. In some areas, it is normal to have large villas, many vacations abroad and summer homes, and thus it is normal to have high greenhouse gas emissions. Prosperity and emissions are intimately linked.

However, a part of the problem is that wealthy people tend to believe that they have low emissions (Nielsen et al., 2024). They are often well educated and climate conscious. They can choose a sweater made of organically grown cotton, afford to buy an electric car or subscribe to demand-grown vegetable boxes. But other aspects of their lifestyle outweigh this – large homes, trips abroad, kitchen renovations, clothes and home electronics. People who are on tight finances, on the other hand, tend to believe that they have high emissions. They certainly cannot afford organic coffee or an electric car. They may find it impossibly expensive to live a climate-smart life. However, the fact is that, on the contrary, it generally costs more to destroy the climate (Wiedmann et al., 2020). The bigger the economic space, the more consumption and the more consumption, the more emissions. Those who have to mend their pants, can't eat meat several times a week and absolutely can't go on vacation, probably already have relatively low emissions.

So far, climate work that has focused on justice or equity has mainly put the underprivileged at the centre and worked to ensure that they are included, listened to and have an impact. This is, of course, important. However, now we are beginning to realise that the major emitters, that is, the wealthy, are just as important to include in the transformation. Not only they have margins, that is, room to reduce, but they also often have a stronger influence at the system level and, not least, set the standard for the desired lifestyle. 'And why should I give up my entrecote when CEO Wall Enberg travels with a private jet' (Wolrath Söderberg, 2023). Thus, their role and responsibility for the transition must be emphasised in both politics, sustainability work and the public discourse.

2.4.3 Justice and responsibility: why the high emitters must lead the transition

When the way of life that we consider normal is threatened, we become anxious, no matter how we set the frame of reference for normality. The idea of abstaining or reducing is then often experienced as unjust or unfair. This is interesting given that justice is increasingly emphasised in research and international climate negotiations. It is the high emitters who have to do the dog's work because they have something to abstain from. Otherwise, we have no chance of transforming at the high pace necessary (Bruckner et al., 2022). But justice is also important for bringing people together. It might be the most critical parameter for political support for new policies. If political policies, taxes and changes are not experienced as just, they risk meeting resistance (Bergquist, 2025; Lindvall et al., 2024; Maestre-Andrés et al., 2019). It can severely undermine democracy if politics are not perceived as legitimate.

Here, we see an awkward tension between different perceptions or definitions of justice – on the one hand, based on data about the extremely unequal distribution of wealth and emissions, and on the other hand, the painful feeling of injustice when you risk losing something. Politics must, of course, deal with the natural anxiety of affluent people expected to decrease or abstain from consumption, but that is not the same as a populism that focuses entirely on the whining of the privileged when they risk having to take responsibility. Just as dangerous is to nurture a victimising myth fuelling the feeling that everything is getting worse and that we are victims, despite that the Swedes purchasing power having more than doubled in 35 years. Such myths feed an infantilising discourse in which citizens are seen mainly as customers or even as giant babies.

There is an important public education task here. We know that knowledge does not in any simple way lead to action (see Chapter 2 about this), but we have nevertheless seen that knowledge about the relationship of one's own emissions to justice plays a role in people actually making lifestyle changes for the sake of the climate (Wormbs & Wolrath Söderberg, 2021).

2.4.4 *The false choice: individuals vs. systems in climate action*

Another underlying assumption has to do with a dichotomy between the individual and the system.

Individuals see themselves as powerless in relation to politics, business or what is called 'the system'. 'It is the system that must be changed. I can do nothing'.

At the same time, we hear from representatives of the system that there is nothing they can do. It is the voters who decide, say politicians. It is the customers, say companies. Thus, the status quo (see Chapter 11 for a discussion on how expectations and responsibility for sustainability transformations are placed on individuals).

Furthermore, the discourse often frames the individual and the system as if nothing exists between them. This is misleading because the transformation occurs in this intermediary space. It is not an empty void but rather a dynamic landscape of groups, families, associations, workplace teams, neighbours and civil movements (Chenoweth & Stephan, 2011). This is also where new norms are formed, where demands for change arise and develop. New norms and paradigms, in turn, are the soil for political change. This becomes clear when looking at historical transformations such as those concerning human rights or gender equality. It does not take very large groups for social tipping points to occur (Centola et al., 2018). Of course, there is no guarantee that movements and new norms will have an impact on politics, but we can be fairly certain that there will be no political change for which there is no pressure or support (i.e. in a democracy).

Individuals in the role of citizens acting together are the major agents of change. However, even at the individual level, people are not powerless. Individuals and households account for/have control over approximately 60% of the Swedish emissions (Swedish EPA, 2025b). The global number is higher (Hertwich & Peters, 2009).

The 'Little me' makes us powerless and victimised. It is a myth that has served fossil fuel interests well. At the same time, there is a kind of counter-myth, namely that this idea that we should see ourselves as individually responsible, is a trick from the fossil fuel industry (see more in Chapter 11). And it really seems that the concept of climate footprint was invented by an advertising agency hired by BP, which then also created the first climate calculator (Franta, 2022). The criticism is that in this way, the spotlight was shifted from the responsibility of fossil fuel producing companies to individuals. Now, this story is sometimes used to enforce the idea that the individual does not matter.

I, however, question whether BP really knew what they were doing. In our studies, we have seen that discovering one's own responsibility for the emissions, especially if it is put in relation to a justice perspective, seems to give people the impetus to change. It seems to work that way also for companies, municipalities and regions. It also seems that the personal transition cannot be separated from collective commitment and participation as citizens, which in turn is an important influencing factor for societal transformation. BP's trick actually seems to backfire against fossil use.

2.5 Implications

Just as with all myths, we need to listen carefully, discern what the reasoning assumes and consider what it does to us. When we examine the myth closely, it releases its suggestive power over us. We can choose to take in what is meaningful in the myth and reject what guides our thinking in problematic ways. So, just paying attention and publicly wrestling with the myth is a way to make the debate healthier.

There is reason to challenge the 'Little me' myth on all levels.

2.5.1 Implications for governments

In Sweden and in several other countries, we see two opposing political trends. One shifts responsibility to individuals – the current politicians in power reject systemic solutions. Traditional liberal ideas, such as that individual liberty should not be at the expense of other freedoms, have been purged of the responsibility perspective and have become the individual's freedom to choose what they want, even at the expense of others and our common environment. The other trend, which paradoxically enough is often driven by the same political parties, says the opposite, that the individual should not have to do anything. In Sweden, we experience something like a fear of touching when it comes to behavioural dimensions and, not least, the idea of having to reduce or abstain for the sake of the climate.

We are in a terrible hurry now. There is a broad scientific consensus and it has been emphasised in the IPCC reports (2022) that technology and innovation will not be enough. Behavioural changes and sacrifice are necessary, specifically from affluent countries and high emitters but it seems to be a political area that politicians neither on the right nor on the left dare to enter, possibly because of confusion – how do we talk about abstaining in a culture of abundance and action points (Wormbs et al., 2024) and probably for fear of losing voter support. But the politicians are mistaken. They underestimate voter support for stronger climate policy (Swedish EPA, 2025c). Research also shows that if politicians are told that they have support for systemic solutions, they tend to actually push for bolder and more radical transformation, such as taxes and policies (Mildenberger & Tingley, 2019). Furthermore, it is a question of raising crisis awareness. We know from history, from wars and natural disasters, for example, that if people understand what is at stake, they tend to have a magnificent power of action and also a willingness to sacrifice. Politicians are not helpless victims of the discourse but can help shape it away from a self-serving individualistic norm to a collective sense of responsibility.

2.5.2 Implications for businesses

For the business community, talking about reduced consumption or encouraging customers to do so can seem self-destructive. Many companies struggle ambitiously and honestly to accomplish more sustainable production. It can feel like an overly painful and hopeless realisation that no matter how hard you try to reduce emissions per garment, armchair or car, it is better if it is not bought at all. But if we do not dare to take the troublesome bull by the horns, we risk only getting part of the way. In the past year, I have met companies that have actually dared to grapple with this problem. These are companies that, for example, instead of striving for customers to love their products so much that they want lots of them, fight for customers to love them so much that they are prepared to have the products repaired over and over again, at an expensive price. There are companies that develop telephones whose components can be repaired and switched out again and again. I also meet companies that see their raison d'être as contributing to the local community and that have re-evaluated their economic goals based on an ideal of sufficiency. But it is difficult in a culture where the goal has so far been more and more.

One challenge is, of course, to meet the customers' 'Little me' thinking – that 'it does not matter if I give up the farmed salmon, because everyone else buys it'. Then it is important to remember that people are open to moral arguments, contrary to what has often been said in the context of sustainability. They are also keen to participate in shared responsibility if they perceive that others are doing so or if their effort is acknowledged. Can you make your customers feel like they are part of a movement? Can you highlight how many people actually make sustainable choices? Can you give a big discount if customers buy vegetables that are starting to get a little dry around the edges? Or turn those who repeatedly make sustainable choices into premium customers.

When the 'Little me' myth loses its hold, something quite uncomfortable happens for businesses. The old excuse that 'we just meet demand' no longer works. If people no longer believe that their own actions are meaningless, they are also far less likely to accept that businesses are just passive players in a bigger system. That card is off the table. Suddenly, companies are expected to take real responsibility not only for their own emissions but also for the kind of behaviours and norms they enable. If it is no longer socially acceptable for individuals to hide behind the crowd, why should it be for companies?

And when customers begin to see themselves as powerful and morally accountable, they start expecting the same from others, including the companies they buy from. That is when integrity becomes non-negotiable. It simply will not do to promote carbon neutrality in one ad campaign and then sponsor luxury flights or meat-heavy festivals in the next. In a world where the 'Little me' has been unmasked, contradictions are harder to ignore – not just by climate activists or critical journalists, but also by ordinary people who now expect businesses to live up to the same standards they hold themselves to or at least try.

Another thing changes, too. Once people stop thinking that 'no one else is doing anything', it becomes possible and necessary to show that they are not alone. This is where businesses can actually make a big difference. By creating social cues that remind us that we are many, not few. That others are already making changes. That our choices add up. And this is not about feel-good marketing. It is about designing systems where customers can see that their choices are part of something bigger. 'Eight out of ten chose bike delivery this week'. 'Together, we saved X tonnes of waste'. That kind of feedback does not just inform, it affirms.

And then there is the question of size. The 'Little me' myth may let the individual off the hook, but once that illusion is gone, something else comes into focus. Namely, the 'Big you'. Big companies, big brands, big polluters. If small actions matter, then big ones matter even more. And if individuals are now expected to act, surely those with far more capacity must lead. Being large is no longer a justification for inertia. It becomes a moral spotlight. So, the question is not whether to act, but how visibly, how boldly and how far beyond the bare minimum a company is willing to go. Because in the absence of the myth, doing something is no longer impressive – it is the baseline.

2.5.3 Implications for the public

Back to the 'Little me'. One conclusion we draw from our research is that it plays a big role for people who really act on their climate knowledge and ambition that they have realised the size of one's own emissions and how this relates to those of others and to the levels we must reduce to (Wormbs & Wolrath Söderberg, 2021).

It is also important to have insights into sizes and proportions when it comes to emissions in general. It is incredibly difficult to figure out for oneself what a ton of carbon dioxide means. We have also become energy blind.[2] When everyone had an approximate experience of how much work a horse could do, we measured in horsepower, but now, with two holes in the wall, we have lost the physical contact with energy. Some scholars talk about energy literacy, which is an understanding of the nature of energy and its role in our daily lives. It is accompanied by a capacity to apply this understanding to problems and make informed decisions. Perhaps we should also talk about emission literacy and resource literacy.

Another insight has to do with who needs to lead the transition. It is those with high emissions. This sounds banal to state, but when we realise that they are, by and large, the same group that is affluent, it immediately becomes more difficult to handle. We tend to end up in a charged political sphere within a right-left scale. It is, however, becoming increasingly clear that issues of justice must guide the transition and that a comprehensive societal transformation is necessary. We, who have historically high prosperity, must do the main part. It will be painful for many. It will not be enough to just tell beautiful stories about a simpler, calmer life. We also need to support each other in the necessary self-reflection and the loss of things we have cherished or taken for granted.

When we start talking about responsibility, we also find ourselves in a moral discourse. In sustainability work, we have learnt that we should avoid moralising in order to get people on board. However, the idea that moral arguments are counterproductive has also proven to be a myth (Bamberg & Möser, 2007). People who change for the sake of the climate, who give up or sacrifice something, often do so for moral reasons (Wormbs & Wolrath Söderberg, 2021). And it is certainly odd when you think about it; we do not think this way, that we should avoid speaking to our sense of responsibility or conscience at all costs, when it comes to other issues, such as the pandemic we have recently gone through, migration or defence issues.

A fourth insight has to do with how we frame our stories about the transition. I mentioned earlier a study that shows that over 80% of the population (in 125 countries) describes themselves as engaged in the climate crisis. Most also indicate that they are willing to make some sacrifices for the climate at least (Andre et al., 2024). At the same time, it turned out that respondents regularly underestimated the willingness of others. The consequence is that it feels less meaningful to change when you are (seemingly) alone in it. Therefore, it appears as an important task to spread the word about those who change – to make people feel others do care and do change, so that they also have to join the movement in order not to become obsolete.

2.6 Main message

Yes, we are small, and our ability to influence such enormous challenges as climate change is limited. But how we see ourselves and talk about ourselves affects whether our impact, so to speak, is smaller or larger than our share. Furthermore, there is no system level that does not also include people in some way. 'Society' is not an animal; it does not have its own soul. It is us, together. Nor is there a vacuum between the individual and 'society' or 'everyone else', but it is there, in the gap between the individual and the world that groups, movements and new norms arise. At a fairly low level, it seems close to the individual. It is when we start to talk differently, act differently in our various collectives, that new ways of thinking and being arise. Therefore, it matters what we choose to buy and what we give up, but perhaps even more that we brag about it. It is contagious.

We, the people, are the ones who decide whether a myth works. We can dispel them by learning to recognise them, putting into words what is happening and refusing to agree with the underlying assumptions. It gains power if many of us do it. New discourses are the soil for new norms, and new norms are the building material for systemic change. In Sweden, it was not so long ago that it was common to punish children corporally. Now, it would be utterly dismaying to hear a parent casually mentioning that they hit their child this morning, and even more absurd hearing 'there are so many children on Earth, so it doesn't matter if I also hit my child'. That's simply not socially acceptable and therefore not viable arguments. We, as citizens and as a collective, have the power to decide what is a viable argument.

Notes

1 The quotes should be read as symbolic examples. Based on the statements of our research subjects, I have attempted to capture and formulate the core arguments in what have been, our could have been, longer and more elaborate reasoning.
2 Energy blindness is a concept used by Nate Hagens in the podcast The Great Simplification. https://www.thegreatsimplification.com/frankly-original/frankly-03-energy-blindness.

References

Alestig, M., Nilsson Lewis, A., & Marbinah, R. (2024). *Sveriges ansvar i klimatkrisen*. Oxfam.

Andre, P., Boneva, T., Chopra, F., & Falk, A. (2024). Globally representative evidence on the actual and perceived support for climate action. *Nature Climate Change*, 1–7. https://doi.org/10.1038/s41558-024-01925-3

Attari, S. Z., Krantz, D. H., & Weber, E. U. (2019). Climate change communicators' carbon footprints affect their audience's policy support. *Climatic Change*, *154*(3), 529–545. https://doi.org/10.1007/s10584-019-02463-0

Bamberg, S., & Möser, G. (2007). Twenty years after Hines, Hungerford, and Tomera: A new meta-analysis of psycho-social determinants of pro-environmental behaviour. *Journal of Environmental Psychology*, *27*(1), 14–25. https://doi.org/10.1016/j.jenvp.2006.12.002

Barros, B., & Wilk, R. (2021). The outsized carbon footprints of the super-rich. *Sustainability: Science, Practice and Policy*, *17*(1), 316–322. https://doi.org/10.1080/15487733.2021.1949847

Benoit, W. L., & Drew, S. (1997). Appropriateness and effectiveness of image repair strategies. *Communication Reports*, *10*(2), 153–163. https://doi.org/10.1080/08934219709367671

Bergquist, M. (2025). Limiting support for environmental policies: Unfairness is a more critical barrier than cost and ineffectiveness. *Ambio*, *54*(2), 350–363. https://doi.org/10.1007/s13280-024-02074-9

Bruckner, B., Hubacek, K., Shan, Y., Zhong, H., & Feng, K. (2022). Impacts of poverty alleviation on national and global carbon emissions. *Nature Sustainability*, *5*(4), 311–320. https://doi.org/10.1038/s41893-021-00842-z

Centola, D., Becker, J., Brackbill, D., & Baronchelli, A. (2018). Experimental evidence for tipping points in social convention. *Science*, *360*(6393), 1116–1119. https://doi.org/10.1126/science.aas8827

Chenoweth, E., & Stephan, M. J. (2011). *Why civil resistance works: The strategic logic of nonviolent conflict*. Columbia University Press.

Circle Economy, & RISE. (2022). *The circularity gap report Sweden* (p. 86). RE: Source.

Eriksson, E., Wolrath Söderberg, M., & Wormbs, N. (2022). Exceptionalism and evasion: How scholars reason about air travel. In K. Bjørkdahl & A. S. Franco Duharte (Eds.), *Academic flying and the means of communication* (pp. 159–183). Springer. https://doi.org/10.1007/978-981-16-4911-0_7

Franta, B. (2022). *Big carbon's strategic response to global warming, 1950–2020*. Stanford University.

Hertwich, E. G., & Peters, G. P. (2009). Carbon footprint of nations: A global, trade-linked analysis. *Environmental Science & Technology*, *43*(16), 6414–6420. https://doi.org/10.1021/es803496a

IPCC. (2022). *Climate change 2022: Mitigation of climate change*. https://www.ipcc.ch/report/ar6/wg3/

Lindvall, D., Sörqvist, P., & Barthel, S. (2024). Overcoming the headwinds: Can policy design shape public acceptance of wind power in Sweden? *Energy Research & Social Science*, *116*, 103674. https://doi.org/10.1016/j.erss.2024.103674

Maestre-Andrés, S., Drews, S., & van den Bergh, J. (2019). Perceived fairness and public acceptability of carbon pricing: A review of the literature. *Climate Policy*, *19*(9), 1186–1204. https://doi.org/10.1080/14693062.2019.1639490

Mildenberger, M., & Tingley, D. (2019). Beliefs about climate beliefs: The importance of second-order opinions for climate politics. *British Journal of Political Science*, *49*(4), 1279–1307. https://doi.org/10.1017/S0007123417000321

Nielsen, K. S., Bauer, J. M., Debnath, R., Emogor, C. A., Geiger, S. M., Ghai, S., Gwozdz, W., & Hahnel, U. J. J. (2024). Underestimation of personal carbon footprint inequality in four diverse countries. *Nature Climate Change*, *14*(11), 1136–1143. https://doi.org/10.1038/s41558-024-02130-y

Nilsson Lewis, A., & Nelson, H. (2023). *Sveriges väg till en jämlik och rättvis klimatomställning*. Text. Oxfam. https://www.oxfam.se/blog/ny-rapport-synliggor-svensk-klimatojamlikhet

Our World in Data. (2025). *Primary energy consumption per capita* [Data set]. U.S. Energy Information Administration. https://ourworldindata.org/grapher/per-capita-energy-use

Swedish EPA. (2025a). *Sveriges utsläpp och upptag av växthusgaser*. Naturvårdsverket. https://www.naturvardsverket.se/data-och-statistik/klimat/sveriges-utslapp-och-upptag-av-vaxthusgaser/

Swedish EPA. (2025b). *Konsumtionsbaserade växthusgasutsläpp per person och år*. https://www.naturvardsverket.se/data-och-statistik/konsumtion/vaxthusgaser-konsumtionsbaserade-utslapp-per-person/

Swedish EPA. (2025c). *Svenskarna positiva till åtgärder för att bromsa klimatförändringen*. https://www.naturvardsverket.se/om-oss/aktuellt/nyheter-och-pressmeddelanden/2025/januari/svenskarna-positiva-till-atgarder-for-att-bromsa-klimat forandringen/?utm_source=chatgpt.com

UN Net Zero Coalition. https://www.un.org/en/climatechange/net-zero-coalition

Wiedmann, T., Lenzen, M., Keyßer, L. T., & Steinberger, J. K. (2020). Scientists' warning on affluence. *Nature Communications*, *11*(1), 3107. https://doi.org/10.1038/s41467-020-16941-y

Wolrath Söderberg, M. (2023). *Gluttony: You have to treat yourself, don't you?* Riksbankens Jubileumsfond.
Wolrath Söderberg, M., & Wormbs, N. (2022). Internal deliberation defending climate-harmful behavior. *Argumentation*. https://doi.org/10.1007/s10503-021-09562-2
Wormbs, N., Eriksson, E., Wolrath Söderberg, M., & Dahlin, M. (2024). The challenge of abstaining in a culture of action points. *Npj Climate Action*, *3*(1), 1–3. https://doi.org/10.1038/s44168-024-00138-w
Wormbs, N., & Wolrath Söderberg, M. (2021). Knowledge, fear, and conscience: Reasons to stop flying because of climate change. *Urban Planning*, 6(2), 314–324. https://doi.org/10.17645/up.v6i2.3974

3

MYTH 2

Infophilia – information alone will change consumer behaviour

Mikael Klintman

3.1 The infophilia myth

'Infophilia' – the notion that steadily increasing the volume and clarity of sustainability information provided to consumers will engender a decisive shift towards ecofriendly behaviours – originates in a rational choice understanding of human decision-making. Over many decades, this assumption has guided countless environmental campaigns, ecolabelling schemes and awareness-raising initiatives, propelled by the belief that once consumers 'know better', they will 'do better' (Ivanova et al., 2016). Yet, as extensive interdisciplinary research reveals, human decisions are shaped by social norms, emotions, ingrained habits, infrastructural constraints and power asymmetries – factors that cannot be surmounted by information alone (Stern, 2000).

This chapter challenges the belief that knowledge, in isolation, suffices to transform consumption patterns at a scale consistent with urgent environmental objectives. While information is vital, focusing almost exclusively on consumer awareness distracts from the structural, infrastructural and collective measures required to facilitate sustainable practices. By exploring the historical evolution of infophilia, its key consequences and the broader range of interventions needed to foster meaningful behavioural and systemic change, this chapter reveals how we might refocus efforts on the material conditions and social contexts that drive unsustainable consumption.

3.2 Origins

The myth of infophilia can be traced to mid-20th-century economic theories emphasising rational choice, wherein individuals are assumed to make

DOI: 10.4324/9781003613718-5

decisions grounded in cost-benefit calculations if given sufficient, accurate data. Embedded in the political and economic transformations of the late 20th century, particularly the rise of neoliberal ideals, the idea that consumer autonomy could solve large-scale environmental problems through informed purchasing gained substantial momentum (Archer, 2013). This framework drew attention away from collective or regulatory interventions and celebrated the market as the primary change arena.

Crucially, under a neoliberal policy umbrella that elevates individual freedom, consumer responsibility and deregulated markets, providing information – through ecolabels, product declarations and educational campaigns – appeared a straightforward, non-coercive solution (Hamilton & Denniss, 2005). By depicting consumers as the ultimate arbiters of environmental reform, governments and industries alike could maintain relatively light-touch regulation, relying on the presumption that knowledgeable shoppers would select sustainable options and thereby influence production and supply chains.

In Western societies, which emphasised individualism, rational self-interest and consumer sovereignty, it proved especially appealing to frame the public as potentially 'moral shoppers' once they had adequate knowledge. Companies developed green marketing strategies highlighting ecofriendly attributes, endorsing that greater transparency and detailed product facts would steer markets towards sustainability. However, early critiques of this approach pointed out that structural barriers – ranging from the limited availability of sustainable products in certain areas to the expense of high-quality, low-impact goods – hindered many from using that knowledge to change habits.

By the early 21st century, infophilia had firmly taken root in public policy and business discourse. Nations enacted voluntary labelling standards; corporations boasted consumer-facing carbon footprints or ethical production tags; and various NGOs published investigative reports detailing product life cycles. Despite these endeavours, unsustainable consumption did not decline in proportion to the wealth of accessible information. Instead, travel grew, fast fashion boomed and disposable consumer goods multiplied. Thus, while infophilia shaped popular narratives and policy frameworks, evidence increasingly suggested it was neither sufficient nor comprehensive enough to address the extent of environmental crises (Nisa et al., 2019).

3.3 Consequences

Over-reliance on informational approaches to sustainability has led to outcomes that often undermine the very objectives infophilia is meant to serve. One of these consequences is the construction of a moralising 'informed consumer' identity. People who fail to adapt their habits are sometimes framed as ignorant or lazy, ignoring structural constraints that limit choices, including socioeconomic barriers or insufficient public infrastructure (Florence et al., 2022). This moralisation also overlooks the complex motives underpinning purchases, such as habit, cultural tradition, or emotional ties, reducing sustainable consumption to an issue of knowledge deficits (cf. Simis et al., 2016).

A second outcome is the commodification of sustainability itself. In focusing on labelling and brand narratives, sustainability becomes 'another product feature' – an attribute that can be marketed and sold (Husic & Cicic, 2009). Consumers, gratified by an ecofriendly label or certificate, might feel absolved of further responsibilities, even if their overall consumption remains high or their lifestyles remain carbon-intensive. Moreover, companies learn to highlight specific environmental indicators while neglecting deeper operational issues.

Infophilia also diminishes attention to community-based interventions and system-level solutions (Stirling, 2014). The emphasis on individual consumer decisions shifts political and corporate discourse away from collective infrastructures – such as comprehensive public transport, shared energy systems, or large-scale waste management. Furthermore, ecolabelled goods can inadvertently exacerbate inequalities when they cater mainly to more affluent demographics.

A related risk involves greenwashing, where organisations promote superficial indicators of environmental responsibility (Ellen MacArthur Foundation, 2017). Companies can deflect scrutiny from the more significant environmental harm embedded in their production methods by giving the impression of corporate virtue through transparent labelling or flashy campaigns. This cycle ultimately fosters distrust as consumers encounter a myriad of contradictory or exaggerated claims.

Finally, the infophilia myth can stall real innovation by allowing governments and businesses to meet public demands for ecoconsciousness primarily through awareness-oriented strategies rather than by implementing transformative policies or reconfiguring infrastructural norms (Fazey et al., 2020). Labelling or consumer education alone cannot dismantle the entrenched systems prioritising continuous economic growth and rapid product turnover (Persson & Klintman, 2020). In turn, the myth of infophilia contributes to a governance style that offloads responsibility onto individuals, offering limited mechanisms to address the systemic drivers of environmental decline.

3.4 Dispelling the myth

Debunking the myth of infophilia requires foregrounding the insights from multiple fields – environmental psychology, sociology, behavioural economics and evolutionary theory – that highlight how essential information rarely suffices to alter day-to-day behaviour or larger structural realities (Klintman,

2013). Below, key lines of argument challenge the assumption that informed consumers alone can catalyse profound, enduring change.

3.4.1 *The gap between knowledge and action*

Decades of empirical studies confirm that awareness does not necessarily lead to behaviour change, an observation often referred to as the 'knowledge–action gap' (Thøgersen & Ölander, 2002). Even when people sincerely believe in cutting down plastic waste or purchasing ethically sourced products, real-life constraints such as cost, convenience, habit and social norms frequently override newly acquired information. This disconnect between knowing and doing manifests across various consumption domains, including energy use, food choices and travel.

One well-documented example pertains to meat consumption and climate concerns. Individuals may acknowledge that high meat intake contributes significantly to greenhouse gas emissions. Yet, they continue with established dietary patterns because of cultural traditions, taste preferences or a lack of affordable and appealing alternatives. In such contexts, the decision goes beyond a lack of facts and involves a reluctance or inability to shift entrenched routines. Hence, while campaigns about livestock's carbon footprint may raise awareness, their capacity to trigger widespread change remains constrained by deeper sociocultural forces.

3.4.2 *Emotional and social dimensions of consumption*

Human decisions are often intertwined with emotional gratification and symbolic identity (Cialdini et al., 1990). Purchases, especially those linked to personal expression – fashion, electronics, vehicles – reflect functional needs and aesthetic, status-related and cultural factors. Replacing one's car with public transport for ecological reasons, for instance, might conflict with emotional attachments to freedom, convenience or the social prestige of a particular vehicle brand. Rational data about emissions can struggle to compete with these deeper drivers, primarily when infrastructure does not adequately support greener modes of mobility.

Furthermore, consumption choices are heavily influenced by social norms and peer pressures. Individuals often emulate friends, neighbours, or influencers rather than adopting purely rational, data-driven decision processes (Schwartz, 2012). As a result, consumer education alone may fail if it does not align with communal norms, networks of trust and the cultural values that shape collective behaviour. Social scientists have noted that people can respond more strongly to signals from peers (e.g. how many neighbours recycle) than from abstract statistics or impersonal messages.

3.4.3 Habitual routines and infrastructural lock-in

Much of daily life operates on autopilot, following well-worn routines that lower cognitive load in a complex world (Shove & Walker, 2014). Whether buying the same brand of washing powder or driving the same route to work, established habits often prevail over new information, however compelling it might be. Incorporating new information can require upheavals in scheduling, budgets or mental effort that hamper the translation of awareness into sustained behavioural shifts.

Moreover, material infrastructures typically shape consumption choices: roads, housing designs, public transport systems, energy grids and local commercial offerings (Mengistie et al., 2017). If energy-efficient public transport is unavailable or unaffordable, the knowledge that 'buses and trains reduce carbon emissions' does not prompt a switch to public transport. Infophilia's emphasis on personal decision-making obscures these infrastructural limitations, placing the onus on individuals to navigate inadequate systems. Without concerted efforts to reconfigure the built environment and introduce robust alternatives, consumer information campaigns alone cannot overcome the path dependencies embedded in existing infrastructures.

3.4.4 Cognitive overload and labelling fatigue

One unintended consequence of infophilia is a deluge of sustainability logos that overwhelms rather than empowers shoppers. A 2024 mapping by the European Commission's Joint Research Centre catalogued 210 distinct sustainability-related food labels circulating on the EU market, visible on about one-fifth of all new packaged-food launches in 2021 (EC, 2023). Independent directories echo this saturation: the Ecolabel Index currently lists 73 food-specific ecolabels active in Europe (Ecolabel Index, 2025). Faced with such a dizzying array, many consumers lack the time, expertise or motivation to distinguish robust schemes from superficial ones – a phenomenon marketing scholars describe as 'label fatigue'. Experimental studies show that when shoppers are presented with more than three competing sustainability logos, deliberation time rises while purchase intention for any labelled item falls (Weinmann et al., 2016).

Proliferation also breeds scepticism. A 2023 16-country survey by the European Consumer Organisation found that 56% of respondents believe there are simply too many green labels and logos to be meaningful (BEUC, 2023). Unless certification bodies converge on harmonised criteria and transparent auditing, adding yet another icon risks amplifying cynicism rather than trust. In this sense, more information can become noise, underlining the limits of infophilia.

3.4.5 The power of framing and cultural interpretation

Behavioural economics and social psychology underscore the importance of framing in shaping responses to information (Thaler & Sunstein, 2008). The same factual content can elicit divergent reactions depending on how it is contextualised – whether it emphasises personal sacrifice, communal benefits, cost savings or moral imperatives (Klintman, 2025). This means the success of an informational campaign may hinge less on the data provided and more on how it resonates with the values, identities or aspirations of the target audience.

Likewise, cultural background affects how sustainability messages are perceived (Hamilton & Denniss, 2005). People raised in societies with strong collective traditions might adopt new habits more readily when messages stress communal well-being. At the same time, individualistic contexts often require appeals to personal benefits or autonomy. When infophilia frames data in universal, purely rational terms, it can neglect local norms, religious values or historical contexts that shape how communities interpret environmental responsibility.

3.4.6 Social practice and collective dynamics

A further critique of infophilia arises from social practice theories, highlighting how ordinary routines evolve through shared norms, cultural habits and material arrangements (Shove & Walker, 2014). Practices such as laundry, cooking, commuting or air-conditioning are not merely products of individual choice but interwoven with institutional, technical and cultural elements. Interventions targeting only consumer education fail to address these interconnections.

For instance, shifting dietary practices away from high-impact foods requires more than awareness of global deforestation or emissions. It demands supportive policies around agricultural subsidies, community-based cooking initiatives and shifting cultural conventions about mealtime. Similarly, encouraging teleconferencing over business flights depends on whether organisations normalise virtual meetings, invest in robust digital infrastructure and adjust performance metrics that previously rewarded in-person attendance. Where practices remain embedded in social and institutional structures, the capacity of information alone to spur shifts is intrinsically limited.

3.4.7 Knowledge resistance and defensive reactions

While traditional models assume people eagerly incorporate new facts, research on knowledge resistance challenges this assumption (Klintman, 2019). When confronted with information that questions entrenched lifestyles, individuals can become defensive, discrediting the source or disputing the data. Attitudes towards climate science, for instance, sometimes become more polarised when campaigns focus only on factual correctness without acknowledging the identity and moral frameworks of the audience (Jasanoff, 2018).

Knowledge resistance stems partly from humans' need for cognitive consistency and in-group belonging. If adopting an ecofriendly behaviour threatens one's sense of self or group identity, the reaction may be hostility rather than open-minded change. In these cases, intensifying informational efforts can inadvertently spark further resistance. Engaging communities through empathetic dialogue and shared projects often proves more fruitful than bombarding them with uncontextualised data that feels confrontational or accusatory.

3.4.8 The weakness of market-driven solutions alone

At the heart of infophilia lies a belief in consumer-led market transformations. Yet certain structural transformations, like decarbonising energy systems or phasing out single-use plastic nationally, typically demand regulation, infrastructure investments and cross-sector collaboration (Stirling, 2014). While green consumer demand can nudge companies, waiting for voluntary shifts overlooks corporate profit motives and investor pressures that discourage adopting radical changes. Even informed consumers might struggle to catalyse large-scale overhauls if polluting practices remain cheaper or more profitable.

Additionally, market-driven changes often prove patchy and slow. Even where consumer demand for ecofriendly goods is substantial, it might not extend to essential sectors like heavy manufacturing or freight transport that remain invisible to average shoppers. A packaging company can brand its recycled plastic, whereas steel or cement industries receive less consumer scrutiny, continuing to emit at high levels. These complexities highlight that, although infophilia frames knowledge as a vehicle for consumer sovereignty, top-down policies frequently prove indispensable for rectifying structural externalities.

3.4.9 Corporate greenwashing and distracted policymaking

Businesses aiming to placate environmentally conscious consumers can engage in greenwashing by emphasising minor 'sustainable' product lines while ignoring more significant corporate impacts (Boström & Klintman, 2019). A supermarket might tout its organic fruit section but still encourage extensive packaging in the rest of its products; a multinational fashion brand may highlight a small 'eco-collection' but maintain a fast-fashion model for the bulk of its inventory. The proliferation of nominally ecofriendly branding and data-laden promotional materials can confound consumer judgments, especially if government oversight is weak.

Policymakers, meanwhile, can become overly enamoured with consumer education programmes, investing public funds in awareness campaigns rather than addressing the more challenging terrain of regulated emissions standards or infrastructural shifts (John et al., 2016). This policy distraction emerges when officials prefer politically palatable approaches, such as marketing sustainability, over interventions that might face opposition from powerful industry lobbies. Consequently, while the myth of infophilia offers the comfort of 'democratic' consumer choice, it may, in practice, stall the political momentum needed for more ambitious legislation.

3.4.10 Lessons from behavioural economics, sociology and evolutionary theory

Synthesising insights from various fields demonstrates that consumption patterns are emergent phenomena shaped by structural, socio-cultural and psychological factors (Caniglia et al., 2021). Behavioural economics emphasises the role of heuristics and nudges, indicating that consumers often need structured defaults or well-designed incentives – rather than mere facts – to adopt more sustainable options (Thaler & Sunstein, 2008). Social psychology points to interpersonal influence, showing that norms spread most effectively through group identity and peer acceptance (Cialdini et al., 1990). Evolutionary perspectives on social motivation argue that people can respond more to immediate social rewards or penalties than abstract knowledge about long-term ecological risks (Klintman, 2013).

In each of these domains, pure information campaigns often appear insufficient. To engender broad changes, a combination of supportive infrastructure, institutional regulations, cultural framing and community leadership is more consequential than simply expanding awareness (Parekh & Klintman, 2020). Infophilia, therefore, is best seen not as misguided in principle – since information is a critical resource – but as an incomplete strategy that, if relied upon exclusively, perpetuates myths about how and why consumers act.

3.5 Implications

Shifting from the myth of 'if only consumers knew more' to actionable change requires a three-part pivot: (1) design rules and fiscal nudges that set sustainable defaults; (2) business models that profit from durability and shared use and (3) community practices that normalise repair, reuse and low-waste habits. The pages that follow translate these insights into concrete steps for the actors who shape everyday consumption – governments, firms and citizens.

3.5.1 Implications for policymakers

Laws, not logos, move material flows at scale. By embedding durability, repairability and clear liability into product markets, governments can unlock climate and resource gains that no label alone can deliver.

This has been seen in, for instance

- France's Repairability Index – since 2021, laptops, smartphones and other electronics must carry a colour-coded 1–10 repair score. Early monitoring shows spare-part availability doubling in several product categories within three years (Ministère de la Transition Écologique, 2024).
- Chile's black stop-sign nutrient warnings – mandatory front-of-pack labels introduced in 2016 cut purchases of high-sugar drinks by 24% in the first two years, demonstrating the power of simple, binary cues (--Taillie et al., 2020).
- EU Right-to-Repair Directive (Directive (EU) 2024/1799) – adopted in 2024, it obliges manufacturers to offer affordable repairs for nine common appliance groups for up to ten years after purchase, giving consumers a statutory right to choose repair over replacement (European Union, 2024).

3.5.2 Implications for businesses

Firms that switch from 'green storytelling' to service- and circular-based offerings capture new revenue streams while future-proofing against stricter regulation. Here are some examples:

- Patagonia's *Worn Wear* – by refurbishing and reselling more than 120,000 garments annually, Patagonia extends product life by up to 60% and opens a profitable second-hand channel (Batten, 2020).
- Signify's 'Pay-per-Lux' contracts – clients pay for light, not bulbs. Signify retains ownership of fixtures, designs them for disassembly and takes them back at the end of use, capturing material value and ensuring upgrades (Ellen MacArthur Foundation, 2022).
- IKEA leasing pilots – in Switzerland and select EU markets, customers can rent *kitchens* or office furniture; returned items are refurbished and re-rented, advancing the retailer's goal to be 100% circular by 2030 (IKEA, 2019).

3.5.3 Implications for consumers and civil society

When infrastructures support it, citizens enthusiastically swap passive eco-labelling for active, communal sufficiency – repairing, sharing and refilling. Here are just a few examples.

- Repair Cafés – more than 3,000 volunteer workshops across 43 countries logged nearly 70,000 electronic repair attempts in the past year, proving an appetite for hands-on fixes (Open Repair Alliance, 2024).
- The Buy Nothing Project – about 12 million participants and 1.6 million app downloads have built hyper-local gift economies where neighbours trade rather than buy goods (Feser, 2025).
- Waitrose 'Unpacked' refill zones – sales of loose and refill products rose by up to 20% when the UK retailer integrated bulk stations directly into aisles, showing that hassle-free design beats information overload (Waitrose, 2021).

Across all three arenas, the pattern is clear: information works best as the *last metre* of change, not the first. Structural incentives, service models and shared norms create contexts in which the 'right' choice is also the easy, affordable and socially rewarded one. Once those conditions are in place, lean, intelligible information – one repair score, one warning label, one QR code – can sharpen decisions rather than drown them in data.

3.6 Main message

The myth of infophilia centres on an overestimation of knowledge as the key driver of environmental reform, suggesting that once consumers understand the ecological impacts of products and lifestyles, they will automatically 'choose green'. Research in social psychology, behavioural economics and sociology shows that while information is essential, real change requires structural, infrastructural and systemic reforms combined with shared cultural norms. Overemphasising consumer awareness can perpetuate greenwashing, obscure inequities and divert attention from necessary regulations and collective action. Moving beyond infophilia involves aligning informed consumers with robust policies, corporate accountability and supportive social contexts, ensuring that sustainable options become both cognitively desirable and practically and normatively ingrained.

References

Archer, M. S. (2013). *Social origins of educational systems*. Routledge.

Batten, D. (2020). *Patagonia Worn Wear Program*. Circular X. https://www.circularx.eu/en/cases/34/patagonia-worn-wear-program

BEUC – The European Consumer Organisation. (2023, December). *The Great Green Maze: How environmental advertising confuses consumers*. BEUC-X-2023–149. https://www.beuc.eu/sites/default/files/publications/BEUC-X-2023-149_The_Great_Green_Maze_How_environmental_advertising_confuses_consumers.pdf

Boström, M., & Klintman, M. (2019). Can we rely on 'climate-friendly' consumption? *Journal of Consumer Culture*, *19*(3), 359–378.

Caniglia, G., Luederitz, C., von Wirth, T., Fazey, I., Martín-López, B., Hondrila, K., & Lang, D. J. (2021). A pluralistic and integrated approach to action-oriented knowledge for sustainability. *Nature Sustainability*, *4*(2), 93–100.

Cialdini, R. B., Reno, R. R., & Kallgren, C. A. (1990). A focus theory of normative conduct: Recycling the concept of norms to reduce littering in public places. *Journal of Personality and Social Psychology*, *58*(6), 1015.

Ecolabel Index. (2025). *All ecolabels in Europe on food*. The independent global directory of ecolabels and environmental certification schemes. https://www.ecolabelindex.com/ecolabels/?st=%3Bcategory%3Dfood%3Bregion%3Deurope

Ellen MacArthur Foundation. (2017). *A new textiles economy: Redesigning fashion's future*. Ellen MacArthur Foundation. https://www.ellenmacarthurfoundation.org/a-new-textiles-economy

Ellen MacArthur Foundation. (2022). *Why buy light bulbs when you can buy light? Signify*.https://www.ellenmacarthurfoundation.org/circular-examples/why-buy-light-bulbs-when-you-can-buy-light-signify

European Commission, Joint Research Centre (JRC). (2023). *Assessment of sustainability labels for food* [Dataset]. http://data.europa.eu/89h/b73d87af-9008-4d59-b578-f0e36c300446

European Union. (2024). *Directive (EU) 2024/1799 of the European Parliament and of the Council of 13 June 2024 on common rules promoting the repair of goods*. Official Journal of the European Union. https://eur-lex.europa.eu/eli/dir/2024/1799/oj

Fazey, I., Schäpke, N., Caniglia, G., Patterson, J., Hultman, J., Van Mierlo, B., & Wyborn, C. (2020). Transforming knowledge systems for life on Earth: Visions of future systems and how to get there. *Energy Research & Social Science*, *70*, 101724.

Feser, K. (2025, January 2). With the new year coming, some Houston shoppers vow to buy nothing. *Houston Chronicle*. https://www.houstonchronicle.com/business/article/buy-nothing-challenge-2025-20007232.php

Florence, K. Y., Acheampong, A., Oteng-Ababio, M., & Tagbor, T. A. (2022). Sustainable consumption and production in Ghana: Social actors and institutional dynamics. *Local Environment*, *27*(1), 94–107.

Hamilton, C., & Denniss, R. (2005). *Affluenza: When too much is never enough*. Allen & Unwin.

Husic, M., & Cicic, M. (2009). Luxury consumption factors. *Journal of Fashion Marketing and Management: An International Journal*, *13*(2), 231–245.

IKEA. (2019). *IKEA will test furniture leasing in 30 markets during 2020*. https://www.ikea.com/us/en/newsroom/corporate-news/ikea-will-test-furniture-leasing-in-30-markets-during-2020-pub1d2281d7/

Ivanova, D., Stadler, K., Steen-Olsen, K., Wood, R., Vita, G., Tukker, A., & Hertwich, E. G. (2016). Environmental impact assessment of household consumption. *Journal of Industrial Ecology*, *20*(3), 526–536.

Jasanoff, S. (2018). Just transitions: A humble approach to global energy futures. *Energy Research & Social Science*, *35*, 11–14.

John, P., Smith, G., & Stoker, G. (2016). Nudge nudge, think think: Two strategies for changing civic behaviour. *The Political Quarterly*, *80*(3), 361–370.

Klintman, M. (2013). *Citizen-consumers and evolution*. Palgrave.

Klintman, M. (2019). *Knowledge resistance: How we avoid insight from others*. Manchester University Press.

Klintman, M. (2025). *Framing: The social art of influence*. Manchester University Press.

Mengistie, B., Mol, A. P., & Oosterveer, P. (2017). Private environmental governance in the Ethiopian pesticide supply chain: Importation, distribution and use. *NJAS–Wageningen Journal of Life Sciences*, *80*, 65–73.

Ministère de la Transition Écologique. (2024). *Indice de réparabilité*. https://www.ecologie.gouv.fr/politiques-publiques/indice-reparabilite

Nisa, C. F., Bélanger, J. J., Schumpe, B. M., & Faller, D. G. (2019). Meta-analysis of randomised controlled trials testing behavioural interventions to promote household action on climate change. *Nature Communications*, *10*(1), 4545.

Open Repair Alliance. (2024). *The rise of community repair: The people and the data creating a movement*. https://therestartproject.org/data-and-insights/research/repair-day-2024/

Parekh, V., & Klintman, M. (2020). The practice approach in practice: Lessons for Civil Society Organizations (CSOs) that work towards sustainable food consumption in Sweden. *Sustainable Production and Consumption*, 1–40.

Persson, O., & Klintman, M. (2020). Framing sufficiency: Strategies of environmental non-governmental organisations towards reduced material consumption. *Journal of Consumer Culture*, 1–20.

Schwartz, S. H. (2012). An overview of the Schwartz theory of basic values. *Online Readings in Psychology and Culture*, *2*(1), 2307–0919.

Shove, E., & Walker, G. (2014). What is energy for? Social practice and energy demand. *Theory, Culture & Society*, *31*(5), 41–58.
Simis, M. J., Madden, H., Cacciatore, M. A., & Yeo, S. K. (2016). The lure of rationality: Why does the deficit model persist in science communication? *Public Understanding of Science*, *25*(4), 400–414.
Stern, P. C. (2000). Toward a coherent theory of environmentally significant behavior. *Journal of Social Issues*, *56*(3), 407–424.
Stirling, A. (2014). Transforming power: Social science and the politics of energy choices. *Energy Research & Social Science*, *1*, 83–95.
Taillie, L. S., Reyes, M., Colchero, M. A., Popkin, B. M., & Corvalán, C. (2020). An evaluation of Chile's law of food labeling and advertising on sugar-sweetened beverage purchases from 2015 to 2017: A before--and---after study-. *PLOS Medicine*, *17*(2), e1003015. https://doi.org/10.1371/journal.pmed.1003015
Thaler, R. H., & Sunstein, C. R. (2008). *Nudge: Improving decisions about health, wealth, and happiness*. Yale University Press.
Thøgersen, J., & Ölander, F. (2002). Human values and the emergence of a sustainable consumption pattern: A panel study. *Journal of Economic Psychology*, *23*(5), 605–630.
Waitrose. (2021, June 1). *Waitrose 'Unpacked' sales grow as demand for refillables rises*. John Lewis Partnership. https://www.johnlewispartnership.co.uk/media/press/y2021/waitrose-unpacks-more-products.html
Weinmann, M., Schneider, C., & vom Brocke, J. (2016). Digital nudging. *Business & Information Systems Engineering*, *58*(6), 433–436.

4

MYTH 3

Shopping is the perfect therapy – consumption offers lasting happiness

Oksana Mont and Ella Baybikova

4.1 Myth

The myth that 'shopping is the perfect therapy' is based on the belief that purchasing items can act as an effective emotional remedy. According to this view, making purchases provides instant comfort, helps reduce stress and can even lead to lasting happiness. Because it seems harmless and self-directed, many people turn to shopping, whether online or in-store, as an acceptable way to cope with boredom or anxiety (Rick et al., 2014).

However, this myth has serious consequences for sustainability efforts. It presents shopping as a normal and sensible way to deal with stress. However, the relief it offers is temporary and often comes at the cost of deeper practices and skills that encourage lasting well-being, such as mindfulness, reflection and strong relationships. Instead of tackling the underlying causes of emotional distress, retail therapy creates a self-perpetuating cycle. Each round pushes individuals towards external goals like status and wealth, while distancing them further from personal growth and meaningful personal and community connections.

Simultaneously, the brief emotional boost that shopping provides often conceals the broader environmental and social costs linked to our consumer habits. It contributes to issues such as climate change, economic inequality and social isolation, all of which cycle back into the stress and insecurity that motivate us to shop initially. This cycle makes it more difficult to adopt sufficiency-focused lifestyles that emphasise contentment and well-being beyond material possessions. Challenging the myth that shopping is the ideal remedy is therefore essential, not only to break individual overconsumption patterns but also to facilitate cultural and systemic transformations towards

DOI: 10.4324/9781003613718-6

sustainable living and collective resilience. But, where does this widespread belief originate from?

4.2 Origins

The concept of 'retail therapy' is linked to the rise of consumer culture after World War II, especially in Western societies. Conspicuous consumption had long served as a way for the wealthy to enjoy leisure and express themselves, as Thorstein Veblen demonstrated *in The Theory of the Leisure Class* (1899/2017). The post-war economic boom expanded these habits to the middle and working classes. Increased stability and access to goods made material comfort widespread. Consumption shifted from basic needs to satisfying desires, enjoying leisure, signalling status and regulating emotions. Baudrillard (1998) observed that shopping became a means of self-expression and emotional management.

A crucial part of this transformation was the growing role of consumption in shaping personal identity. While it has historically been recognised that possessions let individuals express themselves, this gained new importance in the mid- to late 20th century. As societies became more individualised and consumer culture expanded, people increasingly used material goods to communicate status, personality and aspirations (Belk, 1988). This extended beyond luxury items to include personal style, home décor and experience-based consumption like travel. Consumption became a key medium for self-representation, reinforcing social belonging and differentiating individuals. Today, this continues in digital spaces, where online personas and visible consumption on social media reflect and amplify similar identity-signalling behaviours (Belk, 2013).

The rise of dual-income households and changing time use, especially by women, fuelled this shift. As more women entered the workforce, they faced the double burden of paid work and unpaid domestic duties, known as 'the second shift' (Hochschild & Machung, 1989). This created time pressure and stress, making retail therapy a convenient self-care and escape from daily demands. Shopping, once routine, became an act of empowerment, particularly for time-strapped working mothers.

The advertising industry embedded retail therapy into culture by linking consumer goods to emotional rewards. Products were seen as paths to happiness, self-worth and validation (Packard, 1957). Slogans like 'Because you are worth it' reinforced shopping as a way to affirm value and aspirations (Ewen, 1974). Media and popular culture portrayed shopping as a socially acceptable response to life's challenges, especially in women's magazines and TV shows, which depicted it as a playful indulgence to lift spirits and soothe stress.

The rise of e-commerce and rapid tech in the late 20th and early 21st centuries integrated retail therapy into daily life. Online shopping made buying easy, quick and satisfying, with vast choices and fast delivery. However, personalised ads and subtle design nudges can exploit feelings and promote impulsive, sometimes harmful, spending (Gupta, 2022). Algorithms anticipating consumer preferences often target stress, boredom or emotional instability (Roy et al., 2024). These technologies expanded retail access but also deepened its emotional hold. So, what are the consequences of this development?

4.3 Consequences

The belief that shopping relieves stress and lifts moods is increasingly costly. This section shows how retail therapy fosters compulsive consumption, financial strain, environmental impacts and social inequality. These issues interact and reinforce each other, escalating the pressures to shop.

4.3.1 Rise in compulsive buying behaviours and consumption addiction

Retail therapy can temporarily boost mood but may lead to problematic behaviours like compulsive shopping, characterised by an obsession with buying unnecessary items (Müller et al., 2012). This issue is a growing public health concern worldwide. About 5% of US adults struggle with compulsive shopping, especially younger people and women (Black, 2022). International surveys show that 4–19% of the general population, shopping centre visitors and university students exhibit this behaviour (Otero-López, 2022).

Compulsive shopping often has deeper emotional causes. It can serve as a way to avoid uncomfortable feelings or unresolved problems. Research connects this behaviour to low self-esteem, a fragile sense of identity and the gap people perceive between who they are and who they aspire to be (Moulding et al., 2017). For example, someone who feels inadequate might purchase luxury goods to project success or confidence. However, the boost is temporary, and once it wears off, it often leaves individuals feeling worse than before, trapping them in a cycle of emotional spending.

The Internet and e-commerce boost impulsive buying by offering instant gratification through personalised suggestions, flash sales and 'buy now' buttons, prompting quick purchases. These tools target emotional weaknesses, especially when stressed or bored, making it hard to resist spending (Rose & Dhandayudham, 2014). Today, personal data can be used to target shopping during psychological vulnerability (Wynn-Williams, 2025). The COVID-19 pandemic worsened these tendencies, raising stress, isolation and boredom, leading more people to shop online (Zhao et al., 2022). Compulsive buying also increased, causing more financial and emotional strain (Kovács et al., 2022). This shows how global crises can heighten vulnerabilities and promote compulsive spending.

Simultaneously, a growing network of social commerce platforms is driving this trend. The US social commerce market, where consumers interact with brands, browse products and purchase directly via social media platforms like Instagram and TikTok, was valued at $89.1 billion in 2022. It is expected to grow by approximately 30% annually until 2030. Sellers of luxury goods openly admit that their success depends more on evoking emotions than fulfilling practical needs (GVR, 2025).

These developments reveal the complex link between emotional vulnerability, social influence and technology. What starts as a quick indulgence can spiral into regret, disappointment and distress, exposing the darker side of retail therapy in modern culture. It can also cause serious health issues, straining healthcare and social systems and raising societal costs.

4.3.2 Debt and financial strain

Compulsive purchasing often results in financial overextension, with emotional spending leading to unplanned purchases and debt. In 2023, the average US household credit card debt was $7,486, up from previous years (Federal Reserve, 2023). A study from 2022 found that 36% of Americans feel financially insecure due to debt, often stemming from retail spending. Interestingly, guilt and anxiety caused by debt can lead to more shopping as emotional relief, worsening the cycle (Madigan, 2025).

Economic inequality worsens these challenges. Middle- and upper-income people may shop to cope, but those with fewer resources often feel excluded from consumer culture, deepening inadequacy and social divides (Mandel et al., 2017). For low-income consumers, high-interest credit and predatory lending can worsen financial hardship, making retail therapy harmful.

Buy-now-pay-later (BNPL) services like Klarna and Afterpay add financial risk to retail therapy. They make purchases seem manageable by splitting payments, but often hide the true cost and lead individuals to spend beyond their means. A 2023 report found that 29% of UK BNPL users struggled to repay and borrowed to cover payments, increasing financial strain (Citizens Advice, 2023). Younger adults, especially those aged 18–34, are most affected, showing how easy credit tools can become problematic. The impacts of compulsive buying and rising personal debt extend beyond individuals, weakening financial resilience, raising loan defaults and straining banks and social safety nets. Thus, individuals' emotional spending can become a public risk.

4.3.3 Environmental impacts

The environmental impact of retail therapy is equally significant. Increasing consumption places immense strain on natural resources, raises carbon emissions and exacerbates the waste crisis. The production of most consumer goods has shifted to Asian countries owing to lower labour costs. However, this often involves exploitative working conditions, long hours, and leads to severe environmental degradation in the least developed regions (Saxena, 2019). The real cost of inexpensive goods is frequently borne in human exploitation and environmental impact, far from the consumers who enjoy the benefits of shopping.

Environmental and social costs are especially visible in sectors like fashion, where retail therapy impacts are intense. Ultra-fast fashion exemplifies this with brands like Shein and Zara producing cheap, disposable clothing through high-speed models. Zara launches 24 collections annually, while Shein added 315,000 styles in 2022 (Guardian, 2025). These rapid cycles drive constant buying. Over 15 years, clothing purchases increased 60%, but items are worn half as long (McKinsey & Company, 2022).

Rapid consumption drives resource use and waste, causing water pollution, soil degradation, deforestation and biodiversity loss. End-of-life product disposal worsens these issues. The Ellen MacArthur Foundation (2021) states that over 73% of textiles are incinerated or landfilled, with less than 1% recycled. The European Environment Agency (EEA, 2022) reports that the average European produces 530 kg of waste annually, mainly from packaging. High consumption and short product lifespans are key factors.

Retail therapy's environmental impact creates a paradox. On the one hand, climate change heightens social anxiety, especially among young people, with many feeling powerless and overwhelmed by eco-anxiety (Hickman et al., 2021). Ironically, this anxiety prompts individuals to shop for comfort, but that short-term relief worsens environmental damage, perpetuating a cycle: anxiety boosts consumption, which exacerbates the crisis causing it.

The normalisation of shopping as a leisure activity has woven consumption into daily life. In many areas, shopping centres have replaced public spaces like parks or libraries, providing emotional comfort and social opportunities. In the United States alone, over 1,500 enclosed malls were built between 1956 and 2006, establishing them firmly as recreational hubs (Lewis & Dart, 2014). However, in the past decade, retail therapy has shifted from shopping centres to the digital world. By 2024, internet sales comprised more than 17% of global retail; forecasts indicate that this will grow to over 21% by 2029 (Coppola, 2025). The ease of instant access and ultra-fast delivery encourages impulsive buying while increasing emissions from packaging, warehousing and last-mile logistics.

4.4 Dispelling the myth

The idea that shopping provides lasting happiness and stress relief is a myth in consumer culture. Here we present counterarguments, based on recent research in psychology, sociology and sustainable consumption, showing why retail therapy often fails to deliver the emotional benefits promised.

4.4.1 The fleeting happiness of shopping

Like many myths, there is some truth to shopping providing temporary emotional relief. Buying new items offers a quick emotional boost, but it is fleeting and seldom leads to lasting satisfaction. Research on hedonic adaptation shows that people quickly return to their baseline well-being after both positive and negative events (Brickman & Campbell, 1971). In his book *Shiny Objects: Why We Spend Money We Don't Have in Search of Happiness We Can't Buy*, James A. Roberts (2011) explores this phenomenon in detail, introducing the concept of the 'treadmill of consumption' as a pattern of repeated spending driven by the false promise of happiness. Drawing on psychological and sociological research, he explains that while materialistic values are reinforced by cultural norms and marketing messages, they rarely deliver on their emotional promise. The happiness gained through consumption is short-lived, leaving individuals on a treadmill of repeated buying and persistent dissatisfaction.

This cycle of fleeting highs and inevitable lows is also reflected in the way the brain responds to shopping. Retail therapy begins with a desire to feel better, driven by the brain's reward system. In her book *Dopamine Nation: Finding Balance in the Age of Indulgence*, Anna Lembke (2021) explains that anticipating and making a purchase releases dopamine, a hormone linked to pleasure. However, this response is short-lived; dopamine levels plummet afterwards, leaving people feeling drained, irritable or emotionally flat. Lembke compares shopping to compulsive behaviours like gambling and overeating, illustrating a cycle of a brief high followed by a low. Post-purchase crashes often lead to regret, guilt and stress, especially when motivated by emotion rather than necessity. This 'consumption hangover' demonstrates that shopping can be a form of emotional self-sabotage. Koles et al. (2018) reveal that impulsive buying undermines self-esteem, reinforcing feelings of inadequacy. Retail therapy may therefore increase emotional vulnerability instead of fostering resilience. Supportive studies include Sneath et al. (2009), who found that 62% of impulse buyers regret their purchases, and Zhang et al. (2017), who linked compulsive buying, particularly online, to negative feelings and financial troubles. The pursuit of comfort often deepens discomfort.

Online shopping amplifies the emotional cycle by focusing more on the experience of browsing, selecting and waiting, rather than owning. Features like personalised recommendations, flash sales and one-click purchases create a seamless, stimulating environment that encourages continuous engagement. Gamification elements, such as daily check-ins, countdowns and reward points, deepen user involvement. For example, Temu uses casino-style features to promote compulsive behaviour and extend usage (Zhang, 2025). Fast delivery also reinforces this cycle by arriving before the emotional dip subsides, prompting repeated shopping. Consequently, many items remain unopened or forgotten, as shopping becomes a mood regulation tool rather than a material necessity.

This dynamic is neither accidental nor incidental. It is intentionally reinforced by the design of digital retail systems and the logic of consumer capitalism. As Sanne (2005) argues, advertising promotes 'organised dissatisfaction', a strategy that keeps consumers constantly wanting. The emotional promise of products is deliberately made fleeting. Planned obsolescence, ever-changing trends and emotional marketing contribute to a culture where satisfaction is momentary and fades quickly, encouraging renewed desire. The treadmill effect, therefore, is not merely psychological but systemic (Roberts, 2011).

Popular culture promotes the emotional appeal of consumption. In Confessions of a Shopaholic, the protagonist says, 'If everyone could just wear new clothes every day, I reckon depression wouldn't exist anymore'. This humorously suggests that emotional well-being can be purchased. However, studies in positive psychology show that pursuing intrinsic goals like meaningful relationships, personal growth and community contribution leads to higher well-being and resilience (Ryan & Deci, 2019). Retail therapy often channels emotional energy into external rewards but leaves these deeper needs unmet, resulting in short-term regret and long-term dissatisfaction.

4.4.2 Retail therapy perpetuates emotional dependency and weakens self-development

At the core of the retail therapy, myth is the belief that shopping can enhance emotional well-being and personal growth. In reality, using consumption as a coping strategy often results in emotional avoidance and dependency. Instead of tackling the underlying causes of distress, such as stress, insecurity or a lack of direction, it provides a temporary distraction through material possessions. Over time, this pattern can weaken emotional resilience and hinder authentic self-development.

Psychological theories of compensatory consumption explain how this cycle occurs. Dittmar (2005) states that people often buy to bridge the gap between their real and ideal selves. Shopping becomes a way to project confidence, success or attractiveness when these feelings are lacking. Although such purchases may offer temporary comfort, they do not address underlying emotional issues. They trap people in a pattern of seeking external validation, making them emotionally dependent and unchanged.

Anthropological research questions the idea that shopping promotes self-development. Lane (2024), studying professional organising, describes 'wishful shopping', where people buy items symbolising aspirational lifestyles or identities they cannot realistically attain. Overwhelmed by work or emotions, they buy books they will never read or clothes for lifestyles they do not genuinely live. These items represent imagined futures, standing in for the time, energy or courage needed for real change. Social media often worsens self-worth by showcasing curated success and beauty, linking it to materialism. Shopping becomes a performance for validation, heightening comparison, self-doubt and reliance on goods to define identity.

To challenge the myth that shopping supports self-development, we should shift focus from material symbols to psychological practice and social experiences. Research on voluntary simplicity and minimalism shows that releasing dependence on possessions can lead to self-awareness, emotional clarity and autonomy (Schreurs, 2010). People in no-buy challenges describe the experience as freeing, gaining control and identity beyond possessions (Chawla et al., 2023). True self-development is more than making purchases; it involves cultivating intrinsic motivation and investing in ourselves, others and individual and community growth-promoting experiences.

In *The Day the World Stops Shopping*, MacKinnon (2021) describes communities worldwide practising voluntary simplicity. From rural Japan to urban North America, people who consume less often report greater emotional grounding, stronger social bonds and a more profound sense of presence. These findings challenge the idea that well-being depends on material wealth. Japanese traditions offer instructive alternatives, such as Ikigai, or 'reason for being', which emphasises purpose, social connections and meaningful activities. In Okinawa, one of the longest-living populations, Ikigai is rooted in community, daily rituals and personal fulfilment (García & Miralles, 2020). During difficult times, having a clear purpose provides emotional stability that shopping cannot offer.

Complementary traditions emphasise values that oppose disposability and emotional substitution through consumption, serving as positive examples for more materialistic cultures. Wabi-Sabi honours imperfection and the value of what already exists (Juniper, 2011). Kintsugi, repairing pottery with gold, shows that flaws can be beautiful rather than reasons for replacement (Kumai, 2018). These challenge the 'newness' culture underlying modern consumption, suggesting well-being arises from acceptance, continuity and care. Shinrin-Yoku, or forest bathing, encourages quiet immersion in nature without digital distraction. It reduces stress and cortisol levels and improves emotional balance (Hunter et al., 2019). Unlike fleeting retail therapy, forest bathing builds emotional resilience over time, demonstrating how simple practices can meet emotional needs more sustainably than shopping.

4.4.3 Retail therapy increases ownership burdens and time stress

What we buy for comfort or self-expression can become an unseen burden. While purchasing may feel rewarding, owning and maintaining those possessions often adds quite a burden over time. Instead of relief, retail therapy items can cause stress, demanding time and attention and displacing more meaningful activities. What is marketed as self-care often results in greater strain, increasing responsibilities instead of easing them.

Sociological and psychological research shows that consumption shapes our environments and use of time. Items like clothes, gadgets and appliances require storage, cleaning, maintenance and disposal, which can cut into time for leisure, reflection and relationships (Southerton, 2020). For example, owning more clothes involves hours of washing, ironing and decision-making – time that could be used for personal growth, rest and well-being.

These challenges are exacerbated by planned obsolescence, where products are designed with short lifespans. This increases waste and traps consumers in repair and replacement cycles (Mont, 2008). This creates time pressure: the more we own, the more we do. Instead of reducing consumption, many respond by upsizing – buying larger homes or storage to hide clutter. But these strategies do not address overaccumulation. Lane (2024) notes that possessions often carry emotional baggage like guilt or obligation, making them hard to let go of. Items bought for comfort can cause psychological and time strain. Kasser (2002) found that material accumulation is linked to higher stress and lower satisfaction. In contrast, minimalists often report clearer priorities, more free time and emotional clarity. Owning less relieves clutter and the burden of managing it.

Japanese cultural traditions offer a different view on ownership. Rather than linking identity to possessions, these customs, shaped by limited space and frequent natural disasters, emphasise impermanence, care and restraint. The aesthetic of Ma, or intentional emptiness, values objects and the space around them. It opposes the Western idea of comfort through abundance, instead promoting balance, presence and deliberate living (Peters, 2019). These values foster a lifestyle that alleviates material and temporal burdens.

Community initiatives demonstrate that reducing ownership alleviates stress (Mont, 2025). Tool libraries, car-sharing schemes, repair cafés and upcycling efforts help meet needs without full ownership, sharing responsibility and fostering skills, community bonds and sustainability. They challenge the notion that possessing more leads to a better life, viewing ownership as a responsibility rather than a reward. Retail therapy does not end at the checkout; its effects persist, influencing well-being. Debunking this myth promotes a slower lifestyle that values freedom and care over consumption and accumulation.

4.4.4 'Consumption detox': real well-being begins where shopping ends

The final argument that debunks the myth is that more and more people are rejecting the idea that consumption leads to well-being, opting instead to explore the psychological benefits of consuming less. Engaging in a consumption detox, through minimalism, mindfulness or voluntary simplicity, may provide a more sustainable path to emotional health. Many try 30-day no-buy challenges, avoiding non-essential purchases for a month. Many people undertake 30-day no-buy challenges, avoiding non-essential purchases for a month. Although for many, the primary motivation for a consumption detox is often financial, individuals also report additional benefits such as increased appreciation for possessions, mental clarity and a greater sense of control over their lives (Chawla et al., 2023). Research supports these experiences. Kasser (2002) shows that living with less can boost autonomy and emotional health. Minimalism, inspired by methods like Marie Kondo's KonMari, can reduce mental load and improve focus (Callmer, 2019). These lifestyle changes help people find more meaningful, lasting fulfilment by moving away from material validation.

Complementing these lifestyle changes, mindfulness-based practices, often regarded as separate from consumption, can play a powerful role in breaking the cycle of retail therapy. Techniques such as gratitude journaling, yoga, breathwork and meditation are supported by strong clinical evidence as effective methods to manage anxiety and depression (Prathikanti et al., 2017; Kumar et al., 2019; Kaushik et al., 2020). Despite this, such practices are sometimes dismissed as niche or excessively gendered, particularly in male-dominated spheres like politics and corporate leadership. This scepticism has hindered their broader adoption and obscured their potential to foster emotional regulation and resilience – the qualities that shopping cannot provide.

Together, these practices highlight that well-being emerges not from buying but from non-material sources of happiness. Strong relationships, meaningful activities and community involvement foster lasting emotional fulfilment. Spending time with loved ones, pursuing passions or community involvement fosters emotional fulfilment beyond material gains. Positive social interactions release oxytocin, reducing stress and enhancing emotional stability. Thus, reducing consumption is empowering, not a sacrifice. Community initiatives such as no-buy months, decluttering workshops and repair cafés offer simple, collective ways to reconnect with these values, promoting sufficiency, mindfulness, care and intentional living.

Expanding the idea of a consumption detox – through digital breaks or mindful choices – also challenges the notion that well-being is bought. Shopping second-hand, repairing or simplifying homes help reclaim time, lower anxiety and resist consumerism. These steps support sustainability and boost psychological clarity and autonomy. Dismantling retail therapy means rethinking consumption as a comfort-seeking habit masking more profound distress. Embracing mindfulness, sufficiency and social bonds creates a path benefiting both emotional health and environmental sustainability.

4.5 Implications

4.5.1 Implications for policymakers

Policymakers play a crucial role in challenging the origins of the retail therapy myth and reshaping societal expectations regarding well-being. Instead of reinforcing consumption as a way to cope, policy can support preventative strategies that encourage sustainable lifestyles and mental health resilience (Barry et al., 2024). This involves investing in initiatives that promote emotional well-being, such as community-building, access to nature and education about mindfulness, without fostering consumer dependency.

Instead of concentrating mainly on reactive health interventions, policymakers should broaden preventive care strategies that address the root causes of stress, such as financial insecurity, social isolation and limited access to mental health support (WHO, 2023). By tackling these underlying pressures, governments can reduce reliance on consumption-based coping mechanisms. Well-designed programmes that alleviate societal stressors not only enhance individual well-being but may also assist in reducing patterns of compulsive consumption.

Public health policies should include mindfulness, emotional resilience and stress management. Policymakers can support this by endorsing non-material approaches like subsidised yoga, meditation and the arts. Funding for emotional regulation and stress management initiatives offers alternatives to consumer-driven coping. For example, in Sweden, gym memberships benefit from a reduced VAT of 6%, compared to 25%, but this excludes slower practices like yoga and meditation. Updating tax policies to include these activities would encourage sustainable, non-material stress management and reduce emotional dependence on consumption.

A strong sense of belonging and social connection can also reduce reliance on retail therapy. Policymakers can promote this by investing in community support systems like local clubs, volunteer networks and recreational spaces that foster personal growth and fulfilment. Funding parks, libraries and cultural centres offers meaningful experiences that encourage connection and well-being without consumption (Frontier Economics, 2024).

Since financial and social pressures lead to shopping as stress relief, policymakers should focus on reducing economic stress with measures like income stability, affordable housing and stronger healthcare. Policies such as minimum wages, fair labour standards and social safety nets can reduce financial strain that fuels overconsumption (Akenji et al., 2021).

Raising awareness about the psychological impacts of consumerism can empower people to make more mindful choices. Policymakers can support public education campaigns that teach financial literacy, highlight the emotional drivers of consumption and promote mindfulness in everyday decision-making (Daniel et al., 2024). By utilising social media and free platforms like YouTube, these campaigns can reach large audiences with engaging, accessible content that explains both the environmental and psychological costs of overconsumption. Education can be a powerful tool for shifting norms and helping individuals find healthier, more sustainable ways to meet their emotional needs, especially when combined with other policy measures.

Advertising also plays a vital role in perpetuating the retail therapy myth by framing consumption as the key to happiness. To address this, policymakers should enhance advertising regulations, especially for digital advertising and sectors like fast fashion, consumer electronics and other impulse-driven industries. Updated guidelines can help curb manipulative marketing tactics that promote unnecessary purchases. Additionally, transparency standards should be introduced for campaigns that utilise psychological nudges, scarcity cues or emotional appeals to stimulate compulsive consumption. Making these strategies visible enables consumers to make more informed choices and challenges the illusion that buying leads to well-being. Building on this, policymakers should also consider banning fossil fuel advertising entirely, as such bans can undermine the legitimacy of carbon-heavy consumption norms and symbolically shift public discourse towards more sustainable lifestyles (Bouman et al., 2025).

4.5.2 Implications for businesses

Businesses, especially in retail and advertising, influence consumer behaviour and have historically promoted the retail therapy myth. As more people prioritise well-being, sustainability and mindful living, companies stuck in outdated models risk irrelevance. Those who adapt can gain new advantages (Mont et al., 2025). Shifting from immediate gratification to long-term value fosters loyalty and boosts reputation. Marketing focusing on intrinsic values, like personal growth, environmental responsibility and community, can redefine aspirational consumption in a post-retail-therapy world.

Companies in sectors like hospitality, education, digital content and recreation are well-placed to serve a growing market of consumers seeking meaningful experiences over material possessions. By offering services that enhance well-being, such as wellness programmes, skill-building workshops or experience-based packages, these businesses can tap into a profitable and values-driven shift in consumer demand. Retailers, too, can adapt by focusing on durable, high-quality products that support conscious consumption (Elf et al., 2021). Meanwhile, subscription-based and service-oriented models may provide steady revenue without relying on constant production or aggressive sales cycles (Mont, 2025). These strategies not only respond to changing preferences but may also help decouple business success from unsustainable consumption.

Businesses can also support well-being by partnering with educational, mental health and social groups. Collaborations promoting financial literacy, stress management and life skills position companies as well-being leaders. For example, financial firms can create responsible spending products, while tech firms can develop platforms focused on education and connection rather than addiction. This shift is evident; in 2021, major US pharmacy chains started offering mental health services, showing how traditional retailers can embed well-being into their core offerings (Caron, 2021).

As retail therapy loses appeal, businesses must rethink value propositions to stay relevant. If consumer behaviour shifts from impulse buys to well-being choices, success depends on meaningful engagement rather than sales volume. Competitive advantage may come from personalised experiences, sustainable models and products with long-term value (Mont, 2025). Purpose-driven companies can stand out by aligning with consumers' desires for fulfilment, sustainability and emotional health (Annemans et al., 2024). This opens opportunities in wellness, experiential services, sustainable fashion and tech-based well-being tools to redefine aspirational consumption as both profitable and socially responsible.

4.5.3 Implications for the public

Consumers must re-evaluate what truly brings happiness, moving from material fixes to sustainable sources like mindfulness, personal development and community. Recognising psychological triggers behind compulsive buying helps break the cycle and foster genuine well-being. When supported by policy and business, this shift can improve our cultural view of well-being.

Spending on experiences rather than material goods increases happiness, as experiential purchases create lasting memories and satisfaction linked to brain reward systems (Aknin et al., 2018). Activities like cultural events foster connection and reduce reliance on material possessions. However, some experiences, like travel, can harm the environment. To enjoy these benefits responsibly, people may opt for low-impact alternatives like local trips, public transit or nature time. Being mindful of social and ecological impacts can boost well-being responsibly.

Adopting anti-consumption practices allows consumers to oppose retail therapy harms by rejecting unnecessary purchases, avoiding conflicting brands and choosing sustainable options. This reduces material dependence, boosting autonomy, emotional resilience and life satisfaction (Lee & Ahn, 2016). Activities like repair cafés, second-hand shopping or 'buy nothing' movements help align behaviour with sustainability and ease ecological grief

(Lee et al., 2020). Learning new skills for growth, career or community builds resilience, purpose, agency and connection beyond consumption.

As discussed earlier, digital consumption links to impulsive shopping and materialism. Constant exposure to targeted ads, influencer content and algorithms can undermine self-control, reduce self-esteem and lead to unnecessary spending (Anderson et al., 2024). Digital detoxes, like limiting screen time and engaging in offline hobbies, help regain control. Stepping back from digital cues promotes healthier relationships with consumption and fosters mindful spending. Offline activities such as reading, nature, sports or face-to-face interactions offer fulfilling alternatives that do not necessarily rely on material goods.

A digital wellness movement has emerged amid widespread digitalisation, offering tools and guidance to disconnect from technology. Digital wellness retreats, which eliminate device use, provide opportunities for mindfulness, nature and reflection (Jansson & Adams, 2021). Participants often report less stress, better sleep and more emotional resilience – outcomes contrary to digital life's restless consumption. These retreats help recalibrate attention and foster meaningful connections, countering the digital saturation that fuels consumerism.

Yoga also offers a structured path to emotional well-being and self-awareness through practices like breathwork, meditation and deliberate movement. It helps recognise emotional triggers and develop healthier coping strategies. Central to yoga, especially Santosha (contentment), is finding happiness within rather than external validation. Studies show yoga reduces stress hormones like cortisol, regulates dopamine and supports emotional stability (Pascoe et al., 2017). Breathwork like pranayama offers time for reflection, helping individuals pause before acting on emotional urges, such as shopping. Yin yoga's long poses allow tension to surface and be released, providing an alternative to retail therapy. Small habits like mindful breathing before purchasing can strengthen self-control. Daily yoga fosters resilience and nurtures a sense of fulfilment beyond material possessions.

4.6 Main message

The myth that shopping offers emotional relief and happiness masks its true psychological, social and environmental costs. Retail therapy can lead to emotional dependence, impede personal growth and increase stress from handling excess. It distracts from genuine personal fulfilment, such as relationships and meaningful goals, trapping individuals in cycles of avoidance and regret. Challenging this myth is vital for building resilience and fostering societal shifts towards sufficiency, well-being and sustainability. Replacing consumption with practices that encourage emotional independence and connection helps individuals and societies move towards more balanced and meaningful lives.

References

Akenji, L., Bengtsson, M., Toivio, V., Lettenmeier, M., Fawcett, T., Parag, Y., Saheb, Y., Coote, A., Spangenberg, J., Capstick, S., Gore, T., Coscieme, L., Wackernagel, M., & Kenner, D. (2021). *1.5-degree lifestyles: Towards a fair consumption space for all* (p. 209). Hot or Cool Institute.

Aknin, L. B., Wiwad, D., & Hanniball, K. B. (2018). Buying well-being: Spending behavior and happiness. *Social and Personality Psychology Compass*, *12*(5), e12386. https://doi.org/10.1111/spc3.12386

Anderson, K. C., Wallach, K. A., & Grimes, M. (2024). The anti-consumption journey: Unplugging for improved well-being. *Journal of Consumer Behaviour*, *23*(6), 3152–3174.

Annemans, D., Dennis, M., Dedyukhina, A., Gilbert, E., Grosse-Buening, I., & Schlenker, K. (2024). *Reimagining digital well-being. Report for designers & policymakers* (p. 34). KNAW. https://philpapers.org/archive/ANNRDW.pdf

Barry, M. M., Kuosmanen, T., Keppler, T., Dowling, K., & Harte, P. (2024). Priority actions for promoting population mental health and wellbeing. *Mental Health & Prevention*, *33*, 200312. https://doi.org/10.1016/j.mhp.2023.200312

Baudrillard, J. (1998). *The consumer society: Myths and structures*. Sage Publications.

Belk, R. W. (1988). Possessions and the extended self. *Journal of Consumer Research*, *15*(2), 139–168. http://www.jstor.org/stable/2489522

Belk, R. W. (2013). Extended self in a digital world. *Journal of Consumer Research*, *40*(3), 477–500. https://doi.org/10.1086/671052

Black, D. W. (2022). Compulsive shopping: A review and update. *Current Opinion in Psychology*, *46*, 101321.

Bouman, T., Bolderdijk, J. W., & Smith, E. K. (2025). Local fossil fuel ad ban as a catalyst for global change. *Nature Climate Change*, *15*(4), 348–350. https://doi.org/10.1038/s41558-025-02267-4

Brickman, P., & Campbell, D. T. (1971). Hedonic relativism and planning the good society. In M. H. Appley (Ed.), *Adaptation level theory* (pp. 287–305). Academic Press.

Callmer, Å. (2019). *Making sense of sufficiency. Entries, practices and politics* [KTH Royal Institute of Technology]. http://urn.kb.se/resolve?urn=urn:nbn:se:kth:diva-265582

Caron, C. (2021, May 7). Therapy on Aisle 7: Retailers are entering the mental health market. *The New York Times*. https://www.nytimes.com/2021/05/07/well/therapy-pharmacy.html

Chawla, S., Kumar, N., & Gupta, P. (2023). Self-control and compulsive buying behavior: Understanding the mediating role of perceived ill-being. *Cogent Business & Management*, *10*(1), 2286673.

Citizens Advice. (2023, November 30). *15 million people are likely to use unregulated buy now pay later to help ease seasonal spending*. Citizens Advice. https://www.citizensadvice.org.uk/about-us/media-centre/press-releases/15-million-people-likely-to-use-unregulated-buy-now-pay-later-to-help-ease-seasonal-spending/

Coppola, D. (2025, March 20). *E-commerce as share of total retail sales worldwide 2019–2029*. Statista. https://www.statista.com/statistics/534123/e-commerce-share-of-retail-sales-worldwide/

Daniel, C., Chowdhury, R. M. M. I., & Gentina, E. (2024). Mindfulness, spiritual well-being, and sustainable consumer behavior. *Journal of Cleaner Production*, *455*, 142293. https://doi.org/10.1016/j.jclepro.2024.142293

Dittmar, H. (2005). A new look at "compulsive buying": Self-discrepancies and materialistic values as predictors of compulsive buying tendency. *Journal of Social and Clinical Psychology*, *24*(6), 832–859.

Elf, P., Isham, A., & Gatersleben, B. (2021). Above and beyond? How businesses can drive sustainable development by promoting lasting pro-environmental behaviour change: An examination of the IKEA Live Lagom project. *Business Strategy and the Environment*, *30*(2), 1037–1050. https://doi.org/10.1002/bse.2668

Ellen MacArthur Foundation. (2021). *A new textiles economy: Redesigning fashion's future*. https://ellenmacarthurfoundation.org/

European Environment Agency (EEA). (2022). *Waste prevention in Europe: State of play and ways forward*. https://www.eea.europa.eu/

Ewen, S. B. (1974). *The captains of consciousness: The emergence of mass advertising and mass consumption in the 1920s*. State University of New York at Albany. https://search.proquest.com/openview/202680c8f8a5aa32e2b030922f0cfff6/1?pq-origsite=gscholar&cbl=18750&diss=y

Federal Reserve. (2023). *Consumer credit report: Outstanding credit card debt*. Federal Reserve System.

Frontier Economics. (2024). *Culture and heritage capital: Monetising the impact of culture and heritage on health and wellbeing* (p. 202). Frontier Economics. https://assets.publishing.service.gov.uk/media/678e2ecf432c55fe2988f615/rpt_-_Frontier_Health_and_Wellbeing_Final_Report_09_12_24_accessible_final.pdf

García, H., & Miralles, F. (2020). *Ikigai journey: A practical guide to finding happiness and purpose the Japanese way*. Tuttle Publishing.

Guardian. (2025, March 28). *Ultra-fast fashion is taking over – and getting us addicted*. https://webstories.theguardian.com/stories/us/2022/jul/12/ultra-fast-fashion-is-taking-over-and-using-every-trick-in-the-book-to-get-us-addicted-2/

Gupta, S. (2022). *How people buy online: The psychology behind consumer behaviour*. SAGE Publications Pvt. Ltd.

GVR. (2025). *U.S. social commerce market size & share report, 2030* [Grand View Research]. https://www.grandviewresearch.com/industry-analysis/us-social-commerce-market-report

Hickman, C., Marks, E., Pihkala, P., Clayton, S., Lewandowski, R. E., Mayall, E. E., Wray, B., Mellor, C., & van Susteren, L. (2021). Climate anxiety in children and young people and their beliefs about government responses to climate change: A global survey. *The Lancet Planetary Health*, *5*(12), e863–e873.

Hochschild, A., & Machung, A. (1989). *The second shift: Working parents and the revolution at home*. Viking.

Hunter, M. R., Gillespie, B. W., & Chen, S. Y.-P. (2019). Urban nature experiences reduce stress in the context of daily life based on salivary biomarkers. *Frontiers in Psychology*, *10*, 413490.

Jansson, A., & Adams, P. C. (2021). Retreat culture and therapeutic disconnection. In *Disentangling: The geographies of digital disconnection* (p. 253). Oxford University Press.

Juniper, A. (2011). *Wabi sabi: The Japanese art of impermanence*. Tuttle Publishing.

Kasser, T. (2002). *The high price of materialism*. MIT Press.

Kaushik, M., Jain, A., Agarwal, P., Joshi, S. D., & Parvez, S. (2020). Role of yoga and meditation as complementary therapeutic regimes for stress-related neuropsychiatric disorders: Utilization of brain waves activity as a novel tool. *Journal of Evidence-Based Integrative Medicine*, *25*, 2515690X20949451.

Koles, B., Wells, V., & Tadajewski, M. (2018). Compensatory consumption and consumer compromises: A state-of-the-art review. *Journal of Marketing Management*, *34*(1–2), 96–133.

Kovács, L. N., Katzinger, E., Yi, S., Demetrovics, Z., Maraz, A., & Kökönyei, G. (2022). Emotion-focused coping mediates the relationship between COVID-related distress and compulsive buying. *Plos One*, *17*(9), e0274458.

Kumai, C. (2018). *Kintsugi wellness: The Japanese art of nourishing mind, body, and spirit*. HarperCollins.
Kumar, S., Subramaniam, E., Bhavanani, A. B., Sarkar, S., & Balasundaram, S. (2019). Effect of adjunct yoga therapy in depressive disorders: Findings from a randomized controlled study. *Indian Journal of Psychiatry*, *61*(6), 592–597.
Lane, C. M. (2024). *More than pretty boxes: How the rise of professional organizing shows us the way we work isn't working*. University of Chicago Press.
Lee, M., & Ahn, C. S. Y. (2016). Anti-consumption, materialism, and consumer well-being. *Journal of Consumer Affairs*, *50*(1), 18–47.
Lee, M. S. W., Ortega Egea, J. M., & García De Frutos, N. (2020). Anti-consumption beyond boundaries: From niche topic to global phenomena. *Psychology & Marketing*, *37*(2), 171–176.
Lembke, A. (2021). *Dopamine nation: Finding balance in the age of indulgence*. Penguin.
Lewis, R., & Dart, M. (2014). *The new rules of retail: Competing in the world's toughest marketplace*. St. Martin's Press.
MacKinnon, J. B. (2021). *The day the world stops shopping: How ending consumerism gives us a better life and a greener world*. Random House.
Madigan, M. (2025, February 13). My shopping addiction had me spending $1K a month on clothes – Now I'm trying to help others beat it. *New York Post*. https://nypost.com/2025/02/13/lifestyle/my-shopping-addiction-had-me-spending-1k-a-month-on-clothes-now-im-trying-to-help-others-beat-it/
Mandel, N., Rucker, D. D., Levav, J., & Galinsky, A. D. (2017). The compensatory consumer behavior model: How self-discrepancies drive consumer behavior. *Journal of Consumer Psychology*, 27(1), 133–146.
McKinsey & Company. (2023). *The state of fashion 2022* (p. 144). McKinsey & Company.
Mont, O. (2008). Innovative approaches to optimising the design and use of durable consumer goods. *International Journal of Product Development*, 6(3/4), 227–250.
Mont, O. (Ed.). (2025). *Understanding the urban sharing economy: Sustainability and institutionalisation*. Edwar Elgar Publishing Limited.
Mont, O., Elf, P., & Isham, A. (2025). Marketing sustainable lifestyles. In K. Peattie, R. De Angelis, N. Koenig-Lewis, & C. Strong (Eds.), *The Routledge companion to marketing and sustainability* (Vol. 2025). Routledge, Taylor & Francis Group.
Moulding, R., Duong, A., Nedeljkovic, M., & Kyrios, M. (2017). Do you think that money can buy happiness? A review of the role of mood, materialism, self, and cognitions in compulsive buying. *Current Addiction Reports*, *4*, 254–261.
Müller, A., Mitchell, J. E., Crosby, R. D., Cao, L., Johnson, J., Claes, L., & de Zwaan, M. (2012). Mood states preceding and following compulsive buying episodes: An ecological momentary assessment study. *Psychiatry Research*, *200*(2), 575–580.
Otero-López, J. M. (2022). What do we know when we know a compulsive buying person? Looking at now and ahead. *International Journal of Environmental Research and Public Health*, *19*(18), Article 18.
Packard, V. (1957). *The hidden persuaders*. Ig Publishing.
Pascoe, M. C., Thompson, D. R., & Ski, C. F. (2017). Yoga, mindfulness-based stress reduction and stress-related physiological measures: A meta-analysis. *Psychoneuroendocrinology*, *86*, 152–168.
Peters, J. (2019). *The art of Japanese living: How to bring mindfulness and simplicity into your life*. Summersdale.
Prathikanti, S., Rivera, R., Cochran, A., Tungol, J. G., Fayazmanesh, N., & Weinmann, E. (2017). Treating major depression with yoga: A prospective, randomized, controlled pilot trial. *Plos One*, *12*(3), e0173869.

Rick, S. I., Pereira, B., & Burson, K. A. (2014). The benefits of retail therapy: Making purchase decisions reduces residual sadness. *Journal of Consumer Psychology, 24*(3), 373–380.
Roberts, J. A. (2011). *Shiny objects: Why we spend money we don't have in search of happiness we can't buy*. HarperOne.
Rose, S., & Dhandayudham, A. (2014). Towards an understanding of internet-based problem shopping behaviour: The concept of online shopping addiction and its proposed predictors. *Journal of Behavioral Addictions, 3*(2), 83–89.
Roy, B., D'Souza, M. S., Bhattacharjee, S., Acharjee, P. B., Thorat, S., & Bhayani, T. (2024). Role of artificial intelligence in influencing impulsive buying behaviour. In *2024 international conference on trends in quantum computing and emerging business technologies* (pp. 1–5). IEEE.
Ryan, R. M., & Deci, E. L. (2019). Brick by brick: The origins, development, and future of self-determination theory. In *Advances in motivation science* (Vol. 6, pp. 111–156). Elsevier.
Sanne, C. (2005). The consumption of our discontent. *Business Strategy and the Environment, 14*(5), 315–323.
Saxena, S. (Ed.). (2019). *Labor, global supply chains, and the garment industry in South Asia: Bangladesh after rana plaza*. Routledge.
Schreurs, J. (2010). *Living with less: Prospects for sustainability* [Doctoral dissertation, Maastricht University]. https://cris.maastrichtuniversity.nl/en/publications/living-with-less-prospects-for-sustainability
Sneath, J. Z., Lacey, R., & Kennett-Hensel, P. A. (2009). Coping with a natural disaster: Losses, emotions, and impulsive and compulsive buying. *Marketing Letters, 20*(1), 45–60.
Southerton, D. (2020). *Time, consumption and the coordination of everyday life*. Palgrave Macmillan UK.
Veblen, T. (2017). The theory of the leisure class. Routledge. (Original work published 1899)
WHO. (2023). *Health in the well-being economy. Background paper: Working together to achieve healthy, fairer, prosperous societies across the WHO European Region* (p. 52). WHO Regional Office for Europe. https://iris.who.int/bitstream/handle/10665/366228/WHO-EURO-2023-7144-46910-68439-eng.pdf
Wynn-Williams, S. (2025). *Careless people. A story of where i used to work*. Pan Macmillan.
Zhang, C., Brook, J. S., Leukefeld, C. G., De La Rosa, M., & Brook, D. W. (2017). Compulsive buying and quality of life: An estimate of the monetary cost of compulsive buying among adults in early midlife. *Psychiatry Research, 252*, 208–214.
Zhang, W. (2025). Business model innovation of cross-border e-commerce platforms under the 'dual circulation' strategy: Case studies of Shein and Temu. *Journal of Economic and Managerial Dynamics, 1*(1), 16–23.
Zhao, S., Yang, Q., Im, H., Ye, B., Zeng, Y., Chen, Z., Liu, L., & Huang, D. (2022). The impulsive online shopper: Effects of COVID-19 burnout, uncertainty, self-control, and online shopping trust. *Future Business Journal, 8*(1).

5

MYTH 4

The more, the merrier – the road to freedom and well-being is paved with endless choices

Oksana Mont, Amy Isham and Patrick Elf

5.1 The paradox of choice myth

The more, the merrier – or is it?

The idea of limitless choice has become a defining feature of modern consumerism. Historically, choices were constrained by material scarcity, geographic limitations and cultural norms. With industrialisation and globalisation, this shifted towards an era where consumers are presented with abundant options, hoping this will encourage them to consume more. This notion underpins the belief that increasing choices leads to greater freedom and satisfaction. Yet, often, this abundance of choice fuels dissatisfaction rather than contentment, as the fulfilment of one desire frequently leads to the emergence of another. The so-called Paradox of Choice, introduced by Barry Schwartz (2004), argues that too many options can result in decision fatigue, anxiety and reduced satisfaction.

The myth of excessive choice is particularly problematic in the context of sustainable consumption as it encourages overconsumption, waste and unsustainable resource use. Dispelling the myth of limitless choice is crucial for shifting towards strong sustainable consumption and sufficiency-based models, where quality, durability and meaningful consumption take precedence over quantity of stuff and the 'throw-away' ideology. This tension highlights the need to rethink the cultural and economic emphasis on more choices, particularly in light of environmental sustainability challenges caused by extractivism and resource overconsumption[1] and a simultaneous attempt to improve human well-being.

DOI: 10.4324/9781003613718-7

5.2 Origins

From the earliest days of human existence, the drive to acquire more has been a matter of survival by increasing available options in uncertain environments. Those who gathered extra food, secured stable shelter and accumulated resources beyond immediate needs were better equipped to withstand scarcity and unpredictability (Darwin, 1871; Buss, 2019). Over millennia, this survival advantage cemented a deep-seated preference for having multiple alternatives, reinforcing the idea that more options equate to greater security and control (Wilson, 2007). However, what once ensured adaptability in harsh conditions now plays a different role in modern consumer behaviour. The instinct that once motivated humans to seek out diverse food sources or protective materials now manifests in the constant pursuit of product variety and market choices.

At the neurological level, the dopamine system reinforces this drive, making the pursuit of more not just a habit but a deeply ingrained mechanism of reward. When individuals acquire new resources, wealth or social status, their brain releases dopamine, creating a sense of pleasure and reward (Lembke, 2021). However, this system does not generate lasting satisfaction. Instead, it creates the tendency to constantly seek greater rewards as people quickly adapt to what they already have. In this way, the evolutionary tendency to accumulate and maximise options now fuels the belief that more choice leads to greater happiness – driving consumers to crave novelty as existing options cannot excite us anymore.

While these biological tendencies laid the groundwork, the idea that more choice is inherently good evolved significantly after the Enlightenment, as ideas about individual freedom and autonomy gained prominence. Before this period, the concept of choice was constrained mainly by feudal and religious institutions. Philosophers like Thomas Aquinas discussed free will, but choices were primarily framed around moral and spiritual decisions rather than material abundance. The Renaissance saw a gradual shift, with the rise of merchant economies and humanism encouraging greater personal achievement. During the 17th and 18th centuries, philosophers like John Locke argued that personal autonomy was central to societal progress. His *Two Treatises of Government* (1689) positioned freedom of choice as a natural right, reinforcing the notion that expanding individual options was inherently positive.

The Industrial Revolution transformed both production and consumption. For the first time in human history, products that used to be expensive, scarce and handcrafted became mass-produced and cheaper, accessible to a broader segment of the population. As Frank Trentmann explores in *Empire of Things* (2016), Victorian Britain's mechanisation of spinning and weaving in the textile industry drastically lowered production costs, making diverse fabrics available across social classes. Similarly, innovations in ceramics, such as those pioneered by Josiah Wedgwood, created aesthetically appealing yet affordable tableware, enabling middle-class families to engage in new forms of domestic self-expression. The choice was no longer restricted by local availability or personal skills. Waged employment in production facilities also allowed more people to earn and spend money in a market economy.

This transformation laid the foundation for modern retail, culminating in the emergence of department stores in the late 19th century in the United States and Europe. These establishments did not merely provide a wider selection of goods; they redefined shopping by making choices central to the consumer experience. Now, consumers could compare, select and differentiate between goods in ways that were previously unimaginable. More than just retail spaces, department stores quickly became arenas where societal norms and modern identities were shaped and negotiated. Personal consumption was no longer purely functional – it became a means of self-expression and social distinction.

In the 20th century, the Mont Pelerin Society promoted the idea that economic freedom and consumer choice were central to individual autonomy. Expanding market options was seen as key for political and social liberty, with minimal government intervention. Friedman's *Capitalism and Freedom* (1962) positioned marketplace choice as a cornerstone of personal liberty, while Becker's rational choice theory (1976) reinforced the assumption that more choices lead to better outcomes. This emphasis on expanding consumer options was reinforced by advertising and marketing, which framed variety as a symbol of freedom, individuality and social status. As deregulated markets encouraged competition, advertising evolved into a powerful force that shaped consumer expectations, promoting the belief that endless choice was not just beneficial but a beacon of modern life. In this way, Friedman and Becker's theories extended beyond policy, embedding the ideology of choice into consumer culture.

The digital revolution of the 21st century has taken this logic to new extremes, transforming not just the availability of choices but the way they are provided. Online platforms like Amazon, Netflix and Spotify offer vast selections of products and media, but choice is no longer neutral or entirely free. Algorithms now structure and filter decisions, shaping what consumers see, engage with and ultimately select. Nick Srnicek's *Platform Capitalism* (2017) explores how these digital platforms operate not just as marketplaces but as economic systems designed to maximise engagement and extract data rather than empower consumer choice. The once-celebrated freedom of choice has thus become increasingly curated and optimised for profit, raising the question of whether digital abundance truly enhances autonomy or simply reinforces a new form of controlled consumption.

5.3 Consequences

Choice is essential as it helps individuals meet their unique needs in a personalised way, which can be empowering. A wide range of options enables *personal autonomy* and *freedom*, allowing individuals to select products that reflect their preferences, values and lifestyles. This empowerment supports a sense of identity and self-expression, as people in societies shaped by the ideology of consumerism use their consumption choices to communicate who they are. Beyond personal identity, choice enables societal, business and personal *resilience* by encouraging adaptation to change. Consumers who incorporate second-hand purchases, rental services, or subscription-based options in their consumption can better adjust to shifting market conditions. Similarly, individuals who explore alternative consumption patterns, such as minimalism or mindful consumption, often develop greater financial security and psychological well-being, making them less vulnerable to economic downturns. Digital platforms that offer a variety of purchasing options, from in-store to online shopping and flexible payment plans, have also enabled consumers to navigate crises, such as lockdowns or inflation spikes, with greater ease. However, an excess of consumption choices may also have adverse consequences.

5.3.1 Choice overload

Modern consumerism places individuals in a constant state of decision-making, where identity *per se* becomes a product of consumption (Bauman, 2001). However, this endless pursuit of self-definition through market choices can lead to instability and anxiety rather than empowerment.

Excessive choices also reduce *decision-making efficiency*, as individuals spend considerable time deliberating, leading to delays and avoidance. The more options available, the greater the cognitive burden, making it harder to commit to and be content with a choice. This phenomenon, known as choice paralysis, occurs when individuals struggle to navigate an overwhelming number of alternatives (Schwartz, 2004). As a result, they may delay decisions or avoid making them altogether. Indeed, studies indicate that individuals faced with complex decision-making processes feel less in control of their lives, a factor closely tied to subjective well-being (Iyengar, 2010). Repeated choices can also deplete cognitive resources, weakening self-control in subsequent tasks (Vohs et al., 2018). In addition, excessive choice overburdens the brain's deliberate reasoning system, known as System 2 thinking (Kahneman, 2011). As cognitive load increases, individuals rely more on System 1 heuristics – mental shortcuts that simplify decision-making but often lead to suboptimal choices. This effect is particularly evident in high-choice environments, such as online retail, where overwhelming selection often causes consumers to default to the familiar option or rely on algorithm-driven recommendations that further shape their decisions. In addition to slowing decision-making, an abundance of options creates a psychological attachment to multiple alternatives, increasing the difficulty of finalising a choice (Carmon et al., 2003). This concept, known as option attachment, explains why an extensive set of options can prolong the selection process rather than shorten it, delaying necessary purchases or important life choices.

Furthermore, an overabundance of choices *raises consumer expectations*, increasing the likelihood of *disappointment* when the final choice falls short of the imagined ideal (Carmon et al., 2003). Consumers often assume that a perfect choice must exist among numerous options, leading to *post-decision regret* even when they make objectively good choices (Iyengar, 2010). For instance, studies show that individuals choosing between many health insurance plans report higher regret levels, feeling they could have made a better decision (Botti & Iyengar, 2006).

> *When the options are few we can be happy with what we choose since we are confident that it is the best possible choice for us. When the options are practically infinite, though, we believe that the perfect choice for us must be out there somewhere and that it's our responsibility to find it.*

Cognitive and neuroscientific research supports these findings, showing that the brain's ability to process information deteriorates under high-choice conditions (Hu et al., 2024). Individuals selecting from many options exhibit heightened stress responses, including cardiovascular patterns associated with perceived threats, indicating that choice overload places both a psychological and physiological strain on individuals (Saltsman et al., 2019).

5.3.2 Overproduction and environmental harm

Modern consumer culture's emphasis on limitless choice has fuelled overproduction and overconsumption, leading to waste and environmental degradation. The belief that more options lead to better outcomes and more satisfied consumers pushes businesses to flood the market with excessive product variations, catering to perceived consumer demand rather than actual need. The cycle begins in supply chains, where nearly 8% of stock across sectors such as food, beauty, apparel, pharmaceuticals, healthcare and automotive industries goes to waste each year due to expiry or overproduction, amounting to $163 billion worth of lost inventory (Avery Dennison, 2022). In fashion, this problem is particularly pronounced. Fast-changing trends and an overwhelming number of product lines encourage constant purchasing yet lead to stock inefficiencies. An estimated 4% to 9% of all textiles produced for the European market are discarded before ever reaching consumers, amounting to 264,000 to 594,000 tonnes of wasted textiles annually (EEA, 2024).

These figures highlight the scale of structural overproduction, where companies continuously provide consumers more choices than they can realistically process.

New, *ultra*-fast fashion brands, such as Shein and Temu, have further accelerated this trend by flooding the market with cheap, short-lived garments. For instance, over six months in 2021, Shein uploaded 2,000 and 10,000 new items to its app daily (Deighton, 2023). These e-commerce platforms ship approximately 9,000 tonnes of goods daily from China to Western consumers – the equivalent of 88 fully loaded Boeing 777s (Farivar, 2024). This relentless supply chain not only encourages excessive consumption but also results in significant carbon emissions from transportation, exacerbating the environmental impact of overproduction. The fashion industry alone is responsible for an estimated 2% to 8% of global greenhouse gas emissions, a direct consequence of mass production driven by ever-expanding consumer choices. By 2030, its annual carbon dioxide emissions are expected to reach approximately 2.7 billion tonnes, comparable to the emissions produced by around 230 million passenger vehicles in a year (UNEP, 2023).

At the same time, the rise of e-commerce further intensifies the problem, reshaping consumer expectations around availability and convenience (see Chapter 3). The ability to browse thousands of options 24/7 has led to more impulsive purchasing and higher return rates, reinforcing unsustainable consumption cycles. Many unsold or returned items are discarded rather than resold or recycled as retailers prioritise efficiency over sustainability (Roberts et al., 2023). This paradoxical outcome, where excessive choice fuels unnecessary production and waste, highlights the environmental cost of a system designed to maximise variety rather than longevity.

One key driver of these waste-generating practices is planned obsolescence, where manufacturers intentionally design products with short lifespans, encouraging frequent replacements (see Chapter 7). Nowhere is this more evident than in the fashion industry, where clothing lifespans have declined dramatically in recent decades. On average, in the United Kingdom, a garment is worn only seven to ten times before being thrown away (WRAP, 2017).

The scale of this waste is staggering. For instance, the value of products destroyed in the European Union from just textiles and electronics sectors was projected to reach €21.74 billion by 2022, surpassing the entire GDP of Cyprus in 2020 (Ökopol & EEB, 2021). Similarly, in the United States, Americans discard an estimated 300 million pairs of shoes each year, with most ending up in landfills, where they can take 30–40 years to decompose. Meanwhile, approximately 300 million children worldwide have never owned a pair of shoes (Kirk, 2010). On the other hand, more than 18 million children (some as young as 5) work in informal e-waste recycling, which often is detrimental to their health (WHO, 2024). Thus, overproduction is an environmental issue and a reflection of deep social inequalities (see Chapter 8 for a more in-depth discussion on justice).

5.4 Dispelling the myth

The idea that 'more choice is always better' is a pervasive myth. Research across diverse disciplines suggests that an overabundance of choices can lead to adverse outcomes for individuals and societal actors. Below, we present key arguments for when less choice leads to more sustainable and rewarding outcomes.

5.4.1 The illusion of choice as freedom

In contemporary consumer societies, choice is often equated with personal freedom and autonomy. However, this freedom can be illusory, as decision-making is frequently shaped and constrained by external influences. Electronics brands offer slight variations of similar products, and streaming platforms filter content through algorithms that reinforce previous preferences rather than broadening perspectives. The culture industry showcases how mass production creates an illusion of endless possibilities while ultimately serving 'sameness' (Horkheimer & Adorno, 2017), thereby exercising a form of social control in the capitalist system.

This dynamic extends beyond the material goods and culture industry. In service industries and public sectors, choice is increasingly constrained by standardisation. Ritzer's concept of *McDonaldization* illustrates how efficiency, control and predictability now shape not just fast food but also consumer experiences (Ritzer, 1993). From education to healthcare, uniform systems have been designed to prioritise optimisation over personalisation, streamlining processes but reducing individual agency. Although consumers may seem to be choosing between different services or providers, these choices are frequently pre-determined and standardised, leaving them with limited control over their decisions, that is, with little genuine autonomy.

The role of artificial intelligence in shaping consumer decisions enhances this illusion. *Recommender systems* embedded in social media, e-commerce and entertainment platforms claim to personalise user experience, but in practice, they restrict rather than expand choice. These algorithms prioritise content based on past interactions, reinforcing existing habits and filtering out unfamiliar alternatives. AI-generated suggestions thus shift agency away from individuals and towards corporations and digital intermediaries. While users may perceive tailored recommendations as helpful, legitimate concerns emerge that recommender systems may deceive or manipulate consumers and adversely affect their critical thinking (Bonicalzi et al., 2023). The result is not greater freedom but a form of soft manipulation that subtly directs choices while maintaining the appearance of individual control.

As consumers navigate an increasingly complex marketplace, their browsing and purchasing behaviours are continuously monitored. Data on their preferences, past choices and interactions are collected, enabling corporations to refine and tailor (and thus control) the options they present (Salecl,

2019). Faced with an overwhelming array of choices, individuals often turn to external sources for guidance on what to select. This strategy gives power to the source of that advice – whether it be celebrities, popular media, or the growing number of social media 'influencers' (Misuraca et al., 2024). Hence, rather than being able to choose among a number of options autonomously, consumers are guided by actors or corporations that have the power to control decision-making in their own vested interests.

The persistent illusion of choice not only constrains individual autonomy but also shapes consumer motivations in ways that reinforce extrinsic rather than intrinsic drivers. *Self-determination theory* highlights the psychological conditions necessary for genuine flourishing and well-being, emphasising the importance of autonomy, competence and relatedness in decision-making (Ryan & Deci, 2017). However, in consumer environments saturated with targeted marketing, algorithmic nudging and social influence, these psychological needs are systematically undermined. Instead of fostering self-directed choices based on intrinsic values – such as well-being, social connection or ethical commitments – market structures encourage extrinsically motivated consumption tied to status, validation or habit (Moller et al., 2006).

This manufactured dependence on external validation is reinforced by strategic product design and marketing techniques that manipulate perceptions of choice. Studies show that when consumers feel competent and informed, they are more likely to make decisions aligned with their long-term interests (Gilal et al., 2018). However, the complexity of modern consumer environments, that is, the overwhelming number of options, combined with complex pricing strategies and persuasive advertising, often makes decision-making confusing, increasing individuals' reliance on external cues. Relatedness, or the need to feel connected to others, also plays a major role in consumer behaviour. Companies take advantage of this by linking their brands to social identity and belonging, shaping not only what consumers buy but also why they buy it (Pelletier & Sharp, 2008). Kasser (2009) further highlights that when people make choices based on their values rather than external pressures, they experience greater well-being and are more likely to make decisions that support environmental sustainability. Similarly, research has shown that companies, by aligning marketing practices with consumer values and motivations, can promote both long-term satisfaction and brand loyalty (Elf et al., 2021). However, the way consumption is structured often discourages this, leading people to follow patterns that serve corporate interests rather than their own values and motivations.

5.4.2 Less choice – better decisions

Although modern consumer culture promotes the idea that more choice leads to better decisions and lasting satisfaction, research suggests the opposite:

when individuals face fewer options, they make quicker, more confident decisions and report higher levels of satisfaction with their selections. Limiting choice reduces cognitive effort, minimises post-decision regret and improves overall well-being (Schwartz, 2004). Rather than restricting autonomy, simplifying choices can enhance decision-making by allowing individuals to focus on meaningful alternatives rather than being overwhelmed by trivial distinctions.

One of the most cited studies on choice overload, conducted by Iyengar and Lepper (2000), demonstrates how reducing the number of available options improves consumer decision-making. There were two groups of people – one group was to chose among 6 varieties and the second one – among 24 jars of jam. Those offered only six options were ten times more likely to make a purchase (30% vs. 3%) and reported greater satisfaction with their selection. This suggests that too many choices can discourage action and reduce confidence in decision-making.

Similar findings apply to complex financial decisions. Iyengar and Kamenica (2010) examined retirement plan participation and found that when employees were given too many investment options, they were less likely to enrol in any plan. However, when companies simplified choices and provided a curated selection, enrolment rates increased significantly, and participants expressed greater confidence in their decisions. These findings highlight how reducing complexity improves outcomes, particularly in high-stakes decision-making.

In the healthcare sector, Reutskaja and Hogarth (2009) found that patients presented with a limited number of clear treatment options made more confident and informed choices than those confronted with a long list of alternatives. When faced with too much information, patients struggled with indecision and were more likely to delay or avoid making crucial health decisions. This reinforces the idea that well-structured, limited choices support more effective decision-making in essential areas of life.

A compelling real-world illustration of the benefits of fewer choices comes from Gordon Ramsay's programme Kitchen Nightmares. In this television series, Chef Ramsay visits struggling restaurants. Many of them offer an excessive number of dishes, overwhelming both customers and kitchen staff. As a result, chefs struggle with quality because an extensive menu stretches resources, making it impossible to perfect each dish. Ingredients go to waste, preparation is inconsistent and execution suffers. Customers face decision fatigue, as a menu with dozens of choices makes it harder for diners to decide, increasing dissatisfaction with their final selection. Slower service and inefficiency arise because a bloated menu complicates kitchen operations, leading to longer waiting times, frequent mistakes and declining customer loyalty. Ramsay's solution is almost always the same: simplify the menu, focus on fewer dishes and master their execution. Restaurants that adopt this approach typically experience higher customer satisfaction, as diners appreciate a curated selection of well-prepared dishes over an overwhelming variety of mediocre ones. Increased profitability follows as streamlining ingredients and preparation reduces waste, improves margins and attracts repeat customers. This example mirrors what research shows across different domains: when choice is carefully curated, individuals and businesses alike benefit from greater focus, efficiency and quality.

The idea of 'less choice – better decisions' is increasingly recognised in business strategy as *choice editing*. Companies that reduce unnecessary complexity in their offerings often see improved customer engagement and financial performance. Research by Gourville and Soman (2005) shows that companies offering fewer product variations experience higher customer satisfaction and stronger sales. Consumers prefer clearer, well-differentiated choices over overwhelming product lines. Besides, choice editing is also a powerful tool for driving sustainability and ethical responsibility. By deliberately limiting product options to more sustainable and ethical choices, businesses can not only enhance decision-making for consumers but also ensure stronger supply chain oversight, enforce ethical standards and minimise reputational risks. This approach supports compliance with evolving regulations on environmental and social responsibility, helping businesses stay ahead of legal requirements. At the same time, it meets growing consumer demand for ethical and sustainable products by ensuring that only responsible options are available while improving efficiency and competitive advantage (Gunn & Mont, 2014).

5.4.3 The scarcity paradox

The idea that more choice leads to greater happiness is deeply embedded in consumer culture. However, the scarcity paradox – the increased appeal of goods when they are perceived as scarce – challenges this assumption. Scarcity does not diminish value but often enhances it, influencing consumer desire, business strategies and broader economic structures. Historically, scarcity was a condition to be endured; today, in some sectors, it is deliberately engineered to increase or maintain demand.

This section examines how scarcity shapes the perception of value, particularly in the luxury industry and sufficiency-oriented businesses, offering a counter-argument against the paradox of choice. Two types of businesses present distinct types of scarcity in business practices: one designed to enhance exclusivity and another aimed at long-term sustainability and sufficiency.

Luxury brands rely on *artificial scarcity* to enhance desirability. By restricting product availability, limiting production volumes and maintaining high prices, these brands cultivate a sense of exclusivity (Kapferer, 2012, 2015). This scarcity is not due to resource limitations but is a strategic tool to maintain social distinction and signal status, as well as exclude certain social groups from accessing the offers. For instance, high-end fashion brands like Hermès limit the availability of their handbags, such as the Birkin bag, by requiring customers to join waiting lists. Similarly, luxury watchmakers release limited-edition timepieces to increase their perceived value. These strategies ensure that ownership remains exclusive, reinforcing the idea that rarity equates to worth. This carefully managed scarcity draws in consumers who seek differentiation, feeding into the aspirational nature of luxury consumption.

While luxury brands create scarcity to uphold exclusivity, *sufficiency-oriented companies* (organisations further discussed in Chapter 8) embrace scarcity for sustainability and long-term resilience. These businesses intentionally limit production to maintain ethical labour practices, environmental responsibility and financial independence (Gossen & Niessen, 2024). Unlike traditional business models that rely on rapid growth and external investment, sufficiency-driven businesses prioritise stability over expansion. Companies employing sufficiency strategies produce goods according to their actual capacity rather than aiming for mass production and stockpiling (Werner et al., 2025). For instance, some small-scale fashion brands operate on a made-to-order basis, ensuring they do not overproduce or waste resources. Others, like artisanal workshops or cooperatives, focus on localised, slow production, which fosters long-term consumer engagement and strengthens brand authenticity.

Luxury scarcity-based business models and sufficiency-oriented businesses share common features in leveraging scarcity to create value, albeit with different objectives. Both models reject mass production and opt for curated, controlled growth, whether to maintain brand prestige or to uphold sustainability principles. Additionally, both focus on qualitative rarity, for example, craftsmanship and durability. In both cases, excessive availability dilutes value, whether in terms of social distinction or environmental and social integrity. Ultimately, these models challenge the assumption that maximisation of choice – whether of offers, production, or market reach – equates to success or well-being.

5.4.4 More choice is not universally desirable

Cultural context also shapes how people perceive and handle the abundance of choice. Douglas (1986) and Claude Lévi-Strauss (1966) have explored how cultural structures impose boundaries on choice. Often, these boundaries serve to maintain social order and cohesion or the fragile balance of the existing natural ecosystem, as seen in the case of indigenous tribes (e.g. Elf et al., 2025). For example, among the Inuit, elders often guide traditional decision-making, and individual choices are informed by communal wisdom rather than personal preference alone.

The distinction between individualistic and collectivist cultures has been highlighted as particularly relevant for understanding how the abundance of choice is treated (Iyengar, 2010). As previously discussed, in individualistic cultures (e.g. much of North America and Western Europe), autonomy and personal freedom are highly valued. As a result, people in these societies often believe that having numerous options is beneficial and empowering. Yet, for some, the clash between the desire for freedom of choice and the overwhelming nature of large assortments can intensify stress. In these cultures, choice overload might manifest as a conflict between the culturally ingrained drive to seek maximum choice and the emotional burden of sifting through excessive information. Indeed, more recent research exploring discrepancies between the perceived ideal and actual number of choices in different life domains across countries has found that respondents in North America were less likely to report having fewer choices than their ideal number (Reutskaja et al., 2022).

Conversely, collectivistic cultures (e.g. parts of Asia, Africa and Latin America) often emphasise group harmony, shared decision-making and guidance from trusted authorities or community elders. People in collectivistic societies may experience fewer personal pressures to evaluate every possible choice individually because decisions are frequently made within close-knit social circles. Fewer choices are preferred, and people are inclined to defer to experts or family members to make decisions. In Japan, for instance, the concept of 'amae' (mutual dependence) plays a role in how individuals navigate choices, often relying on family and workplace hierarchies to structure decisions (Markus & Kitayama, 1991). These differences in cross-cultural preferences are seen at an early age. Iyengar and Lepper (1999) found that Anglo-American children preferred more choices, while Asian-American children were happier and performed better when their choices were made for them by trusted figures. This reduced individual burden of navigating excessive options can permit people to have more capacity to invest in social relationships and shared activities. Putnam (2000), in his book Bowling Alone, observed that societies with a stronger focus on individualised consumerism experienced declining levels of community participation and social capital.

5.5 Implications

The evidence dispelling the myth of 'the more, the merrier' has implications not only for consumers but also for policy and businesses. Recognising that excessive choice can lead to decision paralysis, dissatisfaction and environmental impact highlights the need for targeted interventions. Stakeholders can take steps to promote sustainable consumption levels by curating options, fostering informed decision-making and designing policies that prioritise well-being over the sheer abundance of consumer choice.

5.5.1 For policymakers

Governments and policymakers play a crucial role in mitigating the negative consequences of choice overload. A growing body of research points to the need for *choice architecture* strategies, such as '*nudges*' (Thaler & Sunstein, 2008), which provide products and services for consumers to facilitate easier and more sustainable consumption patterns and levels. *Choice editing*, where harmful or unsustainable products are removed from the market, is a potent tool to manage unsustainable abundance while steering consumption towards sustainability.

France has taken a leading role in choice editing through two key policies: the French Bill on Ultra-Fast Fashion and the Ban on Fossil Fuel Advertising. The *Ultra-Fast Fashion Bill* aims to curb the environmental and social harms of rapid, high-turnover fashion by limiting excessive production and overconsumption. It does so by restricting the number of new collections companies can introduce each year and mandating stricter sustainability requirements (Holland, 2024). By reducing the sheer volume of disposable clothing, the policy curtails unsustainable consumption opportunities and encourages longer product lifespans.

Similarly, France's *Ban on Fossil Fuel Advertising*, which came into force on 22 August 2022, targets the roots of demand creation by restricting the promotion of products that drive climate change (Frost, 2022). The law prohibits advertisements for fossil fuel-related products, including petrol and diesel vehicles, while controversially exempting gas.[2] By removing market signals that normalise fossil fuel dependency, this measure limits consumer exposure to unsustainable and high-emission goods.

Simplifying sustainable choices through transparent, standardised ecolabels can help consumers navigate markets without being overwhelmed. While *ecolabels* are meant to guide decision-making, their effectiveness depends on design and presentation (Sunstein, 2020). Research shows that too many or poorly structured labels can complicate rather than simplify choices, leading to decision fatigue or disengagement (Sunstein, 2021). Thus, policymakers should ensure that ecolabels are not only clear and standardised but also designed to maximise accessibility and actual behavioural change, for example, by enforcing stricter labelling regulations, limiting the number of competing certifications and ensuring labels use simple, recognisable formats that help consumers make informed decisions without being overwhelmed.

5.5.2 For business

Businesses can address choice overload through three main strategies: curating a more streamlined product offering, providing filtering tools and reducing time pressure.

The first way businesses can manage choice overload is by curating their product offerings rather than providing excessive variety. Many companies assume that offering more choices increases customer satisfaction, but in reality, too many options often lead to frustration and indecision (Dar & Gul, 2025), as well as overconsumption. By focusing on a smaller, high-quality selection, businesses can improve both consumer experience and operational efficiency (Werner et al., 2025). A reduced product range also enhances supply chain transparency and quality control, making it easier for companies to ensure ethical sourcing, minimise environmental impact and avoid reputational risks associated with unsustainable practices in their supply chains. This approach aligns with emerging consumer preferences for durability, repairability and sustainability over excessive consumption. By streamlining their offerings and embracing a sufficiency-oriented approach, businesses can foster more sustainable consumption levels while differentiating themselves in an increasingly crowded marketplace (Mont et al., 2025).

When providing many options is unavoidable, businesses can minimise choice overload by enhancing how options are presented and making decision-making more intuitive. For example, in online shopping environments, filtering features enable consumers to narrow down their selections based on price, sustainability or customer reviews and ratings, reducing the cognitive effort required to evaluate numerous alternatives (Turri & Watson, 2023). These interactive decision aids improve consumer satisfaction by simplifying product comparisons. In physical stores, similar mechanisms can be implemented through store layouts and displays that highlight the most relevant or high-quality options for a given category (Mantrala et al., 2009). With the rise of AI-driven technologies, businesses increasingly use personalised recommender systems that tailor product suggestions based on past consumer behaviour. They can help simplify decision-making for consumers by reducing cognitive effort. However, businesses and consumers should recognise that recommended options are not neutral, as algorithms prioritise certain choices over others. It is, therefore, essential to consider the risks of bias, misinformation and privacy concerns when implementing and relying on these technologies (Paul et al., 2023).

The third way to reduce choice overload is by addressing time pressure, which significantly impacts consumer decision-making. When faced with many options, consumers often experience greater stress when they feel they must make a decision quickly (Misuraca et al., 2024). Businesses frequently exacerbate this pressure through marketing techniques such as flash sales, countdown timers and limited-edition product releases, which create urgency but also contribute to poor decision-making and post-purchase regret. Instead, companies can reduce time pressure by allowing consumers more space to evaluate their options. Extending return periods or trial-based purchasing models can help alleviate decision anxiety and encourage more thoughtful purchases. Subscription models and pre-order systems can also remove the burden of repeated decisions by offering consumers a predictable and stress-free way to access products.

5.5.3 For consumers

Consumers play a crucial role in challenging the assumption that more choice leads to lasting happiness by shifting towards conscious, intentional and sufficiency-oriented consumption. The belief that more options lead to better outcomes has driven excessive consumption, yet research suggests that an abundance of choice often decreases satisfaction and increases stress. Drawing on Iyengar's (2010) strategies – developing expertise in choice elimination, categorising options to make them more manageable and leveraging crowd-based recommendations – consumers can take practical steps to shift from overwhelming decision-making to more satisfying and meaningful consumption. Below, we describe these strategies in more detail.

One way to break free from the illusion that more choice equals more happiness is to develop expertise in choice elimination. The most effective consumers are not those who chase endless options but those who know what truly matters to them and filter out distractions. Rather than feeling obligated to explore every available alternative, consumers can set clear criteria – such as prioritising durability, sustainability or ethical production – before making a purchase. Deliberately limiting choices reduces decision fatigue while fostering a deeper sense of control and long-term satisfaction. The *#deinfluencing* movement, which emerged in early 2023, highlights this shift. Deinfluencers challenge overconsumption by encouraging followers to resist impulse buying, question marketing narratives and invest in fewer, higher-quality products. Instead of being seduced by the novelty of choice, consumers who embrace fewer but better purchases report greater post-purchase satisfaction and reduced stress (Isham et al., 2022).

A second strategy is to organise choices into meaningful categories, reducing cognitive overload while reinforcing a sense of control. More choices do not necessarily mean better choices. Instead, they often create confusion. This is, for example, evident in areas like sustainable food consumption, where an increasing number of ecolabels and ethical certifications can overwhelm rather than empower consumers. Focusing on a few trusted certification schemes, such as organic, fair trade, or regenerative agriculture labels, helps simplify decision-making. Similarly, in fashion, consumers struggling with fast-changing trends can adopt capsule wardrobe principles, building a small, versatile collection of timeless, high-quality clothing instead of continuously chasing new styles. The Swedish concept of lagom, meaning moderation and balance, aligns with this mindset by encouraging people to find satisfaction in just enough rather than endless variety (Elf, 2020). Categorising and limiting options help restore a sense of sufficiency (further explored in Chapter 8), replacing the false security of endless choice with the confidence of well-informed decision-making and contentment.

Finally, crowd-based recommendations can counteract the false promise of infinite choice by redirecting attention towards community-driven knowledge rather than marketing-driven consumption. Seeking peer recommendations, ethical shopping guides and sustainability-focused consumer platforms allows consumers to make informed choices while reducing decision fatigue. Studies show that collaborative decision-making and collective wisdom lead to higher satisfaction and less regret, as consumers base their decisions on shared experiences rather than manipulative marketing tactics (Iyengar, 2010). Digital tools and AI-powered recommendation systems provide another layer of support, tailoring choices based on actual preferences rather than arbitrary trends. However, consumers must remain critical of algorithm-driven suggestions, which can reinforce consumption patterns based on convenience rather than sustainability. Engaging with community-driven networks, such as repair collectives, second-hand marketplaces and ethical brand directories, enables consumers to shift away from the mindset that more choice equals more happiness and towards an approach that values meaning, quality and sufficiency.

5.6 Main message

The myth that more choice equals more happiness has led to unsustainable consumption patterns, environmental degradation, consumer dissatisfaction and decreased levels of well-being. The phenomenon dubbed the Paradox of Choice shows that instead of increasing satisfaction, a surplus of options may also lead to stress and anxiety. In contrast, having fewer, well-curated choices can simplify decision-making and lead to more fulfilling outcomes. By understanding the paradox of choice, policymakers, businesses and consumers can work towards creating systems where fewer, more sustainable choices lead to better outcomes for individuals and society.

Notes

1 By overconsumption, we mean material accumulation, which no longer contributes to well-being but is driven by social norms, advertising, and economic structures geared towards perpetual growth (Jackson, 2009). At the individual level, overconsumption is driven by status-seeking behaviours and the pursuit of an idealised lifestyle, while structurally, it is reinforced by economic systems that prioritise continuous expansion and profit maximisation (Schor, 1998).

2 Despite the proactive nature of the ban, critics argue that the exemption for natural gas allows companies to continue promoting fossil fuels and, in general, leaves much leeway for companies to bypass the restrictions.

References

Avery Dennison. (2022). *The missing billions – The real cost of supply chain waste* (p. 71). Avery Dennison. https://rfid.averydennison.com/content/dam/rfid/en/news-and-insights/insights/white-papers/supply-chain-waste-report-the-missing-billions.pdf

Bauman, Z. (2001). Consuming life. *Journal of Consumer Culture*, *1*(1), 9–29.
Becker, G. S. (1976). *The economic approach to human behavior*. University Of Chicago Press.
Bonicalzi, S., De Caro, M., & Giovanola, B. (2023). Artificial intelligence and autonomy: On the ethical dimension of recommender systems. *Topoi*, *42*(3), 819–832.
Botti, S., & Iyengar, S. S. (2006). The dark side of choice: When choice impairs social welfare. *Journal of Public Policy & Marketing*, *25*(1), 24–38.
Buss, D. M. (2019). *Evolutionary psychology: The new science of the mind* (6th ed.). Routledge.
Carmon, Z., Wertenbroch, K., & Zeelenberg, M. (2003). Option attachment: When deliberating makes choosing feel like losing. *Journal of Consumer Research*, *30*(1), 15–29.
Dar, A. R., & Gul, M. (2025). The "less is better" paradox and consumer behaviour: A systematic review of choice overload and its marketing implications. *Qualitative Market Research: An International Journal*, *28*(1), 122–145.
Darwin, C. (1871). *The descent of man, and selection in relation to sex*. John Murray.
Deighton, J. A. (2023, April 25). *How SHEIN and Temu conquered fast fashion – And forged a new business model*. Harvard Business School. https://www.library.hbs.edu/working-knowledge/how-shein-and-temu-conquered-fast-fashion-and-forged-a-new-business-model
Douglas, M. (1986). *How institutions think*. Syracuse University Press.
EEA. (2024). *The destruction of returned and unsold textiles in Europe's circular economy* [Briefing]. European Environment Agency. https://www.eea.europa.eu/publications/the-destruction-of-returned-and/the-destruction-of-returned-and
Elf, P. (2020). *Supporting sustainable lifestyle change: An evaluation of IKEA's Live Lagom project* [PhD thesis, University of Surrey]. https://openresearch.surrey.ac.uk/view/pdfCoverPage?instCode=44SUR_INST&filePid=13140531660002346&download=true
Elf, P., Ferreira Moura Junior, J., & Kumaruara, A. (2025). Learning to walk lightly through the world: Lessons from amazonian indigenous praxis. *Journal of Tropical Futures*, *2*(2), 81–92.
Elf, P., Isham, A., & Gatersleben, B. (2021). Above and beyond? How businesses can drive sustainable development by promoting lasting pro-environmental behaviour change: An examination of the IKEA Live Lagom project. *Business Strategy and the Environment*, *30*(2), 1037–1050.
Farivar, C. (2024). You're buying so much from Temu and Shein the air cargo industry can't keep up. *Forbes*. Retrieved February 10, 2025, from https://www.forbes.com/sites/cyrusfarivar/2024/05/21/youre-buying-so-much-from-temu-and-shein-the-air-cargo-industry-cant-keep-up/
Friedman, M. (1962). *Capitalism and freedom*. University of Chicago Press.
Frost, R. (2022). France becomes the first European country to ban fossil fuel adverts. *Euronews*.
Gilal, F. G., Zhang, J., Gilal, N. G., & Gilal, R. G. (2018). Integrating self-determined needs into the relationship among product design, willingness-to-pay a premium, and word-of-mouth: A cross-cultural gender-specific study. *Psychology Research and Behavior Management*, *11*, 227–241.
Gossen, M., & Niessen, L. (2024). Sufficiency in business. The transformative potential of business for sustainability. Transcript-Verlag.
Gourville, J. T., & Soman, D. (2005). Overchoice and assortment type: When and why variety backfires. *Marketing Science*, *24*(3), 382–395.
Gunn, M., & Mont, O. (2014). Choice editing as a retailers' tool for sustainable consumption. *International Journal of Retail & Distribution Management*, 42(6), 464–481.

Holland, O. (2024, March 15). French lawmakers approve bill penalizing fast fashion. *CNN*. https://www.cnn.com/2024/03/15/style/france-fast-fashion-bill-intl-hnk/index.html
Horkheimer, M., & Adorno, T. W. (2017). The culture industry: Enlightenment as mass deception. In *Karl Marx* (pp. 405–424). Routledge.
Hu, X., Meng, Z., & He, Q. (2024). Choice overload interferes with early processing and necessitates late compensation: Evidence from electroencephalogram. *European Journal of Neuroscience*, *59*(11), 2995–3008.
Isham, A., Verfuerth, C., Armstrong, A., Elf, P., Gatersleben, B., & Jackson, T. (2022). The problematic role of materialistic values in the pursuit of sustainable well-being. *International Journal of Environmental Research and Public Health*, *19*(6), 3673.
Iyengar, S. S. (2010). *The art of choosing*. Twelve.
Iyengar, S. S., & Kamenica, E. (2010). Choice proliferation, simplicity seeking, and asset allocation. *Journal of Public Economics*, *94*(7–8), 530–539.
Iyengar, S. S., & Lepper, M. R. (1999). Rethinking the value of choice: A cultural perspective on intrinsic motivation. *Journal of Personality and Social Psychology*, *76*(3), 349–366.
Iyengar, S. S., & Lepper, M. R. (2000). When choice is demotivating: Can one desire too much of a good thing? *Journal of Personality and Social Psychology*, *79*(6), 995–1006.
Jackson, T. (2009). *Prosperity without growth. Economics for a finite planet*. Earthscan.
Kahneman, D. (2011). *Thinking, fast and slow*. Farrar, Straus and Giroux.
Kapferer, J.-N. (2012). Abundant rarity: The key to luxury growth. *Business Horizons*, *55*(5), 453–462. https://doi.org/10.1016/j.bushor.2012.04.002
Kapferer, J.-N. (2015). *Kapferer on luxury: How luxury brands can grow yet remain rare*. Kogan Page Publishers.
Kasser, T. (2009). Psychological need satisfaction, personal well-being, and ecological sustainability. *Ecopsychology*, *1*(4), 175–180. https://doi.org/10.1089/eco.2009.0025
Kirk. (2010). *Recycling with sole*. https://www.waste360.com/waste-recycling/recycling-with-sole
Lembke, A. (2021). *Dopamine nation: Finding balance in the age of indulgence*. Dutton.
Lévi-Strauss, C. (1966). *The savage mind*. University of Chicago Press.
Locke, J. (2013). Two treatises of government, 1689. *The Anthropology of Citizenship: A Reader*, *12*(2). https://books.google.com/books?hl=en&lr=&id=PatxDwAAQBAJ&oi=fnd&pg=PA43&dq=Two+Treatises+of+Government+&ots=l7a5UBCZpj&sig=oFDJlHwAu2vmLU9r9zyKZ0mdsSc
Mantrala, M. K., Levy, M., Kahn, B. E., Fox, E. J., Gaidarev, P., Dankworth, B., & Shah, D. (2009). Why is assortment planning so difficult for retailers? A framework and research agenda. *Journal of Retailing*, *85*(1), 71–83.
Markus, H. R., & Kitayama, S. (1991). Cultural variation in the self-concept. In J. Strauss & G. R. Goethals (Eds.), *The self: Interdisciplinary approaches* (pp. 18–48). Springer. https://doi.org/10.1007/978-1-4684-8264-5_2
Misuraca, R., Nixon, A. E., Miceli, S., Di Stefano, G., & Scaffidi Abbate, C. (2024). On the advantages and disadvantages of choice: Future research directions in choice overload and its moderators. *Frontiers in Psychology*, *15*, 1290359.
Moller, A. C., Ryan, R. M., & Deci, E. L. (2006). Self-determination theory and public policy: Improving the quality of consumer decisions without using coercion. *Journal of Public Policy & Marketing*, *25*(1), 104–116. https://doi.org/10.1509/jppm.25.1.104
Mont, O., Elf, P., & Isham, A. (2025). Marketing sustainable lifestyles. In K. Peattie, R. De Angelis, N. Koenig-Lewis, & C. Strong (Eds.), *The Routledge companion to marketing and sustainability* (Vol. 2025). Routledge, Taylor & Francis Group.

Ökopol, & EEB. (2021). *Prohibiting the destruction of unsold goods* (p. 18) [Policy Brief]. European Environmental Bureau.

Paul, J., Ueno, A., & Dennis, C. (2023). ChatGPT and consumers: Benefits, pitfalls and future research agenda. *International Journal of Consumer Studies*, *47*(4), 1213–1225. https://doi.org/10.1111/ijcs.12928

Pelletier, L. G., & Sharp, E. (2008). Persuasive communication and proenvironmental behaviours: How message tailoring and message framing can improve the integration of behaviours through self-determined motivation. *Canadian Psychology/Psychologie Canadienne*, *49*(3), 210.

Putnam, R. D. (2000). *Bowling alone: The collapse and revival of American community*. Simon & Schuster.

Reutskaja, E., Cheek, N. N., Iyengar, S., & Schwartz, B. (2022). Choice deprivation, choice overload, and satisfaction with choices across six nations. *Journal of International Marketing*, *30*(3), 18–34.

Reutskaja, E., & Hogarth, R. M. (2009). Satisfaction in choice as a function of the number of alternatives: When "goods satiate". *Psychology & Marketing*, *26*(3), 197–203.

Ritzer, G. (1993). *The McDonaldization of society*. Pine Forge Press.

Roberts, H., Milios, L., Mont, O., & Dalhammar, C. (2023). Product destruction: Exploring unsustainable production-consumption systems and appropriate policy responses. *Sustainable Production and Consumption*, *35*, 300–312. https://doi.org/10.1016/j.spc.2022.11.009

Ryan, R. M., & Deci, E. (2017). *Self-determination theory: Basic psychological needs in motivation, development, and wellness*. Guilford Press.

Salecl, R. (2019). Consumerism and choice. In Y. Stavrakakis (Ed.), *Routledge handbook of psychoanalytic political theory*. Routledge. http://eprints.bbk.ac.uk/26147/

Saltsman, T. L., Seery, M. D., Kondrak, C. L., Lamarche, V. M., & Streamer, L. (2019). Too many fish in the sea: A motivational examination of the choice overload experience. *Biological Psychology*, *145*, 17–30.

Schor, J. B. (1998). *The overspent American: Upscaling, downshifting, and the new consumer*. Basic Books.

Schwartz, B. (2004). *The paradox of choice: Why more is less*. HarperCollins.

Srnicek, N. (2017). *Platform capitalism*. John Wiley & Sons.

Sunstein, C. R. (2020). Valuing environmental labels. *NYU Envtl. LJ*, *28*, 135.

Sunstein, C. R. (2021). Are food labels good? *Food Policy*, *99*, 101984.

Thaler, R. H., & Sunstein, C. R. (2008). *Nudge: Improving decisions about health, wealth, and happiness*. Yale University Press.

Trentmann, F. (2016). *Empire of things: How we became a world of consumers, from the fifteenth century to the twenty-first*. Penguin UK.

Turri, A. M., & Watson, A. (2023). Product assortment, choice overload, and filtering technology across retail contexts. *The International Review of Retail, Distribution and Consumer Research*, *33*(3), 219–239. https://doi.org/10.1080/09593969.2022.2056904

UNEP. (2023). *Sustainability and circularity in the textile value chain. A global roadmap* (p. 81). United Nations Environment Programme.

Vohs, K. D., Baumeister, R. F., Schmeichel, B. J., Twenge, J. M., Nelson, N. M., & Tice, D. M. (2018). Making choices impairs subsequent self-control: A limited-resource account of decision making, self-regulation, and active initiative. In *Self-regulation and self-control* (pp. 45–77). Routledge.

Werner, A., Elf, P., Lyon, F., & Vickers, I. (2025). Beyond novelty and growth: A virtue ethics enquiry into fashion entrepreneurs' responsible and harmonising practices towards sustainability. *Journal of Business Ethics*, *196*(4), 845–861.

WHO. (2024). *E-waste and child health* [World Health Organization]. https://www.who.int/news-room/facts-in-pictures/detail/e-waste-and-child-health

Wikipedia. (2025). Kitchen nightmares. In *Wikipedia*. https://en.wikipedia.org/w/index.php?title=Kitchen_Nightmares&oldid=1278508681
Wilson, E. O. (2007). *The creation: An appeal to save life on Earth*. W. W. Norton & Company.
Wrap, U. (2017). *Valuing our clothes: The cost of UK fashion*. WRAP

PART II

Organisational level

6

MYTH 5

In tech we trust – the environmental crisis can be engineered away and sustainable consumption attained

Oksana Mont, Marianne Ekdahl and Andrius Plepys

6.1 The techno-optimism myth

In a fire station in Livermore, California, a small lightbulb has been glowing almost continuously since 1901. Known as the Centennial Light, it stands as a quiet testament to the remarkable potential of human ingenuity (Kykta, 2021). If a lightbulb can operate for over a century without being replaced, then perhaps technological solutions are key to addressing the environmental challenges caused by increasing consumption, resource use, and pollution. Innovations in energy-efficient lighting, such as LED bulbs, have indeed demonstrated significant reductions in the energy used per product, reinforcing the idea that tech-driven progress can enable sustainable consumption without sacrifice. Stories like the Centennial Light are often celebrated as proof that the solutions already exist, and we simply need to scale them up and continue with the 'in tech we trust' narrative (Alexaner & Rutherford, 2019). Sustainability can then be framed as a matter of adopting the 'right' technologies and products, rather than questioning how much is consumed, why and under what structural conditions.

Optimism about technology has become the dominant paradigm, shaping mainstream sustainability strategies in policy and business, as green innovations promise profits, GDP growth and competitiveness (Sætra, 2023). However, evidence indicates that absolute decoupling remains rare in most sectors (Haberl et al., 2020). By promoting technology as the primary solution to sustainability challenges, this myth masks the limited ability of technological measures to achieve absolute reductions in environmental impacts, especially without behavioural and structural changes. Even ambitious scenarios of efficiency and electrification fall short of meeting climate targets without lifestyle

DOI: 10.4324/9781003613718-9

shifts, sufficiency strategies and redefined consumption norms (Cap et al., 2024; Golinucci et al., 2025). So, where does this myth originate?

6.2 Origins

Technological advancements have deeply transformed human civilisation, from early tools and agriculture to Enlightenment ideals, shaping societies and driving progress. During the Enlightenment, thinkers like Bacon and Descartes reinforced the belief that technology was the main force behind societal improvement and future prosperity. This optimism reached its peak in the Industrial Revolution of the 18th and 19th centuries, when mechanisation, steam engines and mass production significantly boosted productivity and radically changed economies, societies and households in the Western world (Giedion, 1948). New inventions led to unprecedented economic growth, supporting the idea that human ingenuity could surpass any obstacle.

By the 20th century, technological innovation became synonymous with societal progress. Post-war modernism embraced new materials, household appliances and cars as symbols of prosperity and convenience, while governments invested in technology as a key to improving living standards. At the same time, these advances also contributed to pollution and resource depletion. Even when environmental movements emerged in the 1960s and 1970s, they rarely challenged the fundamental reliance on technology (Mol & Spaargaren, 2000). The prevailing view was that sustainability could be achieved through efficiency improvements – developing energy- and material-saving products, and relying on recycling. Most environmental policies focused on cleaner production, end-of-pipe technologies and efficiency gains (Mol & Spaargaren, 2000).

Significant eco-efficiency gains have demonstrated technology's potential to improve human life. However, the same technology has also caused environmental and social externalities, including air, land and water pollution, deforestation, habitat destruction and greenhouse gas emissions (Park & Labys, 1998). These harms were often regarded as side effects rather than systemic outcomes of a growth-driven model (Kolbert, 2021). The dominant response was to aim for further efficiency improvements instead of rethinking production and consumption systems (IPCC, 2022).

Early technological successes solidified the cultural narrative that technology is both the driver of progress and a sufficient solution to sustainability challenges. The growth of digitalisation and artificial intelligence has strengthened expectations that autonomous systems and algorithmic governance can indeed provide such solutions. Although these developments offer promise, they also risk reinforcing the idea that technology alone can resolve sustainability challenges (see, e.g. Gundeti et al., 2024).

6.3 Consequences

The myth of techno-optimism today has widespread effects on policymakers, businesses and individuals alike. By overemphasising technological solutions, it influences expectations, strategic choices and daily practices in ways that may hinder more transformative approaches to sustainability, overshadow more effective environmental measures, or even create new challenges. The following sections examine how techno-optimism shapes policy, business and everyday practices.

6.3.1 Policy lock-in: how techno-optimism limits policy options

Many sustainability policies tend to prioritise efficiency and product design, assuming that greener products are sufficient (Mont et al., 2022). The UN's sustainable development goal (SDG) 12 exemplifies this by emphasising resource efficiency while overlooking the need to reduce overall consumption levels (Gasper et al., 2019). At best, this results in 'weak sustainable consumption' (Lorek & Fuchs, 2019). Likewise, the EU's ecodesign regulation, often praised, improves product efficiency but has not prevented the increasing volumes of short-lived devices.

The aviation industry offers a clear example of misplaced technological optimism in policy. For decades, policymakers have promised low-carbon aviation through fuel efficiency, biofuels and electric aircraft, but emissions continued to rise. Meanwhile, total revenue passenger kilometres increased ninefold (Peeters et al., 2016). Similarly, hydrogen fuel-cell vehicles were once celebrated as a major step towards decarbonising transport, but they failed despite significant investments. High costs, limited refuelling infrastructure, comparable climate footprints and policy frameworks favouring electric cars led to a 'technology lock-out', relegating hydrogen vehicles to a niche role (Boretti & Pollet, 2024).

Climate mitigation strategies that depend on negative emissions technologies like CCS and BECCS face similar criticisms. They give the false impression of a future technological fix, which justifies delaying urgent action (Anderson & Peters, 2016). Heavy reliance on carbon removal pushes back mitigation efforts and shifts resources away from measures such as rapid fossil fuel phase-out, demand reduction and structural changes in high-impact sectors like energy and transport (Shindell & Rogelj, 2025).

6.3.2 Comfortable consumption: how techno-optimism encourages superficial change

Consumers also play a crucial role in maintaining the myth of techno-optimism. It reassures individuals that they can live sustainably by purchasing eco-efficient products or adopting green technologies, without rethinking their overall consumption (European Commission, 2024). Ethical consumerism and branding strengthen this idea. Even though solar panels or LED lighting may offer some advantages, they seldom challenge high-impact behaviours such as reliance on cars (IPCC, 2022). The charm of techno-optimism lies in its comfort: it enables individuals to see themselves as part of the solution without making significant lifestyle changes.

This comfort aligns with consumer preferences for options that cause minimal disruption. People often favour high-tech, high-cost solutions with modest benefits over low-tech, low-cost measures with much greater potential (Richter et al., 2024). Therefore, electric cars or solar panels are widely accepted, while plant-based diets, smaller homes or giving up private cars meet stronger opposition. The more a change disrupts norms of consumption and personal comfort, the less acceptable it becomes, regardless of environmental benefits.

Techno-optimism also reinforces the notion that sustainable living is a privilege reserved for the wealthy. Electric vehicles, usually costing more than conventional cars, serve both as environmentally friendly choices and status symbols (IEA, 2025a). Other innovations, such as smart home systems or extensive retrofits, require upfront investments that many households cannot afford. Consequently, low-income groups, despite having smaller footprints, are shut out of many 'sustainable' options (Flipo et al., 2025). Sustainability becomes limited to expensive lifestyle upgrades, transforming it into a privilege rather than a shared opportunity.

6.3.3 Business risks of techno-optimism

For businesses, investing in technology is often seen as the most direct way to enhance market offerings, gain a competitive edge and attract environmentally conscious consumers. Innovation promises efficiency improvements, reduced emissions and alignment with regulatory and financial incentives. In this way, techno-optimism presents a compelling narrative: it enables companies to tackle sustainability issues while continuing to grow and operate within existing business models (Sætra, 2023). Many firms have followed this approach, adopting new materials, energy-saving processes and circular practices that sustain operations and enhance their reputation.

However, techno-optimism can also limit corporate sustainability efforts. Companies often concentrate on manageable, measurable areas such as energy efficiency or waste management (Bansal & Song, 2017), while neglecting structural issues like rebound effects and increased consumption, which are often stimulated by efficiency improvements. This selective focus reflects a cultural belief that technology is an inevitable and morally progressive force (Danaher, 2022).

Another risk arises when capital-intensive investments in new technologies cause resource and infrastructure lock-ins (Markard, 2018). Firms that heavily invest in systems like automated sorting technologies or incineration plants are motivated to maximise usage over time to recover costs. These path dependencies can hinder more radical changes, such as decreasing output or adopting service-focused or sufficiency-oriented models. Past investments can, therefore, restrict strategic options and entrench companies in linear production and consumption patterns, even as societal expectations begin to shift (Geels et al., 2017).

6.4 Dispelling the myth

Let us now consider a series of arguments that challenge the common belief that technological innovation alone can resolve today's sustainability crises.

6.4.1 Technology alone cannot offset growing consumption levels

A helpful way to understand technology's role in lowering environmental impact is through the I=PAT equation, which presents impact as the product of Population, Affluence and Technology (Holdren & Ehrlich, 1974). For technological advancements to decrease overall impact, they must more than offset the increases in population and consumption. However, in reality, global resource extraction, carbon emissions and other environmental pressures continue to rise. Seven of the nine planetary boundaries are now crossed, including climate change, biosphere integrity, land use and freshwater use (Richardson et al., 2023).

Population growth contributes to this trend. The world population reached 8 billion in 2023 and is projected to peak at about 10.4 billion by 2086 (UN, 2022). However, population size alone does not determine impact. Affluence, consumption levels and lifestyles also play an equally significant role. High-income groups exert a far greater per capita impact: in 2023, US per capita CO_2 emissions were 14.2 metric tons, compared to 5.4 in the EU and 1.9 in India (IEA, 2024). Rising wealth drives demand for luxury goods, larger homes, frequent travel and energy-intensive lifestyles. This trend is evident in developing Asia: its emissions rose from one-quarter to about half of the global total since 2000, with China alone accounting for roughly 35%. Today, wealthy individuals are the decisive factor: the richest 10% of the global population account for nearly half of all emissions (Chancel, 2022). These lifestyles are further normalised through digitalisation, advertising and social media, which promote affluent consumption as aspirational.

Within the IPAT framework, only technology can, in theory, offset the impacts of population growth and affluence. However, for this to be successful, efficiency gains must produce absolute reductions, not merely lower resource use per unit of consumption. In practice, efficiency improvements are often outstripped by rising consumption (Haberl et al., 2020). Global emissions from energy and industry have risen by around 80% since 1990, while emissions related to consumption increased by 64% (IEA, 2024; Our World in Data, 2024). The International Energy Agency warns that technological progress alone cannot achieve net-zero targets[1] (IEA, 2020). Only pathways combining technological advancement with sufficiency and systemic change offer realistic prospects (Victor, 2023). Even under rapid innovation scenarios, no country is currently on track for the Paris Agreement's 1.5°C goal through efficiency alone. Recent studies support this: Cap et al. (2024) indicate that industrial decarbonisation cannot align household footprints with 1.5°C, while Golinucci et al. (2025) show that sufficiency measures, such as reducing energy demand and consumption, are essential in a decarbonising Europe.

6.4.2 Green technologies are not sustainable by default

Green technologies can reduce emissions but often shift problems elsewhere, creating new resource dependencies, emissions or social impacts (Luderer et al., 2019). This is clear in electrification strategies. Electric vehicles, solar panels, wind turbines and digital infrastructures are essential for decarbonisation, but they depend heavily on lithium, cobalt and rare earths. A typical EV requires six times more mineral inputs than a conventional car, and an onshore wind plant nine times more resources than a gas plant (IEA, 2022). Meeting the goals of the Paris Agreement would require mineral demand to quadruple by 2040 and increase sixfold by 2050 (IEA, 2022). Extraction already has serious impacts: lithium mining in South America depletes water resources; cobalt mining in the Democratic Republic of the Congo is associated with deforestation, toxic waste and child labour (Sovacool, 2019); and rare earth extraction in Bayan Obo, China, has contaminated soil and water with radioactive elements, affecting millions dependent on the Yellow River (Pan & Li, 2016). Life-cycle assessments add further complexity: EVs perform better than petrol cars in reducing climate impact but worse in terms of toxicity, particulate matter and resource depletion (Del Pero et al., 2018). Their benefits only become apparent after extensive use, and battery recycling remains limited and energy-intensive (Fahimi et al., 2022).

Biofuels exemplify problem-shifting. The cultivation of palm oil has led to extensive deforestation in Indonesia and Malaysia, destroying biodiversity and displacing food production (SFO°C, 2023). In Europe, biomass demand has resulted in logging protected forests in Estonia and Latvia, reducing carbon storage (NOAH, 2025). Here, lowering reliance on fossil fuels has come at the cost of ecosystems. The food sector reveals similar contradictions. Ultra-processed, lab-engineered foods are promoted as sustainable alternatives to meat, yet evidence links them to health risks. A UK Biobank study found that every 10% increase in calories from ultra-processed plant-based foods raised the risks of heart disease and coronary heart disease by 5% and 6% respectively (Rauber et al., 2024). Such products may decrease reliance on animal protein but introduce new health risks.

Finally, technologies are never neutral. They mirror the social and structural inequalities of the societies where they are created. Digital innovations, for example, often reinforce racial and gender biases under the illusion of neutrality (Benjamin, 2019). Algorithmic discrimination, insecure digital labour and platform exploitation show how green technologies can entrench injustice just as easily as they address environmental problems.

6.4.3 Efficiency gains are reduced by rebound effects

Another limitation of techno-optimism is its vulnerability to rebound effects, or the Jevons paradox: efficiency improvements often lead to increased consumption, which can offset or even undo environmental gains (Herring & Sorrell, 2009). As early as the 19th century, efficiency gains in coal-fired steam engines resulted in higher coal consumption (Polimeni et al., 2015). This illustrates the classic direct rebound effect, where increased efficiency makes a service cheaper and thus more widely used (Lange et al., 2021). For example, ride-sharing services show a direct rebound effect of 68–77%, as lower costs encourage longer car trips and reduce the use of public transport and cycling (Coulombel et al., 2019). Household energy efficiency tells a similar story: improved home insulation can produce rebound effects of 20–30% as households respond by heating more rooms or increasing indoor temperatures (Herring & Sorrell, 2009). These rebounds do not occur in isolation; rather, they interact with broader structural trends such as rising affluence and consumption levels. These effects combine with wider trends like increased affluence, further limiting the potential for absolute decoupling.

Appliances offer another example. EU washing machines now use about 40% less energy per unit than in 2000, but load capacities have increased, for instance, from around 4.8 kg to 7.6 kg between 1995 and 2020. Still, average loads remain well below capacity, which can offset efficiency improvements (Odyssee-MURE & Enerdata, 2024; EEA, 2024a). This demonstrates engineering progress, but also the trend towards larger, more powerful appliances, which risks causing greater overall use and potentially negating efficiency gains (Vivanco et al., 2016).

Fuel-efficient cars cut emissions per kilometre and also reduce the cost of driving, which encourages longer journeys (Small & Van Dender, 2007). Meanwhile, car weights have increased: European new cars grew from around 1,500–1,650 kg in 2018 to nearly 1,950 kg by 2023, adding almost 400 kg in just seven years (Autocar, 2024). This trend, driven by SUVs, electrification and heavier designs, undermines the benefits of technological efficiency, while creating urban challenges such as pedestrian safety risks and parking shortages (Transport & Environment, 2024).

Beyond direct rebounds, indirect effects happen when efficiency savings are spent elsewhere (Herring & Sorrell, 2009). Tesco's well-known campaign exchanging low-energy bulbs for air miles demonstrates this (Gillespie, 2009). Studies indicate that indirect rebound effects can range from 5% to 200%, especially among wealthier households, where savings often support high-impact goods and services (Andersson & Nässén, 2023). Directing these savings into low-impact areas such as health, education or cultural activities can help reduce the impact (Albizzati et al., 2022).

Psychological rebounds add another layer. Moral licensing causes individuals to compensate for environmentally friendly actions with indulgent behaviours, such as insulating a home while booking a long-haul holiday (Richter et al., 2024). Even those with pro-environmental values are susceptible to this effect, although such values can lessen its impact (Seebauer, 2018). Social norms further strengthen this dynamic: small household energy savings are often seen as a licence for carbon-intensive activities like flying (Sorrell et al., 2020).

6.4.4 *Techno-optimism often neglects shift and sufficiency strategies*

Beyond efficiency, reaching sustainable consumption also requires *'shift'* and *sufficiency* strategies (Creutzig et al., 2018). Shift strategies, such as cycling instead of driving or adopting plant-based diets, reduce impacts but often leave high-consumption lifestyles intact. Sufficiency strategies go further by explicitly reducing absolute demand, for example through smaller homes, less flying or slower travel (see Chapter 8). Only when efficiency, shift and sufficiency are combined do we see a credible sustainability pathway (Alexander & Rutherford, 2019).

Real-world examples demonstrate the limitations of technology without behavioural change. At BedZED in the United Kingdom, efficiency improvements were offset by residents' high energy consumption (Chance, 2009). Masdar City in the United Arab Emirates did not achieve its zero-carbon targets because of low occupancy and reliance on air-conditioning (Cugurullo, 2016). Songdo in South Korea illustrates how digital optimisation could not prevent car-dependent commuting and higher-than-expected energy use (Peyrard & Gelézeau, 2020).

These cases confirm that technology cannot replace changes in behaviour and social norms. Demand-side actions such as living car-free, reducing living space, flying less and adopting plant-based diets provide some of the highest mitigation potential, while sharing-based models could further cut household emissions (Ivanova et al., 2020). Yet, sufficiency remains largely absent from mainstream sustainability discourse, where policies overwhelmingly favour efficiency and circular economy measures, such as extending product lifespans, despite evidence that sufficiency-oriented strategies are essential to achieve absolute reductions in environmental impacts (EEA, 2024b).

6.4.5 The digital revolution has its own ecological backpack

A further misconception of techno-optimism is the belief in the power of the digital revolution. Digital and smart technologies are often portrayed as contributors to sustainability through efficiency, dematerialisation and optimised resource use. However, digitalisation is not inherently low impact. It may support decarbonisation only if it is appropriately governed (IPCC, 2022). 'Smart' household technologies demonstrate the gap between expectations and reality. Laboratory studies show significant efficiency gains, but real-world savings are modest once behaviour and rebound effects are considered. For instance, Brandon et al. (2022) found that smart thermostats delivered only 1–6% savings.

The digital revolution, that is, the spread of artificial intelligence (AI), cloud computing and the Internet of Things (IoT), has increased the demand for electricity, data capacity and critical raw materials (IEA, 2025c). Digital infrastructures already consume significant energy. In 2020, data centres used about 200 terawatt-hours (TWh) of electricity, roughly 1% of global demand; networks account for a further 1.5%, and both are increasing rapidly (IEA, 2025b). Streaming, gaming, blockchain and AI are key contributors. Some large-scale AI search deployments can raise per-query energy use by ten times. Bitcoin mining alone used an estimated 125 TWh in 2023, equivalent to the electricity consumption of the United Kingdom. These figures do not include upstream impacts from manufacturing servers and devices (IEA, 2025b).

Beyond energy, digitalisation has significant material impacts. Global e-waste reached 62 million tonnes in 2022, but less than a quarter was formally recycled, and rates are expected to decline further by 2030 (UNITAR, 2024). Informal recycling poses serious environmental and health risks, while resource recovery remains very low: only 1% of global rare earth demand is met through recycling. Digitalisation has also spurred consumption; especially e-commerce has driven over-ordering, increased returns, and impulse buying (Lehner et al., 2024). Likewise, virtual platforms such as the metaverse still rely on large-scale infrastructure, high energy use and continuous device production.

Finally, digitalisation has social costs. In 2024, one-third of the world's population – 2.6 billion people – remained offline (ITU, 2024). Closing this digital divide is essential for education and development, but if access expands along the energy- and resource-intensive paths of wealthy countries, it risks replicating the same environmental damage (van Dijk, 2020). Therefore, while digital technologies can promote sustainability, without careful governance they may reinforce inequality and worsen ecological pressures.

6.5 Implications

The previous section explored the limitations of viewing technological innovation as the only path to sustainable consumption. It stressed the necessity for a fundamental shift in sustainability strategies, where green technology is one element of the solution, but not the sole answer.

6.5.1 Implications for policymakers

Dispelling techno-optimism requires policymakers to use a broader toolkit. They should promote shift and sufficiency strategies alongside efficiency solutions. Supply-side innovations and supportive policies are necessary but must be paired with demand-side measures targeting consumption. The IPCC (2022) estimates that behavioural, social and structural changes could reduce emissions by 40–70% compared to 2050 projections under current pledges. This involves embedding sufficiency into policies on climate, energy, transport, nutrition and urban development. For instance, national energy plans should combine renewable energy goals with demand-reduction, supported by investments in public transport, less car and aviation infrastructure and incentives for retrofitting and fossil-free heating.

Many policies still rely on information campaigns and voluntary measures, assuming that well-informed individuals will make rational and sustainable choices. Yet research shows that such tools, on their own, achieve only limited effects (Engström et al., 2024). A more effective approach combines regulatory, economic and market-based instruments that actively influence demand. Regulatory tools include minimum durability standards, restrictions on advertising high-impact goods and bans on unsustainable products, such as single-use plastics, combustion engine vehicles or short-haul flights. Economic instruments like carbon pricing, progressive taxation on resource-intensive goods and targeted subsidies can offer flexibility, although public support depends on fairness and transparency in revenue use (Klenert et al., 2018). Choice editing, which involves removing harmful options from the market through regulation, corporate commitments or procurement policies, can further bolster systemic change (Lehner et al., 2016).

Beyond policy instruments, policies must also target the narratives that underpin progress and well-being. Since hedonic adaptation limits the long-term satisfaction from technological improvements (Agar, 2015), well-being cannot rely solely on innovation. Policymakers should promote normalising low-impact lifestyles by supporting imaginaries of sufficiency, care and 'enough'. Adopting vegetarian options in Swedish schools, initially championed by civil society but now mainstreamed through municipal policies, demonstrates how public institutions can shift norms.

Finally, precautionary measures are essential. Technological progress often surpasses regulation, creating gaps where untested innovations can cause harm before oversight is established. Applying the precautionary principle enables action when products or processes may pose risks, even amid scientific uncertainty (European Commission, 2000). This entails shifting from reactive to proactive governance, evaluating whether emerging technologies meet social needs and planetary boundaries. Simultaneously, overly strict enforcement might hinder green innovation (Thierer, 2016). Striking a balance between precaution, adaptive regulation, conditional approvals and risk assessments is vital to prevent harm while supporting long-term sustainability.

6.5.2 Implications for businesses

Similarly to governments, businesses need to expand their range of sustainability strategies beyond efficiency and technological fixes by adopting shift and sufficiency approaches. Debunking techno-optimism involves recognising that long-term competitiveness and resilience rely not only on technological innovation but also on novel business models that operate within planetary boundaries and set production and consumption corridors. This requires differentiating between essential production that directly meets human needs, excess production that fuels planetary overshoot and the vast 'in-between' economy that mixes necessary and unnecessary activities (Bärnthaler & Gough, 2023). Based on this, businesses must assess which activities contribute to essential provisioning systems and which sustain excessive or luxury production with little social value but high ecological cost. This reorientation depends on fostering consumption practices that align with defined corridors and on critically reassessing which products and services genuinely merit provision.

Sufficiency-oriented business models provide a practical entry point for such a shift. They already challenge the dominant growth logic and raise critical questions about which products should be made, under what conditions, and for whose benefit (Gossen & Niessen, 2024). Their strategies include right-sizing production, extending product lifespans, promoting fairer value sharing and reducing profit margins to levels necessary for maintaining operations (Soulis & Mont, 2024). Examples include LilySilk, which avoids overproduction through on-demand models; Radically Open Security, which caps dividends and reinvests profits into social and ecological initiatives; and Kipépéo, a Kenyan slow-fashion brand that offers made-to-order collections with fair pay and community investment. Companies that adopt this orientation might be better prepared for stricter climate regulations, shifting consumer expectations and resource limitations, while also strengthening their legitimacy in a low-carbon future (Heikkurinen et al., 2019).

Beyond the private sector, momentum is also increasing among civil society actors experimenting with justice-focused innovation strategies. Participatory design labs and equity-focused incubators support underrepresented entrepreneurs and prioritise socially beneficial technologies over profit-driven ventures (Benjamin, 2019). Similar initiatives are emerging in housing, where innovation tackles affordability and resilience, and in agriculture, where respect for land rights and smallholders remains central. These examples demonstrate areas where businesses could engage more proactively to strengthen their own strategies.

This trend highlights the need to reorient innovation and rethink the role of businesses within it. Instead of chasing novelty for its own sake or prioritising short-term commercial gains, companies are increasingly expected to work more closely with civil society and learn from existing non-business practices. Ensuring that innovation helps build a regenerative and resilient society involves integrating systematic tools such as life-cycle and social impact assessments directly into the innovation process. This approach aids in early risk identification, reduces burden-shifting and helps avoid the pitfalls of techno-optimism.

6.5.3 *Implications for consumers*

Rethinking techno-optimism involves reevaluating the role of consumers. People are not merely passive recipients of green innovations but can actively help redefine norms, markets and policies. This does not mean that everyone must calculate rebound effects or lifecycle impacts, but it does require supportive conditions that make low-impact living both accessible and attractive.

Moving beyond techno-optimism also brings forward new visions of the good life. Instead of viewing sustainability as a high-tech extension of consumerism, alternative aspirations focus on sufficiency, care and connection. Kate Soper's (2020) alternative hedonism emphasises the pleasures of slower, less resource-intensive living, while degrowth scholarship highlights well-being through autonomy, social bonds and non-market time (Kallis et al., 2020). Such visions require cultural change, where institutions, education and civil society promote low-impact lifestyles as normal. As Jackson (2021, 2025) argues, various pathways can disconnect well-being from material throughput, but this depends on affordable housing, resilient infrastructure and institutional arrangements that protect time sovereignty through secure employment, accessible care and fairer divisions of labour.

Rejecting techno-optimism also expands consumer agency beyond mere market choices. As Maniates (2001) argued, environmental responsibility cannot be limited to shopping decisions. Collective engagement is evident in climate litigation, repair legislation and movements such as the Right to Repair, youth-led lawsuits or land-access projects like 596 Acres. Peer-to-peer sharing and commons-based production, including energy communities, likewise challenge traditional distinctions between producers and consumers (Robra et al., 2023). Consequently, consumption becomes political, expressing values and demanding accountability (Sassatelli, 2007).

This reimagined agency also transforms innovation. Citizens and civil society can scrutinise new technologies by asking who benefits, what unintended effects arise and what justice issues are involved. Winner (1980) demonstrated that technologies embed power relations, and responsible innovation scholarship has expanded this call for collective governance (Owen et al., 2013). Collective governance stresses that decisions about innovation should not be left solely to companies or policymakers but require inclusive processes where diverse actors, for example, citizens, civil society, experts and affected groups, deliberate together on social and ecological impacts. Civil society organisations can support this through citizen juries, ethical audits and deliberative forums. Examples such as France's Citizens' Climate Convention and Denmark's Consensus Conferences show how public reasoning can steer governance. Developing critical literacy and access to reliable information is vital for individuals to challenge risky innovations and support those aligned with long-term ecological and social objectives.

6.6 Main message

In this chapter, we challenge the belief that technology alone can achieve sustainability and support unlimited consumption. Despite decades of technological progress, environmental degradation has worsened. Gains in efficiency have been overshadowed by rising consumption, and many technologies tend to shift environmental impacts rather than reduce them. The problem is not technology per se, but how it is framed in terms of purpose, as well as how it is governed, used and incentivised. True sustainability demands structural change: aligning innovation with production and consumption corridors, prioritising essential over excessive production, reducing overproduction and waste and exercising caution when innovation outcomes are uncertain. It involves systems that focus on provisioning with high social value and low ecological cost and that prioritise long-term societal benefits over short-term private gains.

Note

1 Net-zero targets mean reducing greenhouse gas emissions as much as possible and then making sure any remaining emissions are cancelled out, for example, by planting trees or using technologies that absorb carbon – so the total added to the atmosphere is zero.

References

Agar, N. (2015). *The Sceptical optimist: Why technology isn't the answer to everything*. Oxford University Press.

Albizzati, P. F., Rocchi, P., Cai, M., Tonini, D., & Astrup, T. F. (2022). Rebound effects of food waste prevention: Environmental impacts. *Waste Management*, *153*, 138–146.

Alexander, S., & Rutherford, J. (2019). A critique of techno-optimism: Efficiency without sufficiency is lost. In *Routledge handbook of global sustainability governance* (pp. 231–241). Routledge.

Anderson, K., & Peters, G. (2016). The trouble with negative emissions. *Science*, *354*(6309), 182–183.

Andersson, D., & Nässén, J. (2023). Measuring the direct and indirect effects of low-carbon lifestyles using financial transactions. *Journal of Cleaner Production*, *386*, 135739.

Autocar. (2024). Average weight of new cars rises by nearly 400kg in seven years. *Autocar*. https://www.autocar.co.uk/car-news/new-cars/average-weight-new-cars-rises-nearly-400kg-seven-years

Bansal, P., & Song, H. C. (2017). Similar but not the same: Differentiating corporate sustainability from corporate responsibility. *Academy of Management Annals*, *11*(1), 105–149.

Bärnthaler, R., & Gough, I. (2023). Provisioning for sufficiency: Envisaging production corridors. *Sustainability: Science, Practice and Policy*, *19*(1), 2218690. https://doi.org/10.1080/15487733.2023.2218690

Benjamin, R. (2019). *Race after technology: Abolitionist tools for the new Jim code*. Polity.

Boretti, A., & Pollet, B. G. (2024). Hydrogen economy: Paving the path to a sustainable, low-carbon future. *International Journal of Hydrogen Energy*, *93*, 307–319.

Brandon, A., Clapp, C. M., List, J. A., Metcalfe, R. D., & Price, M. (2022). *The human perils of scaling smart technologies: Evidence from field experiments*. National Bureau of Economic Research. https://www.nber.org/papers/w30482

Cap, S., de Koning, A., Tukker, A., & Scherer, L. (2024). (In)Sufficiency of industrial decarbonization to reduce household carbon footprints to 1.5°C-compatible levels. *Sustainable Production and Consumption*, *45*.

Chance, T. (2009). Towards sustainable residential communities; the Beddington Zero Energy Development (BedZED) and beyond. *Environment and Urbanization*, *21*(2), 527–544.

Chancel, L. (2022). Global carbon inequality over 1990–2019. *Nature Sustainability*, *5*(11), 931–938.

Coulombel, N., Boutueil, V., Liu, L., Viguié, V., & Yin, B. (2019). Substantial rebound effects in urban ridesharing: Simulating travel decisions in Paris, France. *Transportation Research Part D: Transport and Environment*, *71*, 110–126.

Creutzig, F., Roy, J., Lamb, W. F., Azevedo, I. M. L., Bruine de Bruin, W., Dalkmann, H., Edelenbosch, O. Y., Geels, F. W., Grubler, A., Hepburn, C., Hertwich, E. G., Khosla, R., Mattauch, L., Minx, J. C., Ramakrishnan, A., Rao, N. D., Steinberger, J. K., Tavoni, M., Ürge-Vorsatz, D., & Weber, E. U. (2018). Towards demand-side solutions for mitigating climate change. *Nature Climate Change*, *8*(4), 260–263.

Cugurullo, F. (2016). Urban eco-modernisation and the policy context of new eco-city projects: Where Masdar City fails and why. *Urban Studies*, *53*(11), 2417–2433.

Danaher, J. (2022). Techno-optimism: An analysis, an evaluation and a modest defence. *Philosophy & Technology*, *35*(2), 54.

Del Pero, F., Delogu, M., & Pierini, M. (2018). Life cycle assessment in the automotive sector: A comparative case study of internal combustion engine (ICE) and electric car. *Procedia Structural Integrity*, *12*, 521–37.

EEA. (2024a). Product lifespans, monitoring trends in Europe. *Briefing*. European Environment Agency. https://www.eea.europa.eu/en/analysis/publications/product-lifespans-monitoring-trends

EEA. (2024b). *Europe's consumption in a circular economy: The benefits of longer lasting electronics*. European Environment Agency. https://www.eea.europa.eu/en/analysis/publications/europes-consumption-in-a-circular-economy-the-benefits-of-longer-lasting-electronics

Engström, E., Larsson, M., Bradley, K., Dotterud Leiren, M., Ejelöv, E., Finnveden, G., Haugs Langvik, K., Heinonen, J., Larsson, J., & Thøgersen, J. (2024). *Policy options for reducing consumption-based emissions: A Nordic survey*. Nordic Council of Ministers.

European Commission. (2000). *Communication from the commission on the Precautionary Principle* (COM (2000) 1; p. 29). Commission of the European Communities.

European Commission. (2024). *Directive (EU) 2024/825 of the European Parliament and of the Council of 28 February 2024 amending Directives 2005/29/EC and 2011/83/EU as regards empowering consumers for the green transition through better protection against unfair practices and through better information*. https://eur-lex.europa.eu/eli/dir/2024/825/oj/eng

Fahimi, A., Ducoli, S., Federici, S., Ye, G., Mousa, E., Frontera, P., & Bontempi, E. (2022). Evaluation of the sustainability of technologies to recycle spent lithium-ion batteries, based on embodied energy and carbon footprint. *Journal of Cleaner Production*, *338*, 130493.

Flipo, A., Alexander-Haw, A., Breucker, F., & Dütschke, E. (2025). Who is sufficient, and why? A mixed-methods approach to the social determinants of sufficiency lifestyles in the pursuit of decarbonisation. *Consumption and Society*, *4*(1), 55–74.

Fuchs, D. A., & Lorek, S. (2005). Sustainable consumption governance: A history of promises and failures. *Journal of Consumer Policy*, *28*.

Gasper, D., Shah, A., & Tankha, S. (2019). The framing of sustainable consumption and production in SDG 12. *Global Policy*, *10*, 83–95.

Geels, F. W., Sovacool, B. K., Schwanen, T., & Sorrell, S. (2017). Sociotechnical transitions for deep decarbonization. *Science*, *357*(6357), Article 6357.

Giedion, S. (1948). *Mechanization takes command*. Oxford University Press.

Gillespie, E. (2009, April 6). Tesco's 'flights for lights' promotion – every little hurts. *The Guardian*. https://www.theguardian.com/environment/ethicallivingblog/2009/apr/06/tesco-advert-energy-saving-bulbs-flights-greenwash

Golinucci, N., Rocco, M. V., Prina, M. G., Beltrami, F., Rinaldi, L., Schau, E. M., & Sparber, W. (2025). The role of sufficiency measures in a decarbonizing Europe. *Ecological Economics*, *235*, 108645.

Gossen, M., & Niessen, L. (2024). *Sufficiency in business. The transformative potential of business for sustainability*. Transcript-Verlag.

Gundeti, R., Vuppala, K., & Kasireddy, V. (2024). The future of AI and environmental sustainability: Challenges and opportunities. In *Exploring ethical dimensions of environmental sustainability and use of AI* (pp. 346–371). IGI Global.

Haberl, H., Wiedenhofer, D., Virág, D., Kalt, G., Plank, B., Brockway, P., Fishman, T., Hausknost, D., Krausmann, F., & Leon-Gruchalski, B. (2020). A systematic review of the evidence on decoupling of GDP, resource use and GHG emissions, part II: Synthesizing the insights. *Environmental Research Letters*, *15*.

Heikkurinen, P., Young, C. W., & Morgan, E. (2019). Business for sustainable change: Extending eco-efficiency and eco-sufficiency strategies to consumers. *Journal of Cleaner Production*, *218*, 656–664.

Herring, H., & Sorell, S. (Eds.). (2009). *Energy efficiency and sustainable consumption. The Rebound effect*. Palgrave, Macmillan.

Holdren, J. P., & Ehrlich, P. R. (1974). Human population and the global environment: Population growth, rising per capita material consumption, and disruptive technologies have made civilization a global ecological force. *American Scientist*, *62*(3), 282–292.

IEA. (2020). *European Union 2020. Energy Policy Review* (p. 310). International Energy Agency.

IEA. (2022). *The role of critical minerals in clean energy transitions – Analysis* (p. 287). International Energy Agency. https://www.iea.org/reports/the-role-of-critical-minerals-in-clean-energy-transitions

IEA. (2024). *CO_2 Emissions in 2023. A new record high, but is there light at the end of the tunnel?* (p. 24). International Energy Agency. https://iea.blob.core.windows.net/assets/33e2badc-b839–4c18–84ce-f6387b3c008f/CO2Emissionsin2023.pdf

IEA. (2025a). *Trends in electric car affordability – Global EV outlook 2025 – Analysis*. International Energy Agency. https://www.iea.org/reports/global-ev-outlook-2025/trends-in-electric-car-affordability

IEA. (2025b). *Data centres and data transmission networks*. IEA. https://www.iea.org/energy-system/buildings/data-centres-and-data-transmission-networks

IEA. (2025c). *Energy and AI* (p. 304). International Energy Agency. https://iea.blob.core.windows.net/assets/40a4db21-2225-42f0-8a07-addcc2ea86b3/EnergyandAI.pdf

IPCC. (2022). *Climate change 2022. Mitigation of climate change* (p. 2913). IPCC.

ITU. (2024). *Measuring digital development*. Facts and Figures 2024 International Telecommunication Union. https://www.itu.int/itu-d/reports/statistics/facts-figures-2024/

Ivanova, D., Barrett, J., Wiedenhofer, D., Macura, B., Callaghan, M., & Creutzig, F. (2020). Quantifying the potential for climate change mitigation of consumption options. *Environmental Research Letters*, *15*(9), 093001.

Jackson, T. (2021). *Post growth: Life after capitalism*. John Wiley & Sons.

Jackson, T. (2025). *The care economy*. John Wiley & Sons.

Kallis, G., Paulson, S., D'Alisa, G., & Demaria, F. (2020). *The case for degrowth*. John Wiley & Sons.

Klenert, D., Mattauch, L., Combet, E., Edenhofer, O., Hepburn, C., Rafaty, R., & Stern, N. (2018). Making carbon pricing work for citizens. *Nature Climate Change*, *8*(8), 669–677.

Kolbert, E. (2021). *Under a white sky: The nature of the future*. Crown.

Kykta, M. (2021). The incandescent light bulb and the mystery of the centennial bulb. *Information Display*. https://sid.onlinelibrary.wiley.com/do/10.1002/msid.0050001/full/incandescentlightbulbfinal.pdf

Lange, S., Kern, F., Peuckert, J., & Santarius, T. (2021). The Jevons paradox unravelled: A multi-level typology of rebound effects and mechanisms. *Energy Research & Social Science*, *74*, 101982.

Lehner, M., Mont, O., & Heiskanen, E. (2016). Nudging – A promising tool for sustainable consumption behaviour? *Journal of Cleaner Production*, *134*, 166–177.

Lehner, M., Richter, J. L., & Mont, O. (2024). Digitalization: A potential tool for sustainable consumption? In K. Bäckström, C. Egan-Wyer, & E. Samsioe (Eds.), *The future of consumption: How technology, sustainability and wellbeing will transform retail and customer experience* (pp. 189–204). Springer International Publishing.

Lorek, S., & Fuchs, D. (2019). Why only strong sustainable consumption governance will make a difference. In O. Mont (Ed.), *A research agenda for sustainable consumption governance*. Edward Elgar Publishing.

Luderer, G., Pehl, M., Arvesen, A., Gibon, T., Bodirsky, B. L., De Boer, H. S., Fricko, O., Hejazi, M., Humpenöder, F., Iyer, G., Mima, S., Mouratiadou, I., Pietzcker, R.

C., Popp, A., Van Den Berg, M., Van Vuuren, D., & Hertwich, E. G. (2019). Environmental co-benefits and adverse side-effects of alternative power sector decarbonization strategies. *Nature Communications*, *10*(1), Article 1.
Maniates, M. F. (2001). Individualization: Plant a tree, buy a bike, save the world? *Global Environmental Politics*, *1*(3), Article 3.
Markard, J. (2018). The next phase of the energy transition and its implications for research and policy. *Nature Energy*, *3*(8), 628–633.
Mol, A. P. J., & Spaargaren, G. (2000). Ecological modernisation theory in debate: A review. *Environmental Politics*, *9*(1), 17–49.
Mont, O., Lehner, M., & Dalhammar. (2022). Sustainable consumption through policy intervention – A review of research themes. *Frontiers in Sustainability*, *3*.
NOAH. (2025). *No smoke without fire: How the Danish energy transition harms the forests of Estonia and Latvia* (p. 36). NOAH Friends of the Earth Denmark. https://noah.dk/sites/default/files/2025-02/No%20smoke%20without%20fire.pdf
Odyssee-MURE, & Enerdata. (2024). *Energy efficiency trends for households in the EU*. Webinar series on Energy Efficiency. https://www.odyssee-mure.eu/events/webinar/energy-efficiency-trends-household-sector-webinar-november-2024.pdf
Our World in Data. (2024). *Consumption-based CO_2 emissions* [Dataset]. Our World in Data. https://ourworldindata.org/grapher/consumption-co2-emissions
Owen, R., Bessant, J., & Heintz, M. (Eds.). (2013). *Responsible innovation: Managing the responsible emergence of science and innovation in society* (1st ed.). Wiley.
Pan, Y., & Li, H. (2016). Investigating heavy metal pollution in mining brownfield and its policy implications: A case study of the bayan obo rare earth mine, Inner Mongolia, China. *Environmental Management*, *57*(4), 879–893.
Park, S. H., & Labys, W. C. (1998). Industrial development and environmental degradation. *Books*. https://ideas.repec.org/b/elg/eebook/1549.html
Peeters, P., Higham, J., Kutzner, D., Cohen, S., & Gössling, S. (2016). Are technology myths stalling aviation climate policy? *Transportation Research Part D: Transport and Environment*, *44*, 30–42.
Peyrard, S., & Gelézeau, V. (2020). Smart city Songdo? A digital turn on Urban Fabric. *Seoul Journal of Korean Studies*, *33*(2), 493–518.
Polimeni, J. M., Mayumi, K., Giampietro, M., & Alcott, B. (2015). *The myth of resource efficiency: The Jevons paradox*. Routledge.
Rauber, F., Louzada, M. L. da C., Chang, K., Huybrechts, I., Gunter, M. J., Monteiro, C. A., Vamos, E. P., & Levy, R. B. (2024). Implications of food ultra-processing on cardiovascular risk considering plant origin foods: An analysis of the UK Biobank cohort. *The Lancet Regional Health – Europe*, *43*.
Richardson, K., Steffen, W., Lucht, W., Bendtsen, J., Cornell, S. E., Donges, J. F., Drüke, M., Fetzer, I., Bala, G., von Bloh, W., Feulner, G., Fiedler, S., Gerten, D., Gleeson, T., Hofmann, M., Huiskamp, W., Kummu, M., Mohan, C., Nogués-Bravo, D., . . . Rockström J. (2023). Earth beyond six of nine planetary boundaries. *Science Advances*, *9*, eadh2458.
Richter, J. L., Lehner, M., Elfström, A., Henman, J., Vadovics, E., Brizga, J., Plepys, A., & Mont, O. (2024). 1.5° lifestyle changes: Exploring consequences for individuals and households. *Sustainable Production and Consumption*, *50*, 511–525.
Robra, B., Pazaitis, A., Giotitsas, C., & Pansera, M. (2023). From creative destruction to convivial innovation – A post-growth perspective. *Technovation*, *125*, 102760.
Sassatelli, R. (2007). *Consumer culture: History, theory and politics*. Sage Publications.
Seebauer, S. (2018). The psychology of rebound effects: Explaining energy efficiency rebound behaviours with electric vehicles and building insulation in Austria. *Energy Research and Social Science*, *46*, 311–320. Scopus.
SFO°C. (2023). *Mission failed: The limitations of palm oil certifications in preventing deforestation* (p. 46). https://forourclimate.org/research/347

Shindell, D., & Rogelj, J. (2025). Preserving carbon dioxide removal to serve critical needs. *Nature Climate Change*, *15*(4), 452–457.
Small, K. A., & Van Dender, K. (2007). Fuel efficiency and motor vehicle travel: The declining rebound effect. *The Energy Journal*, *28*(1), 25–52.
Soper, K. (2020). *Post-growth living: For an alternative hedonism*. Verso Books.
Sorrell, S., Gatersleben, B., & Druckman, A. (2020). The limits of energy sufficiency: A review of the evidence for rebound effects and negative spillovers from behavioural change. *Energy Research and Social Science*, *64*. Scopus.
Sovacool, B. K. (2019). The precarious political economy of cobalt: Balancing prosperity, poverty, and brutality in artisanal and industrial mining in the Democratic Republic of the Congo. *The Extractive Industries and Society*, *6*(3), 915–939.
Soulis, M., & Mont, O. (2024). Towards sustainable fashion: Exploring sufficiency-oriented business models in French fashion SMEs. In M. Gossen & L. Niessen (Eds.), *Sufficiency in business* (Vol. 2024, pp. 197–223). Transcript.
Sætra, H. S. (2023). *Technology and sustainable development: The promise and pitfalls of techno-solutionism* (1st ed.). Routledge.
Thierer, A. (2016). *Permissionless innovation: The continuing case for comprehensive technological freedom*. Mercatus Center at George Mason University.
Transport & Environment. (2024). *Ever-wider: Why large SUVs don't fit, and what to do about it*. Briefing. https://www.transportenvironment.org/uploads/files/2024_01_Width_limit_for_light_duty_vehicles_final_2024-04-29-155013_zacs.pdf
UN. (2022). *World population prospects. 022 Summary of results* (p. 52). United Nations, Department of Economic and Social Affairs, Population Division. https://www.un.org/development/desa/pd/sites/www.un.org.development.desa.pd/files/wpp2022_summary_of_results.pdf
UNITAR. (2024, March 20). *Global e-waste monitor 2024: Electronic waste rising five times faster than documented e-waste recycling* | UNITAR. https://unitar.org/about/news-stories/press/global-e-waste-monitor-2024-electronic-waste-rising-five-times-faster-documented-e-waste-recycling
van Dijk, J. (2020). *The digital divide*. John Wiley & Sons.
Victor, P. A. (2023). *Escape from overshoot: Economics for a planet in peril*. New Society Publishers.
Vivanco, D. F., McDowall, W., Freire-González, J., Kemp, R., & van der Voet, E. (2016). The relevance of consumption rebound effects for the environmental impact of green consumer products. *Sustainability*, *8*(7), 618.
Winner, L. (1980). Do artifacts have politics? *Daedalus*, *109*(1), 121–136.

7

MYTH 6

Services will save us – sustainability without sacrifice through access, sharing and digitalisation

Emma Johnson and Oksana Mont

7.1 The services-will-save-us myth

Imagine a world where meeting your needs does not require owning things, where the real value of products lies not in possessing them but in the freedom to use them when needed. No more cluttered homes or broken appliances to repair, but on-demand access to whatever you need without the burdens of ownership. Why own cars, furniture or clothing when rental, sharing and subscription services promise the same utility without the commitment? Add digitalisation, and it is easy to believe these services are sustainable by design: less stuff, more efficiency, fewer emissions. This is the vision of a sustainable service economy.

The appeal of a service economy for sustainable consumption depends on the idea that access to services can replace ownership. This chapter discusses four main types of services: traditional services, product–service systems (PSS), sharing and digital services. Each is shown as lowering material use while still offering convenience without needing individual ownership. Renting and leasing, often promoted under the PSS label, offer durability and reuse by enabling consumers to access products like furniture or household appliances without purchasing them. Sharing and collaborative consumption platforms aim to lower overall consumption by enabling shared access to items such as cars, tools and accommodation. Digital services, including cloud storage, streaming and artificial intelligence (AI) solutions, show how virtual consumption can fully substitute for physical products. The core idea of this myth is that services can help economies dematerialise – that is, shift away from resource-intensive production and consumption – while still maintaining modern comforts.

DOI: 10.4324/9781003613718-10

The idea that services can replace ownership and considerably cut material consumption has become prevalent in sustainability talks (IPCC, 2022; EC, 2020). This view has influenced major sustainability strategies among governments, businesses and international organisations. From the European Union's circular economy plans to the fast growth of subscription models and digital services, these efforts rely on the belief that services naturally result in less resource use while maintaining economic growth. However, upon closer examination, the idea that services are immaterial reveals a more complex reality, as their material impacts are often concealed within supply chains, data centres and logistics systems. This chapter explores the often-overlooked resource demands behind seemingly 'immaterial' services. While the service economy may support certain forms of sustainable consumption, understanding its limitations is crucial if absolute reductions in resource use are to be achieved.

7.2 Origins

The idea that replacing product sales with services could reduce environmental impacts emerged in the 1990s amid concerns about pollution and resource depletion. A shift to a 'service economy' offered a way to support growth without harming the planet. Services, discussed in sustainable production and consumption, were promoted by the World Business Council for Sustainable Development (WBCSD, 1996) as part of an eco-efficiency agenda. It was hoped that services would use fewer materials and energy, aiding dematerialisation. However, sceptics like Nørgård (1995) and Graedel (1997) questioned whether services were truly less resource-intensive across their life cycles.

Part of the confusion surrounding the environmental promise of services arises from the broadness of the term, which covers a wide array of phenomena influenced by different schools of thought and underlying assumptions (Heiskanen & Jalas, 2000). Some researchers argued that entire economies could decouple growth from environmental harm by transitioning towards knowledge-based and service-based sectors. Walter Stahel (1997), a pioneer of this idea, envisioned a future centred on services and performance rather than production and waste. He suggested that economies could depend on performance-based business models, such as energy companies offering demand-side management or firms leasing instead of selling goods. Around the same period, the influential Factor 4 book by von Weizsäcker et al. (1997) proposed that it was possible to double wealth while halving resource use with the right innovations. Designers and innovation managers also claimed that consumers do not want products themselves but rather the functions those products provide. It was believed that resource use could be minimised by focusing on function provision.

By the early 2000s, attention had shifted to product–service systems (PSS), business models that integrated products and services in innovative ways.

Research indicated that PSS could reduce the environmental impacts of production and consumption by altering how goods and services are delivered and utilised (Mont, 2002). Across three different types of PSS, these models extended the service logic and reinforced the belief that shifting from ownership to access could promote dematerialisation and sustainability.

In product-oriented product–service systems (PSS), services such as maintenance, repair or financing are bundled with the product. For instance, the purchase of a lawnmower may include an installation service or a financing plan (Tukker, 2004). In use-oriented PSS, the provider keeps ownership, and customers pay for access via renting, leasing or sharing, like paying to use a car or power drill only when needed. Result-oriented PSS charges for a specific outcome, such as 'lighting as a service', where offices subscribe to functional lighting and maintenance without buying bulbs.

In the 2010s, the narrative expanded with the rise of the sharing economy, spurred by digital services. The sharing economy promoted the idea that many goods are infrequently used and could be shared among multiple people rather than owned individually. Early examples, such as neighbourhood tool libraries and community car-sharing schemes, appeared promising. Why should everyone buy a drill that they only use once a year? These models proliferated as peer-to-peer lending and short-term access became easier through digital platforms, surpassing early community-based initiatives. Companies like Airbnb and Uber scaled the concept globally, claiming they reduced waste and underuse by connecting people with underutilised assets.

The increase in digitalisation and virtual infrastructure also boosts the potential of the service economy, making physical goods seem less necessary as many become available online. Platforms such as Netflix and Spotify have replaced physical media, such as DVDs and CDs, with streaming services that are accessible 24/7. Digital services expanded in the 2020s, with streaming, digital twins and AI seen as tools offering sustainability potential to help achieve a low-carbon future. Remote and hybrid work have replaced travel and commuting, especially after COVID-19. Cloud storage replaced physical copies. Governments and companies invest in digital infrastructure, aiming for reduced environmental impact and a dematerialised economy (Tarpani et al., 2024).

These innovations have fuelled a growing belief across industry, academia and policy that services can indeed decouple economic activity from environmental harm. But can they? Let us first consider the macroeconomic consequences of the shift to services.

7.3 Consequences

Expanding services across traditional, PSS, sharing and digital sectors has far-reaching environmental, social and economic consequences. These include environmental impacts linked to infrastructure demands, economic effects tied to value creation and territorial divides and social outcomes related to labour conditions and power concentration.

The environmental impacts of servicisation are often portrayed as beneficial, since a rising service share in the economy can lessen them. Jankiewicz and Szulc (2024), analysing 164 countries between 2015 and 2020, find that a 1% rise in the proportion of services in GDP correlates with a 0.15% improvement in energy sustainability indicators, especially in developed economies with established service sectors. However, overall global material consumption has risen in the last decades, leading to 're-materialisation' rather than dematerialisation of the global economy (Hickel & Kallis, 2020). This trend is evident in the growing ecological footprint of digital infrastructures. Streaming, social media and video conferencing rely on data centres, transmission networks and short-lived consumer electronics, with global data centre capacity expected to double by 2030 due to heightened demand for digital services and artificial intelligence (IEA, 2024). The infrastructures supporting digital services are currently estimated to consume over 40% of the per capita carbon budget compatible with a 1.5°C pathway (Istrate et al., 2024). Already now, the energy use and carbon emissions associated with these infrastructures disproportionately impact regions hosting energy-intensive facilities like data centres (Capello et al., 2023).

The economic effects of expanding services include both new opportunities and systemic risks. Leasing, renting and subscription-based services offer convenience and flexibility. Consumers often gain from more choices and lower upfront costs, while platforms benefit from data control and economies of scale. Subscription models have spread across sectors, from entertainment and cloud storage to transport and meal delivery. Between 2012 and 2021, the subscription economy increased by 337% (Tzuo, 2021). However, the distribution of these changes is very uneven: metropolitan and innovation-intensive regions develop fully fledged digital service economies. In contrast, peripheral regions risk economic marginalisation, which worsens territorial disparities in productivity and entrepreneurship (Capello et al., 2023).

The social effects of a service-driven economy include new forms of consumer engagement and changes in the labour market. Digitalisation has concentrated informational and economic power in the hands of six large corporations – Google, Meta, Netflix, Amazon, Apple and Microsoft – that, by 2022, accounted for nearly half of global internet traffic (Sandvine, 2023). These firms influence what information users access, regulate online markets and monetise personal data (Lehner et al., 2024). While services promoted as empowering may appear beneficial, they often turn attention, time and data into commodities, leading to cognitive overload and financial stress (Lehner et al., 2024). In terms of employment, Capello et al. (2023) observe that platform-based services generate more entrepreneurial and flexible jobs, but mainly in the form of gig labour (Frenken & Schor, 2019). These jobs are often unstable, low-paid and lack social protections, resulting in wage polarisation and greater inequality. Regions with a high concentration of knowledge-intensive services tend to offer better opportunities, whereas poorer areas are left with fewer prospects, widening social and regional disparities (Capello et al., 2023).

7.4 Dispelling the myth

In the previous section, we discussed macro-level consequences related to the rise of the service economy. Here, we examine whether promises of dematerialisation and sustainability of the different types of services have been met or remain unfulfilled.

7.4.1 The illusion of dematerialisation: services are just the tip of the iceberg

Services are like an iceberg: what we see is only the tip. All types of services, however immaterial they might be, still require material and energy inputs, which lead to environmental impacts (Heiskanen & Jalas, 2003). Below the surface lies a vast support system of buildings, equipment, energy infrastructure, logistics and human labour. Many experiences, such as visits to museums, theatres and cultural venues, depend on resource-intensive buildings. Museums need controlled indoor environments to preserve collections, necessitating energy-consuming systems for heating, cooling, lighting and humidity. These spaces are highly carbon-intensive because of their climate control needs (Merriman, 2024). Since they are often visited infrequently and are far from residents, emissions from travel can also be substantial.

Theatre and live performance industries face similar sustainability challenges. Productions are often short-lived, requiring new sets, costumes, props and lighting for each show, many of which are used only once. Touring performances increase emissions by transporting people and equipment between cities and countries. Audience travel also creates a significant impact. For music and cultural festivals, travel-related emissions can account for 80 to 90% of the total carbon footprint, particularly when fans fly in from distant locations (Skolczylas, 2020).

Travel and tourism are major service sectors with significant environmental impacts. Behind experiences are hotels, airports, cruise terminals and recreational facilities, all needing extensive land, water, and energy. Tourism infrastructure can cause deforestation, soil erosion and habitat loss (Gössling & Peeters, 2015). It heavily strains water resources in coastal areas and islands, and risks spreading invasive species and diseases (Gössling, 2002). Globally, tourism contributes about 8% of greenhouse gases, mainly from transport and accommodation (Lenzen et al., 2018). While connecting people with nature, it can also commodify it, turning nature into something to be consumed rather than protected.

Healthcare also significantly impacts the environment, accounting for 8–10% of US and 4% of UK greenhouse gas emissions (MacNeill et al., 2017). Certain areas, like surgical suites, are resource-intensive, using three to six times more energy due to heating, ventilation and sterilisation needs (Robinson et al., 2023). Surgeries rely on single-use tools, sterile packaging and energy-heavy processes. Some anaesthetics are potent greenhouse gases. A single surgery's carbon footprint ranges from 6 to 814 kg CO_2e (Rizan et al., 2020), comparable to a return flight from Berlin to Lisbon at about 846 kg CO_2.

Even seemingly harmless personal care services, such as hair salons, present environmental challenges. Hair washing, drying and styling consume energy and water, while treatments involving chemicals like ammonia or formaldehyde also endanger health and the environment. Salon workers encounter VOC exposure levels that often surpass safety limits, resulting in health problems (Kavi et al., 2024). Daily use of single-use items like gloves, foils and plastic containers also produces substantial waste, often ending up in landfills. This highlights a simple but often overlooked point: traditional services are not immaterial.

7.4.2 More access may mean more use: increased impacts surrounding product use in PSS

Product–service systems (PSS) are often described as a model to reduce environmental impacts by maintaining product ownership with the producer or service provider, rather than transferring it to consumers (Mont, 2004). Instead of purchasing a product, consumers access it when needed through leasing, renting or pay-per-use schemes. The concept is simple: fewer products need to be manufactured if more people share the same product over time, resulting in more efficient resource use. In theory, this model could satisfy people's needs with less production, less waste and longer-lasting products that are repaired and maintained rather than discarded.

In practice, however, many of these models fall short as they can lead to more frequent product use, shorter lifespans and increased environmental pressures. The actual emissions associated with PSS vary widely. Some assessments show they can cut carbon emissions by up to 90%, while others suggest they may raise emissions by a similar amount (Sarasini et al., 2024). How businesses design and manage these models is a primary cause of variability and uncertainty in environmental impact. In sectors like electronics, leased or rented products are often not made to last. They may be intended for quick replacement, sometimes within a year or two, and are marketed through constant upgrades and planned obsolescence, even under the guise of circularity (Watson et al., 2017). Companies are incentivised to maintain consumer interest by introducing novelty and frequent refresh cycles.

PSS are also prone to rebound effects, where efficiency improvements cause increased overall consumption. An analysis of environmental impact assessments found that such models can produce rebound effects ranging from 14% to 216%, meaning that anticipated environmental benefits may be entirely negated or even reversed (Bączyk et al., 2024). PSS can cause direct rebound effects when individuals utilise potential savings of money or time on additional consumption of the same types of goods; energy-saving lights are left on for longer, greatly reducing the projected savings (Alfarisi et al., 2022; Koide et al., 2022).

Indirect rebound effects happen when savings in one area, like time, money or energy, are spent elsewhere. For instance, a consumer saving money by leasing a fridge may use those savings on air travel or clothing. Sometimes, increased efficiency encourages people to work more for premium services, resulting in more consumption. These re-spending and substitution patterns can reduce the environmental benefits of service models (Metic & Pigosso, 2022). Another consequence of improved efficiency is expanding access. As services become more affordable, convenient or available to groups that previously could not afford them, the total user base grows, leading to higher overall consumption. While this can enhance equity and social inclusion, it also amplifies environmental pressures. PSS often adds to existing consumption by renting products consumers might not have bought and combining rental with traditional shopping, especially in high-income contexts. For instance, clothing rental normalises frequent outfit changes and use, raising transport emissions from shipping and returns (Zamani et al., 2017). A study on camera rentals showed environmental impacts rose for new users but declined for those replacing purchasing with renting (Sai et al., 2023).

Even when services lower material inputs per use, they often require new infrastructure that causes environmental impacts. Rental systems for goods rely on storage, logistics and sometimes physical installations like lockers (Martin et al., 2021). PSS products also demand more maintenance, rental garments need laundering and vehicles require servicing. All these activities consume water, chemicals and energy, sometimes more than private ownership does (Monticelli & Costamagna, 2022). Transport, cleaning and maintenance impacts can surpass even those from reduced production (Johnson & Plepys, 2021; Johnson & Mont, 2025).

7.4.3 Sharing is not always caring: how collaborative consumption may fuel new demand

The sharing economy is based on utilising idle resources owned by individuals, access to which are often provided through online platforms on demand

(Mont, 2025). Examples include short-term accommodation rental via Airbnb, ride-hailing services such as Uber and Lyft, and numerous car sharing clubs, clothes libraries and tool sharing sheds. Sharing models assume that utilising underused assets such as spare rooms or cars reduces the need for new production. However, these services often create new markets instead of shrinking existing ones. Airbnb, initially regarded as an improvement in housing use, has driven mass tourism and short-term rentals. Since short-term rentals typically generate higher income per day, property owners often prefer short-term rentals over long-term tenants. This increases housing costs and displaces long-term residents in high-demand cities (Guttentag, 2019). Ride-hailing services were anticipated to reduce private car use and traffic, but often replace walking or public transport in dense areas – up to 83% of trips (Jin et al., 2018). Similarly, shared e-scooters and bike-sharing tend to substitute more sustainable modes such as walking or public transit (Hollingsworth et al., 2019).

A second assumption is that increased access leads to lower overall consumption. The idea is that enabling temporary use instead of ownership will help people to consume less. However, when platforms make goods more affordable, convenient or novel, they tend to generate new demand. This is especially clear in car-sharing services, which are marketed as sustainable alternatives to car ownership. Research shows that they can also attract individuals who might otherwise use public transport, walk or cycle – resulting in more driving overall (Arbeláez Vélez & Plepys, 2021; Plepys & Arbeláez Vélez, 2025). Similar to product–service systems, access can become additive rather than substitutive, offering more ways to consume rather than fewer.

While collaborative consumption is praised for increasing the use of products, this does not automatically reduce environmental impacts. For consumer goods, higher utilisation offers benefits only under certain conditions – when products are durable, are used efficiently and genuinely replace new purchases. In reality, many shared products are not designed for longevity. For instance, shared e-scooters, a symbol of urban mobility, generally last only about three months before breaking down or being retired, compared to owned alternatives (Moreau et al., 2020). Furthermore, digital sharing platforms rely on complex logistics systems, including warehousing, cleaning, digital interfaces and reverse logistics. The indirect environmental impacts of such infrastructure are often overlooked in sustainability assessments, perpetuating the misconception that increased access rather than ownership signals dematerialisation in the economy.

Environmental claims made by sharing platforms are often accompanied by social promises such as community building, empowerment, and increased social cohesion. While such values can arise in small-scale, community-led initiatives, they are not inherent to all sharing platforms. Profit-oriented platforms tend to extract value from users rather than generate it for communities.

Trust and reciprocity are not automatically present in these interactions but depend on context, platform design, and governance structures (Frenken & Schor, 2019). Some sharing platforms operate in legal and regulatory grey zones, avoiding tax obligations, standard safety requirements, and sidestepping established labour protections (Schor & Vallas, 2023). Questions of fairness also emerge regarding who controls these platforms, how profits are distributed and who bears the risks. While platforms claim to empower individuals, their extractive nature often resembles traditional capitalist enterprises, with fewer responsibilities (Mont, 2025).

Most sharing economy models focus on growth, monetising access and offering new ways to consume without reducing consumption. They compete on convenience, speed and novelty, encouraging repeat use and engagement. Some sharing models may yield environmental or social benefits, but they often expand market reach instead of decreasing material demand. Without systemic measures to limit resource use, sharing risks becoming just another form of business as usual disguised as sustainability.

7.4.4 Digital is physical: the hidden material footprint of daily digital services

Digitalisation is another type of service that promises to dematerialise consumption. Like leasing and sharing, digital services are often seen as a sustainable alternative to material goods, providing seamless access to information, communication, entertainment and productivity without the environmental impacts of manufacturing and distribution. However, this view is misleading. Digitalisation tends to redirect material demand to less visible infrastructures such as data centres, transmission networks and electronic devices. All of these require significant amounts of electricity, water and raw materials (Andrae & Anders, 2020).

Data centres in major economies such as the United States, China and the European Union account for about 2–4% of total electricity consumption. This figure already represents more than 20% of the country's electricity use in Ireland, where many data centres have been built. Due to their geographical concentration, data centres can disproportionately impact local electricity systems (Spencer & Singh, 2024). These facilities support a wide range of digital services and are expected to grow rapidly, especially as AI becomes more integrated into everyday platforms (Andrae & Anders, 2020).

AI is particularly energy- and water-intensive during its training, development and use phases, as it relies on extensive hardware and cooling infrastructure (de Vries, 2023). Data centres hosting AI services consume not only large amounts of electricity but also significant volumes of water, both directly for cooling and indirectly through energy production. This can exert pressure on water-scarce regions (Siddik et al., 2021). Generative AI systems such as

ChatGPT are estimated to use around ten times more energy per query than a standard Google search (de Vries, 2023). The surge in AI, cryptocurrencies and online advertising worsens these trends (Ruiz et al., 2022).

Most environmental impacts from digital devices like smartphones, laptops and TVs involve raw material extraction, manufacturing, and logistics. Istrate et al. (2024) state that digital infrastructure accounts for 55% of total electricity consumption. This figure has already exceeded 20% of the limits for mineral and metal use and 20% of total electricity consumption. It has also exceeded 20% of freshwater eutrophication limits per person. Devices are not used indefinitely; obsolescence and software incompatibility force frequent upgrades, leading to over 50 million tonnes of e-waste annually (Forti et al., 2020). Mining for rare earths and conflict minerals raises ethical and environmental issues, emphasising that digital services rely on environmentally and socially problematic supply chains, despite being marketed as immaterial.

Additionally, digitalisation influences consumption patterns by actively reconfiguring them. Lower transaction costs, one-tap payments, and algorithmic personalisation speed up and increase the frequency of purchasing decisions, often encouraging unreflective consumption. Although digital services can support sustainability – by highlighting ecolabelled products or nudging consumers through tailored interfaces – these features are built into systems optimised for engagement and sales rather than moderation (Donato & Adıgüzel, 2022). Platforms are deliberately designed with addictive mechanisms to monopolise user attention, raising screen time and contributing to negative effects on mental and physical well-being (Büchi et al., 2019). The outcome is business models that reinforce throughput and dependency, speed up the pace of life, and increase resource use rather than decrease it (Lange et al., 2023).

7.5 Implications

The previous sections have challenged the idea that services bring about dematerialisation and environmental advantages. Recognising this reality underlines the importance of deliberate and coordinated efforts by governments, businesses and civil society to tackle the challenges arising with the service-based and digital economy.

7.5.1 Implications for governments

To address the environmental impacts of service-based models, public policy needs to adopt stronger regulatory frameworks that focus on limiting material use, energy consumption, and rebound effects. National strategies could incorporate and reinforce the use of social and environmental indicators rather than relying solely on economic metrics when assessing services. Governments have clear opportunities to act at both the city and national levels.

At the city level, authorities can address the environmental and social impacts of traditional services like tourism. Cities manage overtourism with measures such as visitor caps, seasonal restrictions and congestion charges. Barcelona uses demarketing to reduce pressure on its historic centre and promote alternative, off-peak destinations (de Miguel et al., 2023). Venice has introduced entry fees during peak times and encourages longer stays to ease crowding and reduce tourism's environmental impact (Choi et al., 2024). Amsterdam has set limits on how many days visitors can rent accommodation, aiming to ease housing market pressures and reduce neighbourhood disturbances (Mont, 2025). Berlin has imposed restrictions on Uber-like services to safeguard public transportation and cut emissions. These cases show how managing service levels can reduce environmental and social issues.

The increasing energy demands of digital services must be addressed at the national level. Ireland and Denmark are countries that have provided incentives for building data centres, resulting in double-digit growth in national electricity consumption (Spencer & Singh, 2024). Therefore, a change in approach is necessary. Stricter zoning regulations and resource-based taxation should be implemented to account for the real environmental impact of energy and water use in data centres. Incentives should focus on low-impact digital infrastructure, energy efficiency improvements and circular hardware systems. Regulatory frameworks should also establish energy efficiency standards not only for hardware but also for software architecture.

Beyond environmental regulation, governments should invest in service infrastructures that follow sufficiency principles. Market-based reforms are necessary but must be supported by public investment in community-oriented and publicly funded services, emphasising resource conservation over market growth. Examples include maintaining and upgrading public libraries, tool libraries, community laundries, repair cafés and local centres that promote reuse and shared use of existing assets rather than encouraging new production (Mont, 2025).

7.5.2 Implications for service industries and service-oriented business models

The dismantling of the service dematerialisation myth places vital responsibilities on service-oriented businesses. The aim is not to discourage providing services but to reduce the material and energy intensity involved in how services are designed, delivered and consumed. Addressing this challenge begins with rethinking core business metrics. Instead of defining success solely through sales growth, service businesses could measure performance by how effectively they meet essential needs while staying within ecological limits. Indicators can be adjusted to focus less on the number of new users and transactions, and more on product longevity, resource efficiency and employee well-being.

Cultural institutions play essential social and educational roles and can also drive the transition towards environmentally sustainable service models. For example, the Sydney Opera House achieved carbon neutrality through seawater-based cooling, renewable electricity procurement, and comprehensive waste diversion programmes (SOH, 2025). In the tourism sector, approaches such as regenerative tourism aim to minimise harm and actively restore ecosystems and strengthen local communities. On the island of Maui, Hawaii, visitors are encouraged to participate in reforestation projects and cultural heritage preservation, turning tourism into a catalyst for conservation (HTA, 2024). In Copenhagen, the CopenPay programme rewards tourists for ecofriendly actions such as cycling, urban clean-ups, or visiting sustainable sites, offering incentives like free museum entry or local products (WC, 2024). These examples demonstrate how service providers can align operations with environmental objectives while enhancing visitor experiences.

Service-oriented business models need careful design to prevent environmental rebound effects. Sufficiency-oriented rental models can reduce the size of the rebound effects as they emphasise product durability, restrict use frequency and avoid marketing strategies that promote unnecessary demand (Johnson & Mont, 2025). Across the digital economy, high-data default modes should be replaced with low-data options, reserving more resource-intensive digital services, AI applications and cloud computing for when they are genuinely needed. In many cases, streamlined technologies can become the default, with advanced features offered on demand (Madon & Lago, 2023).

7.5.3 Implications for civil society and individuals

Understanding these impacts requires individuals to adopt a more conscious approach to daily services. Instead of assuming that renting, streaming, or subscribing is more sustainable, individuals must question how necessary they are, how often they should be used and how environmentally and socially costly they are. A practical starting point is to reduce the use of high-frequency platforms such as food delivery, fast fashion rentals, ride-hailing and streaming, which increase emissions and material consumption. Effects can be minimised by consolidating deliveries, choosing slower logistics, cancelling unused subscriptions and selecting services that utilise second-hand goods (Mont, 2025).

Shared and collective infrastructures provide valuable alternatives to individual ownership when used thoughtfully. Using books, clothes, tool libraries or community workspaces reduces unnecessary purchases, supports resource efficiency and helps us move away from hyper-individualised consumption. However, even these collective infrastructures must not become vehicles for overuse. Sufficiency-oriented governance is essential (Mont, 2025). Users should handle shared items carefully, avoid unnecessary bookings and promote fair access. This way, shared infrastructures can support sufficiency, social bonds and collective responsibility.

Digital sufficiency is also essential, and it starts with awareness. Individuals can adopt lower-impact practices, such as reducing reliance on cloud storage when local storage is adequate, avoiding unnecessary syncing or updates, and using specific digital tools only on demand rather than keeping them active continuously (Madon & Lago, 2023). Opting for simpler tools and reconsidering whether particular digital solutions are essential can also help regain control over time, attention and energy consumption (Lehner et al., 2024).

Individuals can foster sufficiency-oriented cultures by supporting businesses that embed sustainability and restraint, and challenging those promoting unlimited use. They could participate in conversations and campaigns emphasising care, moderation and enoughness. As Persson and Klintman (2022) note, cultural change starts with shifting narratives to prioritise well-being over throughput. Individuals can help transform the service economy from the bottom up by aligning choices with ecological limits.

7.6 Main message

Services have long been celebrated as the immaterial alternative to resource-intensive economies. Yet evidence shows that traditional services such as tourism and healthcare, as well as digital services, rely on energy- and resource-intensive infrastructures. Product–service systems often generate rebound effects and added logistics that reduce potential environmental savings. Sharing platforms tend to create new demand, platform monopolies and precarious labour conditions. Digital services often shift rather than reduce environmental burdens, reconfigure consumer behaviour and increase digital dependency.

Addressing these realities requires targeted action by various actors. Governments should give more attention to the environmental and social impacts of services. They could incorporate low-impact service provision into urban planning and support local sharing initiatives, such as libraries for books, tools and clothes. Businesses must offer services with durable and environmentally friendly products, take responsibility for supply chain and infrastructure impacts and provide secure employment in platform economies. Individuals can reduce reliance on high-frequency, high-impact services like fast fashion rentals or excessive streaming and opt for services that prioritise local providers and models based on reuse and shared use.

References

Alfarisi, S., Mitake, Y., Tsutsui, Y., Wang, H., & Shimomura, Y. (2022). A study of the rebound effect on the product-service system: Why should it be a top priority? *Procedia CIRP*, *109*(2021), 257–262.

Andrae, G., & Anders, S. (2020). New perspectives on internet electricity use in 2030. *Engineering and Applied Science Letters (EASL)*, *3*, 19–31.

Arbeláez Vélez, A. M., & Plepys, A. (2021). Car sharing as a strategy to address GHG emissions in the transport system: Evaluation of effects of car sharing in Amsterdam. *Sustainability*, *13*(4), Article 4.

Bączyk, M., Tunn, V., Worrell, E., & Corona, B. (2024). Consumer behavior in circular business models: Unveiling conservation and rebound effects. *Sustainable Production and Consumption*, *52*, 283–298.

Büchi, M., Festic, N., & Latzer, M. (2019). Digital overuse and subjective wellbeing in a digitised society. *Social Media + Society*, *5*(4), 2056305119886031.

Capello, R., Lenzi, C., & Panzera, E. (2023). The rise of the digital service economy in European regions. *Industry and Innovation*, *30*(6), 637–663.

Choi, J., Jeon, H., & Asperin, A. (2024). Popularity Paradox in Venice, Italy: A Battle of Priorities. *Journal of Hospitality & Tourism Cases*, 21649987241281375.

de Miguel, S. M., de la Calle Vaquero, M., & Parra, B. M. (2023). Managing overtourism in historic centers through demarketing. *Investigaciones Turisticas*, *25*, 196–219. Scopus.

de Vries, A. (2023). The growing energy footprint of artificial intelligence. *Joule*, *7*(10), 2191–2194.

Donato, C., & Adıgüzel, F. (2022). Visual complexity of eco-labels and product evaluations in online setting: Is simple always better? *Journal of Retailing and Consumer Services*, *67*, 102961.

EC. (2020). *A new circular economy action plan for a cleaner and more competitive Europe* (Communication COM/2020/98; p. 28). European Commission.

Forti, V., Baldé, C. P., Kuehr, R., & Bel, G. (2020). *The global E-waste monitor 2020: Quantities, flows and the circular economy potential* (p. 120). UNU/UNITAR and ITU.

Frenken, K., & Schor, J. (2019). Putting the sharing economy into perspective. In O. Mont (Ed.), *A research agenda for sustainable consumption governance*. Edward Elgar Publishing Ltd.

Graedel, T. E. (1997). Life cycle assessment in the service industries. *Journal of Industrial Ecology*, *1*(4), 57–70.

Gössling, S. (2002). Global environmental consequences of tourism. *Global Environmental Change*, *12*(4), 283–302.

Gössling, S., & Peeters, P. (2015). Assessing tourism's global environmental impact 1900–2050. *Journal of Sustainable Tourism*, *23*(5), 639–659.

Guttentag, D. (2019). Progress on Airbnb: A literature review. *Journal of Hospitality and Tourism Technology*, *10*(4), 814–844.

Heiskanen, E., & Jalas, M. (2000). *Dematerialisation through services – A review and evaluation of the debate* (The Finnish Environment 435, p. 43). Ministry of Environment.

Heiskanen, E., & Jalas, M. (2003). Can services lead to radical eco-efficiency improvements? – A review of the debate and evidence. *Corporate Social Responsibility and Environmental Management*, *10*(4), 186–198.

Hickel, J., & Kallis, G. (2020). Is green growth possible? *New Political Economy*, *25*(4), 469–486.

Hollingsworth, J., Copeland, B., & Johnson, J. X. (2019). Are e-scooters polluters? The environmental impacts of shared dockless electric scooters. *Environmental Research Letters*, *14*(8), 084031.

HTA. (2024, August 20). *Hawai'i tourism authority announces selected organisations for community stewardship and regenerative experiences programs.* Hawaii Tourism Authority. http://www.hawaiitourismauthority.org/news/news-releases/2024/hawai'i-tourism-authority-announces-selected-organizations-for-community-stewardship-and-regenerative-experiences-programs/

IEA. (2024). *World energy outlook.* https://www.iea.org/reports/world-energy-outlook-2024

IPCC. (2022). *Climate change 2022. Mitigation of climate change* (p. 2913). IPCC. https://doi.org/10.1017/9781009157926.001

Istrate, R., Tulus, V., Grass, R. N., Vanbever, L., Stark, W. J., & Guillén-Gosálbez, G. (2024). The environmental sustainability of digital content consumption. *Nature Communications*, *15*(1), 3724.

Jankiewicz, M., & Szulc, E. (2024). The consequences of economy servitization for ensuring energy sustainability—The case of developed and developing countries. *Energies*, *17*(20), 5180. https://doi.org/10.3390/en17205180

Jin, S. T., Kong, H., Wu, R., & Sui, D. Z. (2018). Ridesourcing, the sharing economy, and the future of cities. *Cities*, *76*, 96–104. Scopus.

Johnson, E., & Mont, O. (2025). Actual versus potential impact: Leveraging life cycle assessment to implement business models for sustainability. *Business Strategy and the Environment.*

Johnson, E., & Plepys, A. (2021). Product-service systems and sustainability: Analysing the environmental impacts of rental clothing. *Sustainability*, *13*(4), 2118.

Kavi, L. K., Shao, Y., Ramachandran, G., Louis, L. M., Pool, W., Randolph, K., Thomas, S., Rule, A. M., & Quirós-Alcalá, L. (2024). Airborne concentrations of volatile organic compounds (VOCs) in hair salons primarily serving women of color. *Journal of Environmental Exposure Assessment*, *3*(3).

Koide, R., Murakami, S., & Nansai, K. (2022). Prioritising low-risk and high-potential circular economy strategies for decarbonisation: A meta-analysis on consumer-oriented product-service systems. *Renewable and Sustainable Energy Reviews*, *155*(August 2021), 111858.

Lange, S., Frick, V., Gossen, M., Pohl, J., Rohde, F., & Santarius, T. (2023). The induction effect: Why the rebound effect is only half the story of technology's failure to achieve sustainability. *Frontiers in Sustainability*, *4*, 1178089.

Lehner, M., Richter, J. L., & Mont, O. (2024). Digitalisation: A potential tool for sustainable consumption? In K. Bäckström, C. Egan-Wyer, & E. Samsioe (Eds.), *The future of consumption: How technology, sustainability and wellbeing will transform retail and customer experience* (pp. 189–204). Springer International Publishing.

Lenzen, M., Sun, Y.-Y., Faturay, F., Ting, Y.-P., Geschke, A., & Malik, A. (2018). The carbon footprint of global tourism. *Nature Climate Change*, *8*(6), 522–528.

MacNeill, A. J., Lillywhite, R., & Brown, C. J. (2017). The impact of surgery on global climate: A carbon footprinting study of operating theatres in three health systems. *The Lancet Planetary Health*, *1*(9), e381–e388.

Madon, M., & Lago, P. (2023). "We are always on, is that really necessary?" Exploring the path to digital sufficiency in flexible work. In *Proceedings – 2023 international conference on ICT for sustainability, ICT4S 2023* (pp. 24–34). IEEE.

Martin, M., Heiska, M., & Björklund, A. (2021). Environmental assessment of a product-service system for renting electric-powered tools. *Journal of Cleaner Production*, *281*, 125245.

Merriman, N. (2024). *Museums and the climate crisis.* Routledge. https://api.taylorfrancis.com/content/books/mono/download?identifierName=doi&identifierValue=10.4324/9781003347606&type=googlepdf

Metic, J., & Pigosso, D. C. A. (2022). Research avenues for uncovering the rebound effects of the circular economy: A systematic literature review. *Journal of Cleaner Production*, *368*(July), 133133.

Mont, O. (2002). Clarifying the concept of product-service system. *Journal of Cleaner Production*, *10*(3), 237–245. https://doi.org/10.1016/S0959-6526(01)00039–7
Mont, O. (2004). *Product-service systems: Panacea or myth?* [Doctoral dissertation]. Lund University.
Mont, O. (Ed.). (2025). *Understanding the urban sharing economy: Sustainability and institutionalisation*. Edwar Elgar Publishing Limited.
Monticelli, A., & Costamagna, M. (2022). Environmental assessment of the rental business model: A case study for formal wear. *Environment, Development and Sustainability*, *0123456789*.
Moreau, H., de Jamblinne de Meux, L., Zeller, V., D'Ans, P., Ruwet, C., & Achten, W. M. J. (2020). Dockless E-scooter: A green solution for mobility? Comparative case study between Dockless E-scooters, displaced transport, and personal E-scooters. *Sustainability*, *12*(5), Article 5.
Nørgård, J. S. (1995). Efficient technology in an inefficient economy. In *The energy efficiency challenge for Europe. Summer study proceedings*. The European Council for an Energy Efficient Economy.
Persson, O., & Klintman, M. (2022). Framing sufficiency: Strategies of environmental non-governmental organisations towards reduced material consumption. *Journal of Consumer Culture*, *22*(2), 515–533.
Plepys, A., & Arbeláez Vélez, A. M. (2025). The environmental impacts of car sharing: Direct and indirect effects. In O. Mont & Y. Voytenko Palgan (Eds.), *Understanding the urban sharing economy: Sustainability and institutionalisation* (pp. 87–109). Edwar Elgar Publishing Limited.
Rizan, C., Steinbach, I., Nicholson, R., Lillywhite, R., Reed, M., & Bhutta, M. F. (2020). The carbon footprint of surgical operations: A systematic review. *Annals of Surgery*, *272*(6), 986–995.
Robinson, P., Surendran, K., Lim, S., & Robinson, M. (2023). The carbon footprint of surgical operations: A systematic review update. *The Annals of The Royal College of Surgeons of England*, *105*(8), 692–708.
Ruiz, D., San Miguel, G., Rojo, J., Teriús-Padrón, J. G., Gaeta, E., Arredondo, M. T., Hernández, J. F., & Pérez, J. (2022). Life cycle inventory and carbon footprint assessment of wireless ICT networks for six demographic areas. *Resources, Conservation and Recycling*, *176*, 105951.
Sai, E., Koide, R., & Murakami, S. (2023). Assessing the environmental impacts of product service systems in the digital-devices market: An application of attributional and consequential life cycle assessment. *Sustainable Production and Consumption*, *38*(December 2022), 331–340.
Sandvine. (2023). When Netflix and MAMAA rule the internet. *Phenomena*, *2023*(January), 38.
Sarasini, S., Bocken, N., Diener, D., Velter, M., & Whalen, K. (2024). Reviewing the climatic impacts of product service systems: Implications for research and practice. *Journal of Cleaner Production*, *452*, 142119.
Schor, J. B., and Vallas, S. P. (2023). Labor and the platform economy. In H. Babak, E. Ozlem, D.-C. Rashmi, & B. Yakov (Eds.), *Reengineering the sharing economy. Design, policy, and regulation*. Cambridge University Press.
Siddik, M. A. B., Shehabi, A., & Marston, L. (2021). The environmental footprint of data centers in the United States. *Environmental Research Letters*, *16*(6), 064017.
Skolczylas, N. (2020). *Climate action and the performing arts* (p. 13) [Report from the IETM Galway Satellite Meeting, December 2–3, 2020]. https://www.ietm.org/system/files/publications/ietm_report_galway_satellite.pdf
SOH. (2025). *Sustainability. Sydney opera house*. https://www.sydneyoperahouse.com/about-us/in-the-community/environmental-sustainability

Spencer, T., & Singh, S. (2024, October 18). What the data centre and AI boom could mean for the energy sector. *IEA*. https://www.iea.org/energy-system/buildings/data-centres-and-data-transmission-networks

Stahel, W. (1997). The service economy: 'Wealth without resource consumption'? *Philosophical Transactions A, Royal Society London*, *355*(1728), 1309–1319.

Tarpani, R. R. Z., Mendoza, J. M. F., Piedra-Muñoz, L., & Gallego-Schmid, A. (2024). Circular strategy assessment for digital services: The CADiS framework. *Sustainable Production and Consumption*, *52*, 378–400.

Tukker, A. (2004). Eight types of product–service system: Eight ways to sustainability? Experiences from SusProNet. *Business Strategy and the Environment*, *13*(4), 246–260. https://doi.org/10.1002/bse.414

Tzuo, T. (2021). *Subscription economy index level reaches 337 over nearly a decade as consumer buying preferences shift from ownership to usership*. Zuora. https://www.zuora.com/press-release/subscription-economy-index-level-reaches-437-over-nearly-a-decade-as-consumer-buying-preferences-shift-from-ownership-to-usership/

von Weizsäcker, E. U., Lovins, A. B., & Lovins, H. L. (1997). *Factor four; doubling wealth – halving resource use*. Earthscan Publications.

Watson, D., Gylling, A. C., Tojo, N., Throne-Holst, H., Bauer, B., & Milios, L. (2017). *Circular Business Models in the Mobile Phone Industry* (p. 90). Nordic Council of Ministers. https://norden.diva-portal.org/smash/record.jsf?pid=diva2%3A1153357&dswid=7073

WBCSD. (1996). *Sustainable production and consumption: A business perspective*. WBCSD.

WC. (2024). *Copenhagen launches new green experience economy initiative, CopenPay*. Wonderful Copenhagen. www.CopenPay.com

Zamani, B., Sandin, G., & Peters, G. M. (2017). Life cycle assessment of clothing libraries: Can collaborative consumption reduce the environmental impact of fast fashion? *Journal of Cleaner Production*, *162*, 1368–1375.

8

MYTH 7

It's not worth repairing: the myth of neophilia

Jessika Luth Richter and Hervé Corvellec

8.1 The neophilia myth

Out with the old and in with the new; why repair?

> I brought my bicycle in for repair one day, anticipating it needed a new chain. The mechanic looked at the bicycle with dismay, declaring it old and in need of not only a new chain, but also a new derailer, among several other parts. He said it would likely be nearly half the price of a new bicycle, and it would be better just to buy new than repair the old. Next to the gleaming perfection of the new bicycles available in a variety of colours, my bicycle indeed seemed old – it was bought used more than 10 years earlier, and in the meantime had acquired more scratches, grease marks, and a rusty basket. Red was never my favourite colour anyways – and now it was red with splashes of brown and grey from daily wear and a lot of muddy puddles. A new bicycle promised problem-free performance, at least for a while, and the chance to choose the design, colour, and accessories that matched my tastes. Repairing meant being content with the old bicycle, with its scratches and only some new parts to restore its functionality. Repairing would still require some investment, but it would also be caring and responsible. Was it worth it?
>
> – Jessika Luth Richter

The short personal case above is illustrative of many similar experiences when consumers are faced with a classic decision – repair or replace? The bike storeowner repeated a common belief – it is better to buy new, often even if it is cheaper to repair. It is the myth of neophilia – the love of newness – and with this the myth of the inferiority of repaired products and the futility of

DOI: 10.4324/9781003613718-11

repairing in comparison to new products and buying new. This chapter looks at where this idea that new is better comes from and argues that it is not always so and that keeping the old, and repairing it, can be better value in many ways.

What is neophilia?

> *The city of Leonia refashions itself every day: every morning the people wake between fresh sheets, wash with just-unwrapped cakes of soap, wear brand-new clothing, take from the latest model refrigerator still unopened tins, listening to the last-minute jingles from the most up-to-date radio. On the sidewalks, encased in spotless plastic bags, the remains of yesterday's Leonia await the garbage truck. Not only squeezed tubes of toothpaste, blown-out light bulbs, newspapers, containers, wrappings, but also boilers, encyclopedias, pianos, porcelain dinner services. It is not so much by the things that each day are manufactured, sold, bought, that you can measure Leonia's opulence, but rather by the things that each day are thrown out to make room for the new.*
>
> — Italo Calvino, Invisible Cities, 1974, p. 114

Leonia describes a city in love with newness, a literary focus of neophilia. Neophilia can be situated within a broader myth of progress – a trend to leave the old and promote the new without really questioning whether new is better (Rhodes & Pullen, 2010). Neophilia rises with affluence and consumerism in Western cultures in the 50s and 60s and is related to the rapid technological progress. Consumers in countries like the United States began to feel functional products were outdated or inferior, as manufacturers and advertisers promoted newness as a social ideal (Packard, 1961). Over time, trends in technological progress, combined with the technological complexity to understand exactly what the progress was, developed into an over-trust in the new as an invaluable product feature. Campbell (2014) describes how products are marketed as 'new', with this being a selling point in and of itself, or 'new and improved', which he notes is a contradiction in terms.

There are essentially three potential forms of consumption of new: to replace objects that are needed, to consume products that are innovative or improved, and lastly, for fashion, aesthetic, or novelty reasons less related to the function of the products themselves (Campbell, 2014). All three forms can be driven by not only the needs and desires of consumers but also the product designs and business practices.

The first form of consumption of the new is a more traditional pattern of consumption historically. Objects that are needed require replacing when they are worn out and cannot be further maintained or repaired. They may also require replacement due to changes of consumer needs (e.g. children grow and need 'new' clothing). However, how often these needed objects are replaced is also a function of how quickly they break down, through either the patterns of use or the design of the products themselves.

The other forms of consumption of the new do not relate to the functional obsolescence of products but relate more to the advantages offered by the latest development of technology. Early adopters of the technology might be driven by a desire for novelty or distinction (Rogers, 2003). New products can serve as cultural markers, used to express identity, taste and social status. As Veblen (1899, 1994) argued, much consumption serves a conspicuous role, signalling distinction rather than fulfilling need. The appeal lies in the novelty itself, often shaped by trends, seasonal cycles, and marketing strategies that position newness as inherently desirable (McCracken, 1990).

Neophilia is related to not only consumption but also production practices. Companies not only respond to demand, but they also have a significant role in shaping that demand through advertising, branding, product design and provision of services (Plepys & Arbeláez Vélez, 2025). Practices such as 'planned obsolescence' can be employed by producers to design products to fail and encourage consumption of new products. Obsolescence isn't always so intentional; it can also be simply designing products to be cheaper and lower quality, with a trade-off of less durable products – products with shorter lifespans (Cooper, 2005) – or a changing technological system that makes the products within older systems incompatible (McVeigh et al., 2019; Packard, 1961). Accelerating consumption of newness is driven through accelerating obsolescence through functional failures, innovation, and fashion (Campbell, 2021). In this respect, this is a 'form of consumption of the new that is forced on consumers rather than something that stems from a preference for the new' (Campbell, 2014, p. 36).

Thus, there are systemic drivers of neophilia with both supply and demand having a role to play and reinforcing each other. While some consumption of new is driven by the needs and desires of consumers, these are encouraged by manufacturers through product designs, investments in R&D for new designs, and aggressive marketing that encourage new over existing goods and services. Governments also play a role, often in directly funding new product development and innovation for growth, while continuously undervaluing repair and maintenance (Hickel, 2020; Slade, 2007; Vinsel & Russell, 2020).

8.2 Consequences

The consequence of neophilia is that existing products are discarded in favour of new ones even before these have stopped to function, as part of faster cycles of production and consumption. Such fast cycles require increasing amounts of resources, which come with associated environmental and social impacts.

The textile industry alone contributes approximately 6–8% of global greenhouse gas emissions and uses a significant amount of freshwater – impacts that have accelerated through rapid production cycles, overconsumption and high volumes of textile waste (Niinimäki et al., 2020). Mining for electronics causes widespread harm, including water depletion from lithium extraction in Chile's Atacama Desert, deforestation and toxic pollution from nickel mining in Indonesia, toxic waste from copper mining in Peru and Zambia, and dangerous labour conditions – including child labour – in cobalt mines in the Democratic Republic of Congo (Beiser, 2024).

There are significant amounts of waste generated in producing new products, but also waste generated in their subsequent premature obsolescence. The new becomes old and discarded in faster and faster cycles. The fictional city of Leonia described earlier is a parable for many high-consumption societies today that produce massive amounts of waste that is packaged and taken away, hiding the waste and its impacts from those who generated it (Clapp, 2002). The production and disposal of textiles and electronics contribute significantly to a global ecological crisis, marked by environmental degradation at extraction sites, depletion of finite resources and intensified geopolitical tensions over access to raw materials. In 2022, the European Union generated nearly seven million tonnes of textile waste, with 85% entering mixed household waste streams, ultimately destined for incineration or landfill due to limited separate collection and recycling infrastructure (EEA, 2025), with some of this waste disposed before even being used (EEA, 2024). Similarly, the world produced 62 million tonnes of electronic waste, of which only 22.3% was formally recycled, with much of the remainder stored indefinitely, incinerated or exported to regions with weaker environmental regulations (Baldé et al., 2024). These exports are increasingly problematic: in 2022, the EU shipped 1.4 million tonnes of used textiles to Africa and Asia, where limited recycling capacity and declining product quality have raised concerns about secondary pollution and waste burden in recipient countries (EEA, 2025). Such downstream impacts obscure the broader environmental costs embedded within global supply chains, including the degradation of habitats, rising prices for key resources and the perpetuation of extractive practices that have, in many cases, been linked to armed conflict and structural violence (Baldé et al., 2024).

Devaluing repair

Another significant consequence of neophilia is that it leads to devaluing of repair practices in both production and consumption, and the perception that repair is not worth it. Historically, repair was a common household activity for most people, particularly in rural and working-class communities, who engaged in repair out of necessity. Goods were typically handmade, expensive, and durable, making repair a vital skill for extending their lifespan. Wealthier classes often had the resources to hire skilled artisans or craftsmen for repairs, which elevated repair work into a specialised trade in certain contexts. However, in modern industrialised societies, societal and cultural values often devalue repaired goods, framing them as lesser in quality and status compared to new ones (Gregson et al., 2009).

Krebs and Weber (2021) give a detailed and nuanced analysis of the history of repair and how it changed with the advent of the Industrial Revolution. The rise of cheap, disposable goods made repair uneconomical for some products, as buying new became cheaper and less durable items were increasingly difficult to repair. Doing repair work yourself out of necessity became increasingly stigmatised in highly industrialised societies and perceived as a practice of the economically disadvantaged. While household repair decreased, the Industrial Revolution also created new kinds of repair work, especially for increasingly complex technologies such as machinery, transportation (e.g. trains, automobiles) and household appliances.

At the same time, manufacturing costs have continuously decreased over time due to outsourcing and economies of scale (Campbell, 2021). Meanwhile repair costs in high-income countries remain high because repairs typically require skilled labour in more expensive, local markets. This disparity discourages repair from an economic perspective, perpetuated by common heuristics, such as the '50% rule': if the repair cost is half or more of the cost of a replacement, then the product should be replaced (Scott & Weaver, 2014).

To sell products for cheap prices, modern products are increasingly designed for obsolescence, without durability or repair in mind (Cooper, 2010). Many academics (e.g. Perzanowski, 2021; Svensson-Hoglund et al., 2021) note that this makes repair increasingly difficult or unattractive for consumers. It is easier, and often less expensive, to buy cheap new clothing than to repair or upcycle cheap used clothing.

Neophilia supports business and policy decisions that prioritise innovations that maintain rapid rates of product renewal over innovations that support more sustainable and repairable designs, which in turn reinforces neophilia over repair among consumers. Manufacturers also use proprietary parts and specialised tools, such as unique screws, glued components and software-restricted hardware, all of which, in the worst case, prevent owners from accessing and fixing their own devices or at least make it more difficult and expensive. An example of this is the pentalobe (five-sided star) screw that replaced common Philips head screws in many Apple products from 2009. There were no screwdrivers outside the Apple technician's toolkit for this, so companies like iFixit reverse-engineered one (Clapp, 2018). Despite its wider availability now, it is another step in more specialised knowledge needed to replace a battery in a laptop or phone.

FIGURE 8.1 iPhone 6s pentalobe screws, lightning connector (proprietary) port and home button with Touch ID (proprietary).

Source: Raimond Spekking/CC BY-SA 4.0 (via Wikimedia Commons).

Manufacturers have increasingly restricted repairability by embedding proprietary technology, implementing software locks and designing products in ways that make self-repair difficult or impossible (Perzanowski, 2021) – see Figure 8.1. Even if you have easily repairable hardware, software can still impede a repair or make the repaired item less functional. For example, replacing the home button on an iPhone 6 while preserving the Touch ID functionality requires using an Apple-authorised repair provider, as independent repairers lack access to the necessary software tools to repair the Touch ID sensor. This was a design choice by Apple to prevent unauthorised access to biometric data and protect against tampering. Some customers who used independent repairers for replacing cracked screens or a home button found their phone was disabled by subsequent Apple software updates (so-called error 53) and were wrongly denied help with the error (Knaus, 2017). While the iPhone 14 was designed to be physically easier to repair, access to software continues to impede functionality of repaired phones (Wiens, 2023). The practice of using software locks, or restricting necessary software, is not isolated to Apple. In January 2025, John Deere was sued by the US Federal Trade Commission (FTC) for restricting access to its essential repair software, making it available only to authorised dealers, which has forced farmers to rely on more expensive, manufacturer-approved repairs. The FTC alleged that this practice gives Deere an unlawful monopoly over repair services and the result is increased costs and barriers for repairing farm equipment. Ironically, the practice has also resulted in many farmers seeking to buy or keep older farming equipment instead.

The increased consumption of more complex products like electronics and digitalised products has also influenced the ability to repair, and who can repair, such products. As a result, consumers are becoming more dependent on authorised repair services while independent repair shops struggle to compete. While offering maintenance and repair services is part of many business models, the practice of premature obsolescence may still at the core of the business model. Packard (1961) describes customers in the 1950s who were reluctant to replace whole appliances at the time were increasingly encouraged to purchase, rather than repair, parts of those appliances. At the same time, more complex product designs increased the complexity of repairs and types of spare parts needed while replacement part costs were also rising, if they were available at all. The barriers to repair described in the 1950s, including difficulty sourcing spare parts and information as well as the increasing complexity of knowledge and skills required align with more recent studies of the barriers to repair described in more recent times (see, e.g. Svensson-Hoglund et al., 2021). Many of these design barriers affect independent repairers, forcing consumers to use original manufacturer repair services.

However, even original manufacturers face challenges in offering repair services while being reliant on shorter product cycles. In 2019, Tim Cook, the CEO of Apple, announced lower-than-expected profits in a letter to investors. He cited several factors for the reduced profits, including lower iPhone sales and the impact of Apple's battery replacement program, which had allowed customers to extend the life of their existing devices rather than upgrading to newer models and resulting in fewer new iPhone sales than expected, impacting the company's revenue and threatening shareholder value. This message was reiterated by Apple's Vice President of Corporate Law, who stated in 2019 that 'for each year since 2009, the costs of providing repair services has exceeded the revenue generated by repairs' (U.S. House of Representatives Committee Repository, 2019, p. 9). The case of Apple illustrates the difficulties for many businesses: they make their main profit from the sale of new products, and they have difficulty making profits from offering spare parts and repair services without undermining their main revenue stream.

Incentivising the production of new over the repair of existing production also has implications for production, economic and labour markets where these activities occur (or do not). Production is often globalised, whereas repair is most often local. If devalued, the knowledge and skills of repair can be lost in local communities, which then are vulnerable when global supply chains are disrupted. This became apparent during the COVID-19 pandemic, as supply chains for new products were disrupted at the same time demand for certain products increased (e.g. functioning ventilators for hospitals and computers for students at home) and repair skills became necessary to keep these functioning but also to restore function to older devices to meet demand (Svensson-Hoglund et al., 2023).

8.3 Dispelling the myth

Unpacking the myth, we can readily find many exceptions to the preferences for new products. For example, according to an EU survey, a majority of EU citizens only replaced their digital devices because they were broken (~37%), not functioning well (30%), or had apps stop working (19%). A smaller number of respondents wanted new devices for their new features (~15%) or just to have the latest device on the market (~5%) (EU Commission, 2019). In some cases, it seems, we are not all neophiliacs.

While there are some who may define themselves by their desire and enthusiasm for new innovations, innovation diffusion theory suggests the number of innovators and early adopters of new technology is quite small (Rogers, 2003). The desire for novelty is also balanced by the comfort and safety of familiarity (McAlister & Pessemier, 1982). Conversely, late adopters of new products are driven more by demonstrated advantages and even these can relate more to social pressure and institutional factors, rather than a demonstrated desire or preference for new. For example, as ICT became widely adopted, this increased the social and institutional pressures on others to adopt it to be able to, for example, respond to emails and access public services. (Rogers, 2003).

So new is certainly not always desired by all; neither is it inherently beneficial for all. For example, the use of information and communication technology (ICT) is not inherently beneficial, and especially in the early 2000s, as Selwyn (2003) shows, there were individuals who resisted adopting new ICT. Reasons ranged from older adults who did not see the relevance to those who struggled with technological complexity, feared data privacy risks or preferred face-to-face interaction.

Even desires for novelty can be met without purchasing new products, as the rise of vintage fashion, antique furniture and refurbished products exemplifies. The majority of consumers surveyed in the EU indicated they would buy secondhand media (e.g. book, DVDs, etc.) and furniture, and young people surveyed were more likely to consider secondhand for a range of product groups (EU Commission, 2014). As one of Europe's fastest-growing companies in 2022, Swappie, a Finnish company specialising in the refurbishment and resale of pre-owned iPhones, reflects the increasing mainstream appeal of reuse in the electronics sector. Between 2017 and 2020, the company recorded a compound annual growth rate of over 477% (Statista, 2024).

This example of company-level growth also aligns with global trends. While the new smartphone market contracted in 2022, the refurbished smartphone market grew by 5%. In 2024, more than 309 million refurbished smartphones were shipped worldwide, and the pre-owned smartphone market was valued at approximately $62.66 billion in 2024 (Clausnitzer, 2025).

In second-hand, vintage and antique stores, consumers can find replacements for broken or worn products but also fulfil the desire for novelty with older products that may be more unique than mass-produced, contemporary alternatives. Furthermore, the unpredictability of second-hand shopping itself introduces an element of discovery and excitement, satisfying a consumer's pursuit of the unfamiliar and the unexpected (Campbell, 2014).

8.3.1 New is not (necessarily) better than old

Consumers are surrounded by advertising messages about new and improved products, encouraging them to buy because they are better than what they have, or they are helping the economy. However, for consumers, the claims of improvement of these products are most often over-stated and they represent only incremental improvements, if any at all (Campbell, 2014). New products promise problem-free functionality, but products often have lifetimes shorter than what consumers anticipate (Cooper, 2004). Many newer products, particularly clothing, electronics and many appliances, are often designed with a focus on cheaper materials that have resulted in decreasing durability over time (Slade, 2007). This is a trend despite protection of legal guarantees that in the EU protect consumers against faults for two years. In practice, many consumers are unaware of legal guarantees and exercising such rights can be difficult in practice with the onus on consumers to prove the fault after the first six months; more are only aware of voluntary warranties offered by product manufacturers (EU Commission et al., 2015). Increasingly, refurbished products like electronics and appliances come with warranties and continue to build trust in the quality and grow the market for reused and refurbished products. A study by Google found that search interest for the topic 'used goods', including the terms 'second hand' and 'pre-loved', was up over 70% in the year 2023 compared to the year before. The study included a survey that found that 41% of consumers bought refurbished technology because it is cheaper, 35% because they can get a better product for less and 15% because it's better for the environment (Breatnach & Puttini, 2024).

The value of new products also declines quickly in many cases. For example, cars can lose 40% of their economic value in the first three years (U.S. Bureau of Labor Statistics, 2024). On the other hand, some older products gain value with age. Empirical studies on consumer attachment to durable goods show that people often form emotional connections with objects they own, particularly when these items have personal meaning, are associated with significant life events or have been customised over time (Mugge et al., 2006, 2010). Objects can shift also from being seen as non-durable or worthless to being reclassified as durable and valuable once they are no longer common or are perceived as culturally or historically significant (Thompson, 1979). Repurposing or customising existing goods allows individuals to transform familiar objects into something personally novel, fulfilling the need for creative self-expression.

In pursuing the new, consumers can be driven to spend money on products they do not really need. In the end, this is consumption that does not contribute to well-being and, in many cases, undermines it (Jackson, 2005). Short lifetimes and faster product cycles can be inconvenient if one considers not only the expense and time in shopping and deciding but also time of learning how to use a new product. This is particularly evident in the case of information and communication technologies (ICT), where even minor hardware or software changes may require users to adapt to new interfaces, settings or functions (Selwyn, 2003). In research of individuals who did not adopt ICT readily, these continual changes can present significant barriers to use, particularly for less technologically confident individuals, who may experience frustration, reduced productivity or even exclusion from digital environments as a result (Selwyn, 2003). Thus, beyond the financial and material implications, rapid product turnover can create cognitive and emotional burdens that discourage meaningful engagement with technology and reinforce digital inequalities.

Much of what is framed as consumer preference for new is often a structural outcome of systemic pressures (Campbell, 2014). If it is in their interest, companies will shape consumer demand towards maintaining and repairing rather than buying new (see Chapter 11 on this). Packard (1961) gave some evidence of this in describing the late 1950s in the United States as not only a consumerist culture but also 'The Repairman's Paradise' (p. 128) because many companies saw new opportunities in selling products that required regular servicing or spare parts. Products like washers, dryers, refrigerators and televisions at the time required an average of at least one service call within the first year after purchase (Packard, 1961, p. 130). However, still today, many businesses successfully operate maintenance and business models based less on new sales than on subsequent revenues from maintaining and repairing the initial products. For example, the agricultural equipment manufacturer John Deere has pursued the provision of repair services, resulting in more of their profits stemming from the repair of their equipment than from the sale of new equipment; however, it also does so by aggressively limiting competition (Rimmer, 2025). There remain many businesses devoted to the provision of repair services as well, which indicates there is value and profitability to repair from a business perspective. According to data from the European Topic Centre on Circular Economy and Resource Use, the turnover in the EU's repair sector increased from €20.9 billion in 2012 to €25.6 billion in 2017, before decreasing to €21.5 billion in 2020. The sector's share of the total EU economy ranged between 1.6% and 1.9% during this period (European Topic Centre on Circular Economy and Resource Use, 2022). The bulk of this turnover was attributed to the repair of computers, peripheral appliances, personal and household goods, communication equipment, and consumer electronics. The data excludes the automobile industry. In 2021, there were over 5.4 million enterprises engaged in the maintenance and repair of vehicles, employing over 29 million people and a net turnover of nearly €11 billion (Eurostat, 2024).

Today, purchasing products comes with the expectation that any needed servicing, at least in the first six months, would be covered by the legal guarantee, but this still falls well short of the expected lifetimes for such products (Dalhammar et al., 2023). Packard (1961) observed that the downside of many repair and maintenance business models for consumers was the expense and hassle of organising repair services, which he notes made some consumers happier to stick with their older, simpler models requiring less servicing. He describes some consumers in the late 1950s intentionally buying older automobiles that they could still maintain and repair themselves rather than new automobiles where this was becoming harder to do oneself. Indeed, in more recent times, manufacturers have had near monopolistic control of repair services for farming equipment, which has pushed many farmers to buy 40-year-old equipment instead so that they could maintain and repair it more easily (Gault, 2020) – again demonstrating another way in which newer products are not better than older, more repairable products, but also that systemic factors not only push for new, but may increasingly limit repair of existing products.

For many products, repairability is often intentionally limited, creating the perception that repair is futile, when in reality it could be viable if designed differently. Companies like Fairphone and Patagonia demonstrate how repair can be economically and environmentally viable for a business and products can be designed to last and be repaired. Still, there are limitations for products that are part of bigger technical systems – as evidenced by the fact that even Fairphones will become increasingly difficult to use as they age past the seven years of software support. Keeping them alive requires knowledge of open-source software options, which may not be compatible with the demands of newer apps, data storage and technological systems without some adaptation of user expectations and behaviour.

From the consumer experience, research on repair experiences reveals a myriad of barriers – from independent repair services being barred from advertising in Google searches (DeBellis, 2020) to consumers not having the knowledge of where to access or not having the skills (Svensson-Hoglund et al., 2021) – all part of the repair experience beyond the barriers with the product itself.

Even when the consumer gets to the repair shop, the repairman might also have an incentive to sell a new product, like the bicycle repair shopowner in the case at the beginning of the chapter. He relied on the persuasive 50% heuristic to make the argument that new was better than old and repair was not worth it. However, the repaired city bike would be just as functional as a new one – it is not a product where significant innovations are easy to argue. Even a professional repairman was not arguing the value of repair. What is the value of repair?

8.3.2 The value of repair

Whether repair is 'worth it' depends on not only the perceived value of the item to be repaired but also the value of repair in itself. Informal rules like the 50% rule mentioned earlier naturally favour repair towards products that have a higher upfront cost, but it primarily focuses narrowly on economic concerns. In reality, there are also many non-monetary factors such as convenience, knowledge, access and skills that are also considered in mental calculations of the value of repair (Svensson-Hoglund et al., 2022).

Repairing has sustainability benefits, such as reducing waste and conserving resources. While there are cases where the sustainability benefits are not so clear – as in repairing older inefficient appliances or containing toxic chemicals – for non-energy using products and even for energy-using products where efficiency improvements are slowing or where they are used seldom anyways – the overall sustainability benefits of extending the lifetime through repair outweigh the inputs of materials through repair (André et al., 2019) or the trade-offs with energy use (Dalhammar et al., 2021).

The sustainability value of repair extends far beyond its material and environmental benefits; it also encompasses social, psychological and cultural dimensions. Repairing objects strengthens individuals' relationships with their possessions, fostering a sense of attachment and care. Van der Velden (2021) explores this in the context of community repair, arguing that repair is not merely a technical act but a form of social-material entanglement where objects and people are interconnected. Through the practice of tinkering and shared repair, individuals cultivate a deeper appreciation for their belongings, which in turn supports a sustainable circular economy by extending product lifespans and encouraging responsible consumption habits (van der Velden, 2021).

Beyond personal fulfilment, repair can also have an empowering effect on individuals and communities, offering opportunities for skill development, collective learning and social bonding. Bradley and Persson (2022) highlight the role of DIY community repair spaces, such as repair cafés, in enabling individuals – especially marginalised groups – to participate in sustainable practices that reinforce social inclusion and non-consumerist forms of citizenship. Their study of Swedish repair initiatives illustrates how community repair fosters a sense of agency, allowing individuals to regain control over their material environments while simultaneously challenging the mainstream circular economy discourse, which often prioritises corporate-led solutions (Bradley & Persson, 2022). These spaces create an environment where repair becomes a shared social experience rather than a solitary technical process, strengthening local communities and reducing dependence on commercial repair services.

Repair skills can be an important resource for a resilient local community. This is particularly evident in vulnerable communities and in times of economic disruption. For examples, repair of ventilators during the COVID-19 pandemic was essential for ensuring the continued operation of healthcare facilities despite severe medical equipment shortages (Cobra et al., 2023). Svensson-Hoglund et al. (2023) also examine the case of ventilators as one of several examples – including also tractors for farmers, laptops for students, etc. – of repair as a resource for resilience. In each case, the ability to repair was directly linked to the continuity of vital services and livelihoods, illustrating that repair is not only a technical process but also a fundamental mechanism for social and economic stability.

Repair can serve as a form of resistance against, and alternative to, a high consumption consumer culture (Bradley & Persson, 2022). It is something even some manufacturers recognise, with Rose Marcario, the CEO of Patagonia, writing in 2015 that 'repair is a radical act' in a culture where 'replacement is king' (Marcario, 2015). Repair practices contribute to an alternative vision of the circular economy, one that is not solely focused on economic efficiency but instead prioritises sustainability, resilience and community well-being (van der Velden, 2021). By engaging in repair, individuals actively challenge the notion that products should be short-lived and disposable, instead asserting their right to maintain and sustain the objects they own.

How much time, money and effort to invest in repair depends on the levels of ambition and the philosophy of both the repairer and/or owner and, on a larger scale, the values of an economy or society. For individuals, Scott and Weaver (2014) show that those consumers with a propensity towards repair are often motivated by attachment to their products and practice care. In their study, they show that motivation for consumers who repair was connected to more intrinsic values such as care than on extrinsic values such as saving money.

Such intrinsic values are also influenced by culture; some cultural practices are observed to embody repair and care as central tenets. For example, kintsugi, the Japanese art of repairing broken ceramics with gold, is not only about the act of repair but also about that the act symbolises an appreciation for longevity and imperfection. It is connected the principle of 'mottainai' – the regret experienced from waste – through which the act of repair not just restores but also conspicuously transforms the object and becomes part of its history. Thus, repair is elevated to a craft of conspicuous care (Keulemans, 2016).

Finally, repair can be seen as an integral part of progress and a form of innovation itself. The concept of 'broken-world thinking' incorporates breakdown, decay and repair as fundamental to how technology operates (Jackson, 2014). In this view, technology is always in a state of decay, requiring constant maintenance and adaptation. Rather than viewing repair as an interruption to progress, Jackson reframes it as an ongoing and creative process essential for sustaining technological systems. Broken-world thinking also notes a shift in mindset, away from a future-oriented vision of technology towards the present realities of sustaining and adapting systems amid breakdown. In this framework, repair not merely is about restoring functionality but also is an act of reconfiguration and survival, shaped by social, political and cultural factors. It reveals power structures, dependencies and inequalities embedded within technological systems. Rather than being secondary to innovation, repair is understood as a co-constitutive force that keeps technology operational and society functioning. This reframes our understanding of technology, emphasising the importance of sustaining, fixing and adapting what already exists rather than solely prioritising the pursuit of the new.

8.4 Implications

8.4.1 Implications for citizens

The implication of a system that dispels the myth of novelty over repair is one where repair is a default behaviour as it is preferable to buying new. This implies that newer products may become either more expensive and repair the same or less expensive. Campbell (2014) argues that internalising externalities, for example, environmental degradation and exploitation that are part of current manufacturing process, is a necessary part of sustainable consumption. This will make newer products more expensive for consumers, but having those products also be designed to be repairable, then extends the utility of those products and can lower the total costs of ownership, even as the upfront purchase price increases. However, the implication remains that products overall would increase in costs along with quality, and this, in turn, might imply decreased levels of consumption overall.

On a deeper and broader level, favouring repair over new as a value implies a 'mending mindset' where imperfection and wear are embraced as attributes of the products that are (continue to be) used and part of their own life story. This also implies a re-orienting of repair as not just a means to keeping products functioning longer but also a way of caring for products. Doing this requires time and money that are often spent in oneself and one's local community. Repair becomes situated in the local community and caring for products the norm.

8.4.2 Implications for businesses

Dispelling the myth of neophilia would have major impact on businesses. It would question the value of novelty and innovation for its own sake and push instead for strategies for innovation, design, production and sales that not necessarily associated with new. Proprietary design solutions are challenged by open-source ones to allow third parties to correct eventual initial defaults and develop new features and applications. Companies would need to develop reverse logistics systems to manage the return of products; they would also need to offer repair services able to provide cost-competitive solutions, even for older products that would require maintaining stocks over older parts – two emerging demands that might question the spatial scope of their operations.

There are many examples of products that are already designed with repairability in mind. For instance, electronics like Fairphone and Framework demonstrate that repairable design is both feasible and beneficial for consumers and manufacturers. Many industrial and commercial products, such as heavy machinery, medical devices and certain electronics, have long been engineered for durability and modular repair, where companies provide replacement parts, repair manuals and dedicated service networks (Stahel, 2016). Repairable design supports waste reduction and contributes to the circular economy, in which materials and products remain in use for as long as possible, promoting sustainability in line with the UN's Sustainable Development Goals.

Companies who produce products can also capitalise on integrating to their business models the possibility of selling again repaired items. Such a possibility could build on their current trust capital and be reinforced by the opportunities for consumers to see and test reused and refurbished products (Abdulla et al., 2024).

8.4.3 Implications for policymakers

For policymakers, there is a need to develop and enforce policies that stimulate and allow the production of durable, easily repairable and upgradable products, as well as the expansion of repair services. Right to repair policies such as those implemented in the EU can change these dynamics in making product designs more repairable by assuring access to the spare parts, manuals and software necessary for repair, and make repair generally more accessible and affordable (Svensson-Hoglund et al., 2021). The Right to Repair Directive adopted in the EU in 2024 ensures consumers have the legal right to choose repair. Repairability and durability indexes like those adopted in France and Belgium, and being developed on the EU level, also give information for consumers to identify and choose more repairable and durable products in the first place.

There is also a need to consider who should be encouraged to offer repair services. Perzanowski (2020) argues that the trends towards manufacturer control of repairs is detrimental to consumer rights and calls for regulatory or legislative action to restore the right to repair, ensuring that people can fix their own devices rather than being forced into more costly and restrictive manufacturer-controlled repair systems. Policymakers should consider how more open systems of repair can be supported and encouraged.

There is a need to recognise repair practices themselves as innovative and of value to society. This recognition should come with more investment in repair skills and education to promote these skills as an important resource for a sustainable economy and resilient local communities (Vinsel & Russell, 2020). For example, repair should be recognised as an integral part of a sustainable supply chain for public services like healthcare, rather than a temporary crisis response. Institutionalising repair strategies within public policies could strengthen resilience in health systems (Cobra et al., 2023).

A thriving repair sector is an important source of value creation in a sustainable and resilient economy. The repair sector can be further supported through VAT reductions on repairs, as in countries like Sweden, which can also make repairs less expensive for consumers. Consumers can also be incentivised, for example, through repair voucher subsidies that have already been implemented in some local and national levels in Austria (covering 50% of the repair costs for household appliances) or use of extended producer responsibility fees to cover repairs, as in France (Dalhammar et al., 2023).

8.5 Main message

The myth of neophilia – the belief that new is inherently better – continues to dominate consumer culture, business models and policy priorities. While it may drive short-term economic activity, it also results in the erosion of local repair knowledge and care practices, and massive social and environmental costs, including escalating resource extraction, and mounting waste. This overvaluation of novelty not only rests on but also further contributes to premature obsolescence. It also represents a loss of opportunity by undermining the value of more sustainable, resilient and community-based alternatives. Contrary to the narrative that consumers simply prefer new, evidence suggests most replacements are driven by systemic constraints, not desire. A shift away from neophilia invites us to reframe repair not as a sign of deficiency, but as a form of conspicuous care, social resilience and sustainable living.

To realise this shift, institutional and cultural support for repair must be expanded. Citizens can reclaim agency by embracing a 'mending mindset' and resisting the cultural pressure to discard what still holds value – practising repair not just for functionality but also as an act of responsibility and meaning. Businesses must rethink innovation as more than newness, investing instead in repairable, durable products and repair services that meet real human and environmental needs. Lastly, governments should institutionalise repair through supportive policies – such as right to repair legislation, repair subsidies and investment in repair skills – as core strategies for sustainability and resilience. Repair should be understood not only as an act of fixing but also as a social, economic and ecological practice that warrants greater recognition and support.

References

Abdulla, H., Abbey, J. D., Atalay, A. S., & Meloy, M. G. (2024). Show, don't tell: Education and physical exposure effects in remanufactured product markets. *Journal of Operations Management*, *70*(2), 243–256. https://doi.org/10.1002/joom.1248

André, H., Ljunggren Söderman, M., & Nordelöf, A. (2019). Resource and environmental impacts of using second-hand laptop computers: A case study of commercial reuse. *Waste Management*, *88*, 268–279. https://doi.org/10.1016/j.wasman.2019.03.050

Baldé, C. P., Kuehr, R., Yamamoto, T., McDonald, R., D'Angelo, E., Althaf, S., Bel, G., Deubzer, O., Fernandez-Cubillo, E., & Forti, V. (2024). *The global e-waste monitor* (pp. 1–147). United Nations University (UNU), International Telecommunication Union (ITU) & International Solid Waste Association (ISWA).

Beiser, V. (2024). The true cost of Black Friday. *TIME*, *11–29*. https://time.com/7198911/black-friday-real-cost/

Bradley, K., & Persson, O. (2022). Community repair in the circular economy – fixing more than stuff. *Local Environment*, *27*(10–11), 1321–1337. https://doi.org/10.1080/13549839.2022.2041580

Breatnach, G., & Puttini, C. (2024). Refurbished tech: How marketers can drive sustainable change. *Think with Google*. https://www.thinkwithgoogle.com/intl/en-emea/consumer-insights/consumer-trends/refurbished-tech-sustainable-shopping-trends/

Campbell, C. (2014). The curse of the new: How the accelerating pursuit of the new is driving hyper-consumption. In *Waste management and sustainable consumption*. Routledge.

Campbell, C. (2021). The desire for the new: Its nature and social location as presented in theories of fashion and modern consumerism. In C. Campbell (Ed.), *Consumption and consumer society: The craft consumer and other essays* (pp. 7–27). Springer International Publishing. https://doi.org/10.1007/978-3-030-83681-8_2

Clapp, J. (2002). The distancing of waste: Overconsumption in a global economy. In T. Princen, M. Maniates, & K. Conca (Eds.), *Confronting consumption* (pp. 155–176). MIT Press.

Clapp, K. K. (2018). *Bit history: The Pentalobe*. iFixit. https://www.ifixit.com/News/9905/bit-history-the-pentalobe

Clausnitzer, J. (2025). *Swappie*. Statista. Retrieved May 6, 2025, from https://www.statista.com/topics/11868/swappie/

Cobra, R., Moroni, I. T., Rodrigues, V. P., Fradinho, J. M. S., & Mascarenhas, J. (2023). Repair as a circular strategy for increasing resource availability and health system resilience during a crisis. *Health Policy and Technology*, *12*(3), 100778. https://doi.org/10.1016/j.hlpt.2023.100778

Cooper, T. (2004). Inadequate life? Evidence of consumer attitudes to product obsolescence. *Journal of Consumer Policy*, *27*(4), 421–449. https://doi.org/10.1007/s10603-004-2284-6

Cooper, T. (2005). Slower consumption reflections on product life spans and the "throwaway society." *Journal of Industrial Ecology*, *9*(1–2), 51–67. https://doi.org/10.1162/1088198054084671

Cooper, T. (2010). The significance of product longevity. In *Longer lasting products*. Routledge.

Dalhammar, C. J., Maitre-Ekern, E., Richter, J. L., Svensson-Hoglund, S., & Milios, L. (2023). Policies with lasting impact. In *Durable economies: Organizing the material foundations of society* (Vol. 10, p. 159). transcript Verlag. https://www.degruyter.com/document/isbn/9783839463963/html?lang=en

Dalhammar, C., Milios, L., & Richter, J. L. (2021). *Increasing the lifespan of products: Policies and consumer perspectives*. Energimyndigheten.

DeBellis, A. (2020, October 30). Banning the fix: Google continues blocking third-party repair ads. *PIRG*. https://pirg.org/articles/banning-the-fix-google-continues-blocking-third-party-repair-ads/

EU Commission. (2019). *Attitudes towards the impact of digitalisation on daily lives – March 2020 – Eurobarometer survey*. https://europa.eu/eurobarometer/surveys/detail/2228

European Commission. (2014). *Attitudes of Europeans towards waste management and resource efficiency* (Flash Eurobarometer 388). Publications Office of the European Union. https://op.europa.eu/en/publication-detail/-/publication/e3932343-3c82-4a5f-8a1a-e22eafd050a6

European Commission, Directorate-General for Justice and Consumers (European Commission), Deloitte consortium, IPSOS, & London Economics. (2015). *Consumer market study on the functioning of legal and commercial guarantees for consumers in the EU: Final report*. Publications Office of the European Union. https://data.europa.eu/doi/10.2838/813430

European Environment Agency (EEA). (2024). *Many returned and unsold textiles are incinerated or landfilled in Europe*. https://www.eea.europa.eu/en/newsroom/news/many-returned-and-unsold-textiles

European Environment Agency (EEA). (2025). *Circularity of the EU textiles value chain in numbers*. https://www.eea.europa.eu/en/analysis/publications/circularity-of-the-eu-textiles-value-chain-in-numbers

European Topic Centre on Circular economy and resource use. (2022). *An overview of Europe' s repair sector* (6/2022). EEA. https://www.eionet.europa.eu/etcs/etc-ce/products/etc-ce-products/etc-ce-report-6–2022-an-overview-of-europes-repair-sector

Eurostat. (2024). *Statistics | Eurostat*. Enterprises in Wholesale Trade, Repair of Vehicles and Motorcycles (NACE Rev.2, G) by Size Class of Turnover. https://ec.europa.eu/eurostat/databrowser/view/sbs_part_wtsct/default/table?lang=en

Gault, M. (2020, January 7). Farmers are buying 40-year-old tractors because they're actually repairable. *VICE*. https://www.vice.com/en/article/farmers-are-buying-40-year-old-tractors-because-theyre-actually-repairable/

Gregson, N., Metcalfe, A., & Crewe, L. (2009). Practices of object maintenance and repair: How consumers attend to consumer objects within the home. *Journal of Consumer Culture*. https://doi.org/10.1177/1469540509104376

Hickel, J. (2020). *Less is more: How degrowth will save the world*. Random House.

Jackson, S. J. (2014). Rethinking repair. In T. Gillespie, P. J. Boczkowski, & K. A. Foot (Eds.), *Media technologies: Essays on communication, materiality, and society* (pp. 221–240). The MIT Press.

Jackson, T. (2005). Live better by consuming less?: Is there a "double dividend" in sustainable consumption? *Journal of Industrial Ecology*, *9*(1–2), 19–36. https://doi.org/10.1162/1088198054084734

Keulemans, G. (2016). The Geo-cultural Conditions of Kintsugi. *The Journal of Modern Craft*, *9*(1), 15–34. https://doi.org/10.1080/17496772.2016.1183946

Knaus, C. (2017, June 5). Apple 'error 53' sting operation caught staff misleading customers, court documents allege. *The Guardian*. https://www.theguardian.com/technology/2017/jun/05/apple-error-53-sting-operation-caught-staff-misleading-customers-court-documents-allege

Krebs, S., & Weber, H. (2021). *The persistence of technology: Histories of repair, reuse and disposal*. transcript Verlag. https://library.oapen.org/handle/20.500.12657/50815

Marcario, R. (2015, November 25). *Repair is a radical act – Patagonia stories*. https://eu.patagonia.com/se/en/stories/repair-is-a-radical-act/story–17637.html

McAlister, L., & Pessemier, E. A. (1982). Variety-seeking behavior: An interdisciplinary review. *Journal of Consumer Research*, *9*(3), 311–322.

McCracken, G. D. (1990). *Culture and consumption: New approaches to the symbolic character of consumer goods and activities*. Indiana University Press.

McVeigh, M. K., Dalhammar, C., & Richter, J. L. (2019). *Planned obsolescence: Built not to last*. European Liberal Forum (ELF); Fores.

Mont, O., & Andrius Plepys, A. (2008). Sustainable consumption progress: Should we be proud or alarmed? *Journal of Cleaner Production*, *16*(4), 4. https://doi.org/10.1016/j.jclepro.2007.01.009

Mugge, R., Schifferstein, H. N., & Schoormans, J. P. (2006). A longitudinal study of product attachment and its determinants. *European Advances in Consumer Research*, 7, 641–647.

Mugge, R., Schifferstein, H. N. J., & Schoormans, J. P. L. (2010). Product attachment and satisfaction: Understanding consumers' post-purchase behavior. *Journal of Consumer Marketing*, *27*(3), 271–282. https://doi.org/10.1108/07363761011038347

Niinimäki, K., Peters, G., Dahlbo, H., Perry, P., Rissanen, T., & Gwilt, A. (2020). The environmental price of fast fashion. *Nature Reviews Earth & Environment*, *1*(4), 189–200. https://doi.org/10.1038/s43017-020-0039-9

Packard, V. (1961). *The waste makers*. Longmans, Green and Co Ltd.

Perzanowski, A. (2020). *Consumer perceptions of the right to repair* (SSRN Scholarly Paper ID 3584377). Social Science Research Network. https://papers.ssrn.com/abstract=3584377

Perzanowski, A. (2021). *The right to repair: Reclaiming the things we own*. Cambridge University Press. https://doi.org/10.1017/9781108946926

Plepys, A., & Ana María Arbeláez Vélez. (2025). 'The Environmental Impacts of Car Sharing: Direct and Indirect Effects'. In *Understanding the Urban Sharing Economy: Sustainability and Institutionalisation*, edited by Oksana Mont and Yuliya Voytenko Palgan. Elgar Understanding Series. Edwar Elgar Publishing Limited, pp. 87–109.

Rhodes, C., & Pullen, A. (2010). Editorial: Neophilia and organization. *Culture and Organization*, *16*(1), 1–6. https://doi.org/10.1080/14759550903558011

Rimmer, M. (2025). Tractor rage: Intellectual property, agriculture, competition policy, and the right to repair. *IIC – International Review of Intellectual Property and Competition Law*, 1–38. https://doi.org/10.1007/s40319-024-01538-5

Rogers, E. M. (2003). *Diffusion of innovations* (5th ed.). Free press.

Scott, K. A., & Weaver, S. T. (2014). To repair or not to repair: What is the motivation. *Journal of Research for Consumers*, *26*(1), 43–44.

Selwyn, N. (2003). Apart from technology: Understanding people's non-use of information and communication technologies in everyday life. *Technology in Society*, *25*(1), 99–116. https://doi.org/10.1016/S0160-791X(02)00062–3

Slade, G. (2007). *Made to break: Technology and obsolescence in America*. Harvard University Press. https://doi.org/10.4159/9780674043756

Stahel, W. R. (2016). The circular economy. *Nature*, *531*(7595), 435–438. https://doi.org/10.1038/531435a

Statista. (2024). *Recycling and reusage of consumer tech*. https://www.statista.com/study/114718/recycling-and-reusage-of-consumer-tech/

Svensson-Hoglund, S., Nordbeck, P. C., Richter, J. L., & Russell, J. D. (2023). *The role of repair as a resource for resilience: Case Studies on the effects of repair outcomes of essential products*. PLATE.

Svensson-Hoglund, S., Richter, J. L., Maitre-Ekern, E., Russell, J. D., Pihlajarinne, T., & Dalhammar, C. (2021). Barriers, enablers and market governance: A review of the policy landscape for repair of consumer electronics in the EU and the U.S. *Journal of Cleaner Production*, *288*, 125488. https://doi.org/10.1016/j.jclepro.2020.125488

Svensson-Hoglund, S., Russell, J. D., & Richter, J. L. (2022). A process approach to product repair from the perspective of the individual. *Circular Economy and Sustainability*, 1–33. https://doi.org/10.1007/s43615-022-00226-1

Thompson, M. (1979). *Rubbish theory: The creation and destruction of value – new edition*. Pluto Press. https://doi.org/10.2307/j.ctt1rfsn94

U.S. Bureau of Labor Statistics. (2024). A consumption measure for automobiles. *Monthly Labor Review*. Retrieved from https://www.bls.gov/opub/mlr/2024/article/a-consumption-measure-for-automobiles.htm

U.S. House of Representatives Committee Repository. (2019). *Questions for the record from the Honorable David N. Cicilline, Chairman, subcommittee on antitrust, commercial and administrative law of the committee on the judiciary, questions for Mr. Kyle Andeer, Vice President, Corporate Law, Apple, Inc.* https://docs.house.gov/meetings/JU/JU05/20190716/109793/HHRG-116-JU05–20190716-SD036.pdf

van der Velden, M. (2021). 'Fixing the world one thing at a time': Community repair and a sustainable circular economy. *Journal of Cleaner Production*, *304*, 127151. https://doi.org/10.1016/j.jclepro.2021.127151

Veblen, T. (1899). The theory of the leisure class. In *The collected works of Thorstein Veblen. Vol. 1* (pp. 1–404). Reprint, Routledge, 1994.

Vinsel, L., & Russell, A. L. (2020). *The innovation delusion: How our obsession with the new has disrupted the work that matters most*. Currency.

Wiens, K. (2023). *We are retroactively dropping the iphone's repairability score*. iFixit. https://www.ifixit.com/News/82493/we-are-retroactively-dropping-the-iphones-repairability-score-en

9

MYTH 8

Sufficiency means the end of modern life, comfort and joy – people will never choose less

Josefine Henman and Oksana Mont

9.1 The sufficiency-means-deprivation myth

> *People will never choose less – sufficiency means the end of modern life, comfort, and joy.*

A widespread myth in sustainable consumption is the belief that people are inherently driven to accumulate more and more material possessions. This assumption fuels resistance to sufficiency – which, simply put, is about living well within limits rather than constantly seeking more. Though sufficiency has gained traction in recent years, making its first appearance in an IPCC report in 2022 as a key strategy for ensuring well-being within planetary boundaries (Creutzig et al., 2022), it is still widely misunderstood. Many equate it with deprivation, scarcity or sacrifice. This narrative frames sufficiency as a step backwards, conjuring images of hardship and outdated living conditions rather than a viable path towards sustainable consumption.

This chapter is informed by interviews with leading scholars in the field of sufficiency. Their reflections and insights will be interwoven throughout the text, helping us to challenge the assumption that more is always better and to explore alternative perspectives on what it truly means to live well.

9.2 Origins

The myth that sufficiency entails regression to pre-industrial lifestyles stems from the deeply rooted ideology of growth. Within capitalism, progress is often equated with the accumulation of wealth and possessions. Accumulation is, in other words, ingrained in our dominant social paradigm (Gorge

DOI: 10.4324/9781003613718-12

et al., 2015; Kilbourne et al., 1997). This paradigm makes the concept of sufficiency, which questions the idea that 'more is better', an ideological outlier and a fertile ground for misconceptions.

But myths do not persist on their own. Powerful capitalist forces have a vested interest in keeping them alive. As one leading sufficiency scholar notes:

> *It suits the capitalist economy extremely well to have this myth in circulation because it depends on ever-expanding growth. . . . The capitalist economy is driven by growth, so it actually needs to propel consumption constantly and increase it in order to keep going. And the wealthiest are in the position to want that to continue, obviously.*
>
> *(Interviewee 2)*

Consumer culture, particularly in affluent societies, plays a pivotal role in perpetuating the myth. The desire to establish social position through spending – commonly referred to as comparative consumption or 'keeping up with the Joneses' – has long shaped consumption patterns. Historically, people compared themselves with neighbours of similar economic standing. Still, over the last few decades (a development taking off already with the advent of mass production in the 1920s and reinforced by the neoliberal shift of the 1970s and 1980s and the rise of individualism), reference points have shifted dramatically.

Economist Juliet Schor highlighted this phenomenon already back in 1999 in her book *The Overspent American: Why We Want What We Don't Need.* Schor argued that we increasingly measure ourselves against individuals with vastly higher incomes, resulting in intensified spending habits and heightened aspirations. She described this 'new consumerism' as being

> *created by the escalated lifestyles of the most affluent and the need that many others felt to meet that standard . . . . If you missed the upscaling in your own neighbourhood and workplace or at the mall, you could watch it on TV.*
>
> *(Schor, 1999, p. 18)*

What drives this system of competitive consumption, she argued, are deep class inequalities.

Nearly three decades later, we can add the rise of social media to Schor's argument, exposing millions to the extravagant lifestyles of influencers and celebrities. The digital age has further reinforced the fantasy of insatiable demand and endless accumulation. If the 20th century was about keeping up with the Joneses, the 21st century is about keeping up with the Kardashians. Unlimited consumption, once seen as excessive or even morally questionable, has become aspirational, making sufficiency appear not only undesirable but also antithetical to modern life.

9.3 Consequences

Affluent consumers today are drowning in stuff – the sheer volume of possessions has surged to unprecedented levels. In the United States, the average person buys a new piece of clothing every 5.5 days, while in Europe, clothing purchases rose by 40% between 1996 and 2012 (Niinimäki et al., 2020). Meanwhile, millions of unused smartphones sit forgotten in drawers, locking away valuable resources (ETC CE, 2023). Beyond buying more, purchases are also getting bigger: SUV sales hit a record high in 2023, making up 48% of global car sales – so significant that, if SUVs were a country, they would rank as the fifth largest emitter of CO_2 worldwide (IEA, 2025). On a broader scale, household consumption in the EU increased by 26% between 2000 and 2019, with household goods and appliances alone rising by 47% (ETC CE, 2023). The International Resource Panel warns that material use has tripled in the past 50 years, with high-income countries consuming six times more resources per capita than low-income ones (UNEP, 2024).

Yet, all this consumption is not making people any happier. As the famous quote goes: 'We buy things we don't need with money we don't have to impress people we don't like'. There is a tendency to seek more yet feel no lasting satisfaction (discussed further in Chapter 3 on retail therapy). Psychologists call this process hedonic adaptation – we get stuck on the hedonic treadmill, always chasing the next thing. Or, as Oscar Wilde put it: 'There are only two tragedies in life: one is not getting what one wants, and the other is getting it'.

In addition to causing detrimental effects on social and ecological systems, the misconception that sufficiency would mean an end to modern life also fuels a systematic unwillingness to take action at the scale or pace required to address unsustainable consumption. It influences not only individuals in their role as consumers but also decision-making at the societal level. Fear of being seen as naive or utopian discourages policymakers from bold strategies. The relatively obscure and unpopular nature of sufficiency as a concept makes it difficult to discuss openly. It reinforces the false belief that endless economic growth is the only viable model (discussed further in Chapter 9 on economic growth and well-being).

> *[The myth] has consequences for policy at different levels of society. It makes it very important to prioritise growth-creating initiatives and strategies, stimulate increased consumption and increased production, so that the cake simply grows.*
>
> *(Interviewee 4)*

This, in turn, prevents meaningful conversations about alternatives. Consumption policies remain limited to weak sustainability approaches (Fuchs & Lorek, 2005), focusing on small adjustments rather than systemic change (discussed further in Chapter 12 on strong sustainability policies). Governments shy away from the many ways in which they could influence consumption through regulation and innovation. The myth thus narrows the scope of what is perceived as possible.

> *Because of this myth being so common, it is really not talked about in society. Sufficiency as a term is not popular. We were told that for a research project, we should not call it anything linked to sufficiency, that that is a no-go term because it will be very poorly perceived. So it is a massive problem. If even talking about sufficiency is seen as something negative and something that people will be very unhappy with, then obviously, it will not be taken up by politics or businesses. So yeah, I think that is a big barrier to anything happening on sufficiency.*
>
> *(Interviewee 1)*

9.4 Dispelling the myth

As we have seen, the belief that more is always better is deeply ingrained in consumer culture and reinforced by structural factors that encourage accumulation. In the following sections, we challenge this narrative and explore how sufficiency provides a meaningful counterpoint to the current consumerism-based economic system, inviting a reconsideration of what constitutes a fulfilling life.

9.4.1 Sufficiency as two meanings of enough

First of all – the idea that sufficiency means regressing to pre-industrial living is a misinterpretation of the concept. Sufficiency is not about deprivation. It is not about having too little. It is about ensuring that everyone has enough while questioning overconsumption and excess wealth. Enoughness in two senses (Spengler, 2016): not too little, not too much. For those living in poverty, sufficiency means 'more'. For the middle and upper classes, it often requires 'less'. In this way, sufficiency is a relevant concept across socio-economic groups – but in different ways. At its core, it is a question of justice.

A helpful way to think about these two sufficiency dimensions is through the concept of consumption corridors – a range bounded by minimum and maximum thresholds. As Doris Fuchs (one of the authors of Chapter 12 of this book) puts it in *Consumption Corridors: Living a Good Life within Sustainable Limits* from 2021:

> *Consumption corridors describe a space between minimum consumption standards that provide every individual with the ability to live a good life, and maximum consumption standards that keep individuals from*

> *consuming in quantities or ways that hurt others' chances to do the same. Such corridors combine the pursuits of a good life and of justice within planetary boundaries.*
>
> *(Fuchs et al., 2021, p. 4)*

Here, a natural question arises: How would we define such socially and ecologically sustainable consumption levels? Indeed a complex task, as consumption needs and impacts vary across cultures, geographies and socio-economic contexts. But the aim is not to define rigid, universal limits. What is needed – and increasingly urgent – is to initiate collective conversations about how we can move towards sustainable consumption corridors. As Fuchs et al. (2021) emphasise, societal limits on consumption must be 'envisioned and developed via lively democratic debate within robust forms of civic participation' (p. 45).

One starting point for discussing the minimum thresholds of consumption is found in the work of Chilean economist Manfred Max-Neef. He argues that while 'wants' can vary endlessly, human 'needs' are universal, finite and remain constant across cultures and historical periods (Max-Neef, 1991). He identifies nine fundamental needs: subsistence (physical health and survival), protection (safety, care and security), affection (relationships and love), understanding (knowledge and education), participation, idleness (rest and play), creation (creativity), identity and freedom (autonomy and choice).[1]

Reflecting on this list, if sufficiency means ensuring that everyone's needs are met – that is, ensuring that every human being on this planet is healthy and safe and surrounded by loving relationships and has access to education and decision-making, time for rest and play, space for self-expression and creativity, and a sense of belonging, freedom of choice – does that sound like regression and deprivation? Far from it. It is a vision of a life rich in meaning, connection and autonomy – a vision that speaks of abundance rather than scarcity (Plomteux, 2024). This challenges the assumption that material accumulation is the key to well-being. What matters is not how much we consume but the extent to which our needs are met.

Max-Neef uses the term 'needs satisfiers' to talk about the means by which our needs are fulfilled. These satisfiers vary widely across different social, cultural and economic contexts. This means that needs can be met in ways that require little material consumption – or in ways that demand excessive resources and environmental harm.

This brings us to the upper limits of consumption. In today's growth-driven consumerist society, there is a tendency to confuse 'needs' with 'wants'. We see a 'needs escalation' – where luxuries become normalised as necessities. Take SUVs, for example. Once designed for off-road use, they were rare just a few decades ago. Today, they dominate urban streets, and many consider them an essential part of daily life. But are they really? A similar shift can be seen in access to hot water. Once a privilege reserved for nobility, requiring extensive resources and labour to heat, hot water has gradually transitioned from a luxury to an assumed necessity in most households (Trentmann, 2016). While access to warm water is undoubtedly a matter of hygiene and well-being, the expectation of unlimited hot water on demand illustrates how consumption norms evolve, often without consideration of their sustainability.

What is clear is that consumption levels and associated environmental impacts are intrinsically tied to wealth. The wealthiest people around the world are contributing disproportionately to environmental breakdown. The carbon budget is being massively used by a tiny percentage of wealthy people – since the 1990s, the richest 1% have burned through more than twice as much carbon as the bottom half of humanity (Khalfan et al., 2023).

> *The top 10% – and, above all, a global elite of around 1% – are driving a global productive system that is based on selling more, destabilising the environment for everyone, with the worst effects suffered by the poorest. So we have got a situation which is being defended as free and democratic, but that is actually exacerbating inequalities and ultimately undermining the actual livelihood of the majority of people around the world.*
>
> *(Interviewee 2)*

Philosopher Ingrid Robeyns, author of *Limitarianism: The Case Against Extreme Wealth* (2024), proposes introducing a cap on how much wealth a person could have. She argues that we should not allow unlimited inequality. Money over a certain level should be seen as excess money. While she acknowledges that conditions (e.g. pension systems) vary across countries, Robeyns even suggests specific limits to wealth:

> *In a country with a socioeconomic profile similar to the Netherlands, where I live, we should aim to create a society in which no one has more than €10m. There should not be any decamillionaires.*
>
> *(Robeyns, 2024, p. xix)*

This kind of wealth is extreme. Through their private jets, yachts, investments and excessive consumption, the super-rich are indeed responsible for a disproportionately large share of greenhouse gas emissions and resource use. But even beyond the top 1%, consumption patterns fall outside the sustainable consumption corridor. For example, while the wealthiest 1% were responsible for 15% of global emissions from 1990 to 2015, the wealthiest 10% accounted for over half (Kartha et al., 2020). To be clear, an annual income of $38,000 (€36,600) is enough to place someone in the world's richest 10% (Nielsen et al., 2021; Kartha et al., 2020) – meaning that this category includes many of the authors of this book (and perhaps you as well).

Again, the point here is not necessarily to define what people should buy or not. Instead, it is about initiating a discussion about what kind of society we would like to have. A society that recognises the reality of finite resources and planetary limits. A society that no longer tolerates unlimited consumption – that is not necessarily satisfying any needs – while the vast majority of people do not have enough to fulfil theirs, let alone live dignified lives – a society that does not permit unlimited inequality. Sufficiency is about questioning what is 'enough', about increasing our literacy of what is 'essential' and what is 'excess'. It is about shifting from accumulation to distribution – about living well within limits.

And what is more: after a certain point, more wealth does not bring more well-being. In fact, the opposite is often true. This is what we will turn to next.

9.4.2 Sufficiency as alternative hedonism

In 1974, Richard Easterlin, then a professor of economics at the University of Pennsylvania, conducted experiments showing that beyond a certain level of affluence, additional wealth no longer contributes to increased happiness (Easterlin, 1974). This phenomenon, now known as the 'Easterlin Paradox', has been confirmed in numerous studies across various countries and contexts, with consistent results (see, e.g. Dittmar et al., 2014; Galbraith et al., 2024). However, it has also been questioned. Recent research such as Killingsworth et al. (2023) suggests that in some contexts, such as the United States, happiness may continue to rise with income, even at higher levels. Still, the relationship between income and well-being remains weak, non-linear, and shaped by cultural and structural factors. More importantly, the broader insight holds: once basic needs are met, accumulating more wealth does not reliably contribute to well-being. In the words of Millward-Hopkins and Fisch-Romito (2025), in addition to being socially unfair and ecologically unsustainable, overconsumption beyond a certain income level becomes 'useless'. And many of us passed that point long ago. Accumulating more possessions is not a recipe for pleasure. Then what brings us happiness, if not more things?

The British philosopher Kate Soper has long advocated for the importance of non-material sources of pleasure. Through the lens of 'alternative hedonism', she challenges the common belief that scaling back consumption is an act of sacrifice. Instead, she argues that this shift can lead to a richer and more fulfilling life, emphasising joy and well-being that come from pursuits beyond material wealth (Soper, 2020).

Soper also emphasises that our commitment to a growth-driven economy (explored further in Chapter 9) often undermines genuine satisfaction. She draws attention to the many downsides of consumer culture – chronic stress, ill health, congestion, pollution, excessive waste, constant noise, and so on – all of which detract from, rather than enhance, quality of life. These negative consequences reveal the urgent need for a different approach – one that reimagines happiness in terms of well-being and fulfilment rather than consumption. In the words of another leading sufficiency scholar, we interviewed:

> *It is about redefining what constitutes a good life and realising that there can be a greater joy and, above all, meaningfulness in steering towards sufficiency, both at the individual level and at the societal level.*
>
> *(Interviewee 3)*

Embracing sufficiency invites us to reconsider what brings us happiness. It calls for a shift towards non-material abundance: more joy, more creativity, more time, more connection, more love, more care. Privileging time over money, freedom over stuff. Freeing ourselves from the pressures of consumer competition and the need to 'keep up with the Joneses'. Yes, we might need to let go of some comforts and joys – but that will leave room for others. Shifting away from consumerism is not about deprivation – it is about liberation.

Buddhism offers an interesting perspective here. It starts with a fundamental truth: suffering is an inherent part of life. But what causes suffering? According to Buddhism's Second Noble Truth, the root cause is craving – craving for wealth, possessions, status and fame. As the ecological economist Tim Jackson writes in *Post Growth* (2021): 'To be ruled by our cravings is to intensify our suffering . . . Suffering can only be alleviated, the Buddha insisted, by freeing ourselves from craving' (pp. 160–164). Here lies a powerful counterpoint to consumer capitalism, which thrives on the constant stimulation of desires. As Jackson points out, the solution cannot, of course, be to make us all find ways to overcome our cravings. But there is something to learn from this ancient philosophical wisdom: true fulfilment does not come from more consumption – it comes from freeing ourselves from the endless cycle of wanting more.

In other words, the belief that sufficiency means giving up joy is fundamentally flawed. On the contrary, embracing sufficiency and questioning our cravings can lead to a deeper, more fulfilling life. And this realisation is gaining traction:

> *I see some signs that there is a cultural shift. Partly because people are very worried about the environmental impact of the current consumer regime. Partly because they're worried about the gaping inequalities it has created. And partly because there is a sense that it is not all gratifying of their own needs and desires anyway.*
>
> *(Interviewee 2)*

Many feel that something is amiss in contemporary society. Consumerist norms ring hollow. As one of our interviewees put it, there is a growing sense of 'consumption fatigue'. A growing awareness that more consumption does not bring greater happiness. In response, people are beginning to seek fulfilment in alternative ways: through community, creativity and reconnecting with nature. And demanding policies supporting this shift. Let us explore this in more detail.

9.4.3 Sufficiency as a citizen demand

One of the most persistent misconceptions about sufficiency is that people simply do not want it. The assumption goes: no one would voluntarily choose to live with less, and certainly not support policies that ask them to do so. But emerging empirical evidence tells a different story. In the spring of 2023, we organised five co-creation workshops as part of the research project *EU 1.5° Lifestyles* – a collaborative effort involving researchers across six European countries. The overall aim of the project was to explore the individual and systemic changes required to align lifestyles within the European Union with the 1.5° target of the Paris Agreement. Now, a few years into the project, we wanted to learn more about how individuals and households experience significant lifestyle changes. What are the perceived consequences of turning towards sufficiency living? To investigate this, we invited participants who had made such changes to share their experiences in workshops held in Sweden, Germany, Latvia, Spain and Hungary. Together, we examined the consequences of four specific lifestyle shifts: giving up car ownership, flying, meat consumption and excess living space (Lehner et al., 2024; Richter et al., 2024).

What we found was that while challenges and undesirable consequences also were acknowledged, participants described a wide range of positive outcomes. Those who had stopped flying spoke of a deepened connection to their local surroundings and a stronger sense of belonging. Giving up car ownership reduced stress – no longer worrying about parking or traffic – and led to greater social interactions and a more active lifestyle. Participants who had shifted to a meat-free diet noted health benefits, as well as an increased awareness of sustainable consumption overall. Downsizing living space brought a sense of freedom – decluttering and managing fewer possessions meant more time for leisure, outdoor activities and personal care. This reduced stress improved their mental health and perceived overall quality of life. For some, smaller living spaces enabled them to move to more central locations with better infrastructure and amenities, which in turn strengthened their social connections and engagement within their neighbourhoods (Richter et al., 2024). These findings suggest that embracing sufficiency indeed can lead to greater well-being. Of course, there are challenges, too. These must be addressed. But across all case countries, positive experiences were reported, as well as solutions for mitigating adverse effects.

Another interesting finding from the *EU 1.5° Lifestyles* project was how people's views tended to shift as they engaged in discussions with others (Vadovics et al., 2024). At an earlier stage of the project, we conducted similar co-creation workshops as described earlier, but with members of the general population (i.e. with individuals who had not necessarily made low-carbon lifestyle changes). From these workshops, we observed how the participants' perspectives evolved during group discussions. While some individuals initially expressed reservations about certain lifestyle changes, such as living in smaller spaces or giving up meat, these perceived barriers were often challenged or softened through collective dialogue. The group discussions fostered a sense of shared understanding.

It seems we should not underestimate the power of interpersonal interactions in reshaping attitudes. Consumption is deeply social (as discussed earlier), and so is the process of reconsidering it. It seems that sufficiency ideas are easier to embrace after deliberation. We do not often have time for this in the busyness of everyday life. But when pausing, taking the time to think and talk about what truly matters, it seems our views and values change. In other words, when people really engage with the issues, sufficiency does not seem as extreme – it seems logical, necessary and even desirable.

This can also be seen elsewhere, beyond the *EU 1.5° Lifestyles* project. In recent years, Climate Citizen Assemblies have emerged across Europe as a model of citizen participation in climate policy. Across the continent, randomly selected citizens – representing the society in terms of gender, age, socioeconomic status, etc. – have spent a day discussing the future of the planet. Participants receive briefings from experts, engage with diverse perspectives and develop policy proposals. In addition to being highly relevant from a democratic perspective, these assemblies provide valuable insights into public attitudes towards sufficiency: public support for sufficiency is higher than commonly assumed. In a recent study, a team of researchers analysed the proposals stemming from the Climate Citizen Assemblies and compared them with national governments' energy and climate strategies. Forty percent of all measures recommended by the assemblies were found to be sufficiency-related (Lage et al., 2023). Ideas such as reducing livestock numbers in agriculture, extending product guarantees and limiting advertisements for certain kinds of products were particularly popular. Compared to the national energy and climate plans, the citizen assembly proposed a significantly higher share of sufficiency policies. As the group of researchers point out:

> *[T]his indicates that sufficiency policies are not per se lacking legitimacy in current European societies. In contrast, in a mini-public such as the [Climate Assemblies], even comparably far-reaching sufficiency policies are seen by a majority as a legitimate and inevitable part of climate mitigation.*
> *(Lage et al., 2023, p. 8)*

One of our interviewees reinforced this point:

> *This suggests a realisation that people want to limit inequalities, the extreme gaps that allow the extremely rich to have the lifestyles that they have. . . . If there's a democratic conversation, sufficiency as an idea is very strong. There's power in the concept of sufficiency; it is something that is intuitively simple for most people to understand.*
>
> *(Interviewee 3)*

The empirics discussed earlier show that the belief that people never want to settle – or vote – for sufficiency is not necessarily true. On the contrary, when given the chance to deliberate and reflect, many citizens support sufficiency and sufficiency policies. And it is indeed striving for sufficiency on the societal level, rather than merely on the individual level, that sets us on the right path.

9.4.4 Sufficiency as a social organising principle

Thinking of sufficiency primarily as a matter of personal restraint – a lifestyle choice for the environmentally conscious individual – overlooks the fact that individual behaviour is profoundly shaped by the systems in which we live. Yes, people's lifestyles and choices do matter – research has shown that for humanity to remain within planetary boundaries, individuals and households must indeed make changes (Cap et al., 2024). However, focusing solely on the individual obscures the systemic picture: our behaviours are embedded in broader social, economic and institutional structures. These structures dictate what is possible, accessible and encouraged. In other words, while personal lifestyle changes are valuable, they are insufficient on their own to address the systemic nature of today's ecological crises and social injustices.

A transformation of existing societal structures and provisioning systems is essential to enable living within the sustainable consumption corridor. As part of the *EU 1.5° Lifestyles* project, we identified seven key structural barriers that undermine the sustainability of provisioning systems for food, mobility, housing and leisure. These barriers include the economic growth paradigm, policy incoherence, vested interests, the externalisation of environmental costs, dominant narratives of the good life, inequality and insufficient integration of environmental concerns in educational systems (Hirth et al., 2023; Kreinin et al., 2024).

To overcome these barriers, sufficiency can guide us – not just as a lifestyle choice but as a social organising principle. This view has been strongly advocated for by Thomas Princen, author of the seminal book *The Logic of Sufficiency* (2005). Princen argues that our current societal logic – efficiency – often undermines ecological and social systems. While efficiency aims to maximise output and minimise costs, it often leads to unintended consequences such as resource overexploitation, ecological degradation and deepening inequalities. In response, he proposes a 'logic of sufficiency', which prioritises moderation and balance. Rather than understanding sufficiency as an individual ethical stance, Princen sees it as a foundational principle that can guide how societies collectively structure their economies, institutions and relationships with the environment. This means redesigning systems – economic, political and cultural – to enable sustainable and just living conditions. Turning our attention to how shared norms, policies and institutions can create the conditions for sufficiency at a societal level.

Since the publication of Princen's book, this work has been further developed. For instance, building on literature in the fields of sufficiency, political ecology, degrowth, ecological economics and sustainable consumption, Callmer and Bradley (2021) outline a framework for sufficiency politics, built around four central elements: politics of limits, of less, of slower and closer and for well-being (see Table 9.1).

TABLE 9.1 Framework for sufficiency politics.

Element of sufficiency	*Key concepts*
Politics of limits	Recognising ecological and social limits Limiting affluence Social protection floor Caps and rationing Maximum income Recognising limits to economic growth
Politics of less	Less market Decrease the influence of the market and strengthen alternative forms of provision Prevent clutter (restrictions to prevent unnecessary consumption)
Politics of slower and closer	A slower pace of production and consumption Redefinition of work, work-time reduction policies More time and more autonomy over one's time Localised production and consumption systems, repair
Politics for well-being	Redefining progress and alternative measures of prosperity Cultural reorientation towards non-materialist values and acceptance of rationing measures Politics for the 'the good life' Satisfaction of human needs and more equitable distribution of resources

Source: Reproduced from Callmer and Bradley (2021) with email permission.

Examples of specific sufficiency policies include, for instance, carbon budgets, work-time reductions and 15-minute-city planning. Clearly, these policies wouldn't result in a loss of comfort and joy – quite the opposite. As one of our interviewees pointed out:

> *Many of us do not feel well in today's society despite high material standards. I think there is much to be gained from combining policies to reduce inequality with policies for a slower-paced society and more social security. And that can be combined with taking ecological limits into account.*
> *(Interviewee 3)*

What is important to keep in mind – and this is something that we could see also in the *EU 1.5° Lifestyles* project (Lehner et al., 2024) – is that people become more open to sufficiency when they realise it is not about individual sacrifices but about systemic changes that make sufficiency easy and desirable. This is why public infrastructure – including, for instance, shared spaces, repair hubs and cultural venues that do not evolve around consumption – and provisioning systems matter so much. Guaranteeing and extending the public and collective provision of essential goods and services has been argued to be essential for people to embrace sufficiency on the individual level. Public luxury, one could call it (Gough, 2022).

The logic of sufficiency is also making its way into business and corporate strategy. Increasingly, companies are exploring what sufficiency might look like at the business level. Laura Niessen and Nancy Bocken, researchers at the Maastricht Sustainability Institute, have identified 16 sufficiency-oriented strategies that businesses can adopt to reduce overconsumption, extend product lifespans, and foster mindful consumer behaviour (Niessen & Bocken, 2021). For example, designing for durability and repairability ensures products last longer, while life extension services such as repair, refurbishment and resale reduce waste. Product-as-a-service models replace ownership with rental or pay-per-use schemes, discouraging unnecessary purchases. Moderating sales strategies, such as avoiding discounts or commission-based selling, helps shift business goals away from volume-driven growth. Open-source creation and personalised production enable localised, customised solutions that reduce excess production. Businesses can also promote mindful consumption by questioning purchasing habits, as seen in anti-Black Friday campaigns.

Another perspective on sufficiency in business is to set limits to growth deliberately. The Danish consultancy firm Post Growth Guide advocates for defining clear boundaries – such as legally limiting customer and product categories, wages, finance options, company size, and working hours – in order for companies to avoid greenwashing and go beyond mere compliance. The aim is to help businesses not just adapt to but also actively contribute to solving the ecological and social challenges of the 21st century (Feldthus & Haumann, 2024).

In other words, while you may adopt sufficiency thinking in your personal life, the strength of the concept rather lies in applying it at the societal level. Sufficiency as an organising principle can help us carve out policies for social and ecological well-being and reimagine business models that thrive within environmental limits. In many ways, this move beyond efficiency is not just necessary – it is an evolutionary step forward.

9.4.5 Sufficiency as evolution

What if consumerism is not the peak of civilisation? What if there is an alternative? Developmental psychology suggests that human consciousness develops through distinct stages. Each development stage reveals a markedly different understanding of the world. The progression moves from ego-centred thinking, focused on personal survival and gratification, to world-centred and ultimately holistic perspectives – that is, increasingly complex and inclusive ways of engaging with reality. Think of the trajectory of human life: from the simplicity of childhood to the rich and multifaceted consciousness of adult maturity (see e.g. Erikson, 1998; Kohlberg et al., 1983).

Similarly, the evolution of humanity can be seen as characterised by such distinct developmental stages. In his book *Reinventing Organisations* (2014), Frederic Laloux traces this history, showing how every major societal transition – whether from foraging to agriculture or from industrialisation to the digital age – has brought fundamental shifts in how we live and organise. Against this background, Laloux argues that organisations as we know them today simply reflect our current worldview – our current stage of development – and that we are standing on the brink of another transformation.

Indeed, throughout history, organisations have evolved alongside societal shifts. Early forms of organisation, Laloux (2014) argues, relied on dominance and fear to maintain power. As societies formalised, stability and control took precedence, which led to the rigid, top-down hierarchies still seen today in government agencies and public institutions. The rise of capitalism then introduced machine-like, efficiency-driven, competitive models, shaping the corporate world as we know it. More recently, culture-driven organisations have emerged, which emphasise shared values and empowerment. Now, we are witnessing another shift – towards viewing organisations as living systems. An organisational breakthrough that will move us beyond today's rigid hierarchies towards more purposeful, self-managed and collaborative ways of organising. A growing recognition that traditional hierarchies may no longer serve the challenges of the present and future.

What does this have to do with sufficiency? Well, at higher stages of development, there is a noticeable shift towards sufficiency values. For instance,

Princen (2005) argues that self-managed teams are more likely than traditional hierarchies to sense what is 'enough'. And the dominant 'achiever' mindset of today – one that glorifies material success, competition and endless growth – is not a fixed truth. It is simply a reflection of our current stage of development. And just as humanity has outgrown previous worldviews, we can – and must – evolve beyond this one.

That does not mean rejecting everything from the past. The roots of sufficiency run deep. Many religious traditions have long stressed the sacredness of simplicity and moderation, and throughout history, sufficiency values have been embraced by many cultures and philosophies. For instance, the Greek philosopher Epicurus (341–270 BC) cautioned that while pleasure is the basis of contentment, extravagance is unlikely to bring us joy. Lao Tzu wrote in the *Tao Te Ching* (c. 260 BC): 'He who knows he has enough is rich'. We have much to learn from the past to advance beyond consumerism. As one of the sufficiency scholars put it:

> *I believe we need to challenge what I sometimes call contemporary chronocentrism, by which I mean the view that we have nothing to learn from the past, but progress is always about further development of what modernity has to offer already. We would benefit from looking towards the past as well to learn. I mean, I think we need to get a more complete and nuanced view of what we mean by prosperity.*
>
> *(Interviewee 2)*

And we must not only look backwards. Around the world, many communities already live in ways that align with the logic of sufficiency – even if they do not use the term themselves. Consider, for instance, indigenous perspectives such as Buen Vivir in Latin America, which questions consumerism and economic growth while offering at the same time alternatives beyond it (Chuji et al., 2019). And within everyday life, around the world, we find echoes of sufficiency: in families where fairness and enoughness are negotiated through sharing and caring, in neighbourhood repair cafés, in communal gardens. Sufficiency is not a foreign or futuristic ideal – it is already being practised. Recognising and learning from these diverse sources of wisdom is part of moving forward.

9.5 Implications

Let us imagine that we have left the myth behind – the belief that more always equals better, that we must endlessly accumulate and that our needs must constantly escalate. Reaching this point would require us to reimagine societies, curing the widespread lack of imagination of other ways of living and opening up dialogue on new understandings of prosperity. As we have argued throughout this chapter, sufficiency is about fairness, redefining the good life, and meeting collective challenges. It is an evolution demanded by citizens and grounded in justice.

What is the first step to implementing sufficiency as the guiding principle of society and economy? One starting point could be to have governments, regions, and municipalities analyse their strategies through a sufficiency lens. The Sufficiency Manifesto (European Environmental Bureau, 2024), signed by 70+ NGOs pushing for sufficiency to anchor the EU's strategic agenda, offers a model for this approach:

> *Sufficiency needs to be at the heart of the next EU mandate . . ., the European Commission should present an EU strategy for sufficiency, based on a thorough analysis of the EU's sufficiency potential and identification of the current legislative gap across sectors, and propose an action plan aiming to ease the achievement of the 2030 targets and set Europe on the right path to 2040 and 2050.*
>
> *(European Environmental Bureau, 2024, p. 6)*

When it comes to specific sufficiency-oriented policies, showing us how this principle can be applied in practical ways, there are many real-world examples we could point to. The City of Zurich's 2000-watt society is one such policy. Approved by referendum back in 2008 with overwhelming support, it sets a goal of reducing energy consumption to 2,000 watts per person by 2040, equivalent to the energy use of Zurich residents in the 1960s and aligned with the planetary boundaries (Stadt Zurich, 2025). The interim target of decreasing energy consumption to 4,000 watts per person by 2020 has been achieved. However, challenges remain in meeting the ultimate goal. France offers another example of sufficiency in action with its 2023 ban on short domestic flights where viable train alternatives exist. While the ban has been criticised for its limited scope, targeting only a few routes and excluding connecting flights (BBC, 2023), it can nevertheless be seen as an attempt to bring transportation into the sustainable consumption corridor. Limiting unnecessary consumption of air travel sends an important political signal, which broader measures will hopefully follow. A third example comes from Melbourne, Australia, where community-driven sharing initiatives have reshaped access to household goods. The Brunswick Tool Library allows members to borrow tools instead of purchasing them, which promotes repair and skill development. The space also functions as a hub for DIY enthusiasts, by offering workshops on, for example, woodworking and maintenance. Similarly, there are toy libraries across Australia and in many other countries, from which parents can borrow toys, teaching children the value of shared resources over ownership. Non-commercial public spaces such as tool and toy libraries thus foster creativity, learning and community. And by replacing individual ownership with shared access, these spaces embody sufficiency principles: they promote abundance in shared experiences and shared resources rather than in material possessions.

For businesses, debunking the myth of sufficiency opens the door to embracing sufficiency strategies, such as those identified by Laura Niessen and Nancy Bocken (2021) and outlined earlier. Some companies have already taken this leap. One example is Commown, a French cooperative that offers sustainable, repairable electronics for rent to both individuals and businesses. Another example is Vitsœ, a manufacturer of modular, repairable furniture designed for long-term use. Uniquely, Vitsœ trains its sales staff to undersell to help customers purchase only what they truly need. Both these companies publicly advocate for reduced consumption, trying to challenge the norm of overconsumption. They are part of a growing movement of businesses proving that sufficiency is not just possible but desirable.[2]

What about individuals? For many of us, especially in affluent societies, the truth is clear: we need to consume less. We are living above our means, far beyond the sustainable consumption corridor. This shift is not easy – it requires letting go of familiar ways of living and ingrained habits. The Swedish art project *Avskedsbyrån* (The Farewell Bureau), set up as a funeral parlour, frames this process as a form of grieving. To move on, we need to say goodbye to certain objects and patterns of behaviour that no longer serve us:

> *The importance of grief in moving on in life cannot be underestimated. . . . With commitment and reverence, we must ensure that we bid a dignified and final farewell to the excesses of consumer culture.*
>
> *(Avskedsbyrån)*

At the same time, let us remember that letting go is not just an act of loss – it is also an act of liberation. As we have argued throughout this chapter, sufficiency is not about deprivation, but about freeing ourselves from the constant pressure to accumulate. It is about making space – for connection, for meaning, for time, for well-being. While sufficiency may ask us to say goodbye to certain comforts or habits, it also invites us to rediscover forms of abundance that consumer culture tends to obscure: shared resources, community, care, creativity.

9.6 Main message

In this chapter, we have challenged the belief that people are inherently driven to accumulate endlessly and would never accept sufficiency. Indeed, consumerist culture exerts strong social pressures to consume, and accumulation is deeply ingrained in our dominant social logic. But that sufficiency would mean an end to modern life, a regression to pre-industrial lifestyles, giving up on comfort and joy – that is simply not true. It would, on the contrary, move us beyond the status quo, towards a future where prosperity is measured not by what we own, but by how well we live within the planetary limits. A future where alternative hedonism flourishes. Where we privilege time over money, freedom over material possessions, and meaningful connections over excess

For policymakers, this requires embedding sufficiency into the very design of societal planning, infrastructures and policies, to shift norms and expectations towards sustainable consumption levels. For businesses, sufficiency means moving beyond volume-driven sales models and exploring setting limits to growth, to prioritise long-term well-being over short-term profit maximisation and ever-increasing material throughput. For people and communities, sufficiency means embracing the logic of well-being, care and freedom it offers – by nurturing a culture of enoughness, supporting businesses that challenge overconsumption and demanding policies that make sustainable, fair and joyful lives not only possible but also easy. Sufficiency is an invitation to take an evolutionary leap – together.

Notes

1 Alongside Max-Neef's, there are other similar frameworks of fundamental needs, such as Martha Nussbaum's (2003) capabilities approach, and Len Doyal and Ian Gough's (1984) theory of human need.

2 For further inspiration, Laura Niessen has created a database of companies across various sectors that have adopted sufficiency strategies. As of this writing, the database features 160 businesses, including Commown and Vitsœ, with more being added regularly.

References

Callmer, Å., & Bradley, K. (2021). In search of sufficiency politics: The case of Sweden. *Sustainability: Science, Practice and Policy*, *17*(1), 194–208. https://doi.org/10.1080/15487733.2021.1926684

Cap, S., De Koning, A., Tukker, A., & Scherer, L. (2024). (In)Sufficiency of industrial decarbonization to reduce household carbon footprints to 1.5°C-compatible levels. *Sustainable Production and Consumption*, *45*, 216–227. https://doi.org/10.1016/j.spc.2023.12.031

Chuji, M., Rengifo, G., & Gudynas, E. (2019). Buen Vivir. In A. Kothari, A. Salleh, A. Escobar, F. Demaria, & A. Acosta (Eds.), *Pluriverse: A post-development dictionary* (pp. 111–114). Tulika Books.

Creutzig, F., Roy, J., Devine-Wright, P., Díaz-José, J., Geels, F. W., Grubler, A., Maïzi, N., Masanet, E., Mulugetta, Y., Onyige, C. D., Perkins, P. E., Sanches-Pereira, A., & Weber, E. U. (2022). Demand, services and social aspects of mitigation. In *IPCC, 2022: Climate change 2022: Mitigation of climate change. Contribution of working group III to the sixth assessment report of the intergovernmental panel on climate change* [P. R. Shukla, J. Skea, R. Slade, A. Al Khourdajie, R. van Diemen, D. McCollum, M. Pathak, S. Some, P. Vyas, R. Fradera, M. Belkacemi, A. Hasija, G. Lisboa, S. Luz, & J. Malley, Eds.]. Cambridge University Press. https://doi.org/10.1017/9781009157926.007

Dittmar, H., Bond, R., Hurst, M., & Kasser, T. (2014). The relationship between materialism and personal well-being: A meta-analysis. *Journal of Personality and Social Psychology*, *107*(5), 879–924. https://doi.org/10.1037/a0037409
Doyal, L., & Gough, I. (1984). A theory of human needs. *Critical Social Policy*, *4*(10), 6–38. https://doi.org/10.1177/026101838400401002
Easterlin, R. A. (1974). Does economic growth improve the human lot? Some empirical evidence. In *Nations and households in economic growth* (pp. 89–125). Elsevier. https://doi.org/10.1016/B978-0-12-205050-3.50008-7
Erikson, E. H. (with Erikson, J. M.). (1998). *The life cycle completed (extended version)* (1st ed.). W. W. Norton & Company, Incorporated.
ETC CE. (2023). *Consumption and the environment in Europe's circular economy*. European Topic Centre on Circular economy and resource use.
European Environmental Bureau. (2024). *Manifesto: A resilient and resource-wise Europe: Sufficiency at the heart of the EU's future*. European Environmental Bureau. Retrieved February 5, 2025, from https://eeb.org/wp-content/uploads/2024/03/sufficiency_manifesto.pdf
The Farewell Bureau. (n.d.). Retrieved February 6, 2025, from https://www.arsmoriendi.se
Feldthus, M., & Haumann, O. (2024). *Setting limits to growth: How to make better business decisions in the 21st century* (1st eBook ed.). Post Growth Guide.
France bans short-haul flights to cut carbon emissions. (2023, May 23). Retrieved February 5, 2025, from https://www.bbc.com/news/world-europe-65687665
Fuchs, D., Sahakian, M., Gumbert, T., Giulio, A. D., Maniates, M., Lorek, S., & Graf, A. (2021). *Consumption corridors: Living a good life within sustainable limits*. Routledge. https://doi.org/10.4324/9780367748746
Fuchs, D. A., & Lorek, S. (2005). Sustainable consumption governance: A history of promises and failures. *Journal of Consumer Policy*, *28*(3), 261–288. https://doi.org/10.1007/s10603-005-8490-z
Galbraith, E. D., Barrington-Leigh, C., Miñarro, S., Álvarez-Fernández, S., Attoh, E. M. N. A. N., Benyei, P., Calvet-Mir, L., Carmona, R., Chakauya, R., Chen, Z., Chengula, F., Fernández-Llamazares, Á., García-del-Amo, D., Glauser, M., Huanca, T., Izquierdo, A. E., Junqueira, A. B., Lanker, M., Li, X., . . . Reyes-García, V. (2024). High life satisfaction reported among small-scale societies with low incomes. *Proceedings of the National Academy of Sciences*, *121*(7). https://doi.org/10.1073/pnas.2311703121
Gorge, H., Herbert, M., Özçağlar-Toulouse, N., & Robert, I. (2015). What do we really need? Questioning consumption through sufficiency. *Journal of Macromarketing*, *35*(1), 11–22. https://doi.org/10.1177/0276146714553935
Gough, I. (2022). Two scenarios for sustainable welfare: A framework for an eco-social contract. *Social Policy and Society*, *21*(3), 460–472. https://doi.org/10.1017/S1474746421000701
Hirth, S., Kreinin, H., Fuchs, D., Blossey, N., Mamut, P., Philipp, J., Radovan, I., & The EU1.5°Lifestyles Consortium. (2023). Barriers and enablers of 1.5° lifestyles: Shallow and deep structural factors shaping the potential for sustainable consumption. *Frontiers in Sustainability*, *4*, 1014662. https://doi.org/10.3389/frsus.2023.1014662
IEA. (2025). *SUVs are setting new sales records each year – and so are their emissions*. Retrieved February 5, 2025, from https://www.iea.org/commentaries/suvs-are-setting-new-sales-records-each-year-and-so-are-their-emissions
Jackson, T. (2021). *Post growth: Life after capitalism*. Polity.
Kartha, S., Kemp-Benedict, E., Ghosh, E., Nazareth, A., & Gore, T. (2020). *The carbon inequality era: An assessment of the global distribution of consumption emissions among individuals from 1990 to 2015 and beyond*. Oxfam, Stockholm Environment Institute. https://doi.org/10.21201/2020.6492

Khalfan, A., Nilsson Lewis, A., Aguilar, C., Persson, J., Lawson, M., Dabi, N., Jayoussi, S., & Acharya, S. (2023). *Climate equality: A planet for the 99%*. Oxfam International. https://doi.org/10.21201/2023.000001

Kilbourne, W., McDonagh, P., & Prothero, A. (1997). Sustainable consumption and the quality of life: A macromarketing challenge to the dominant social paradigm. *Journal of Macromarketing*, *17*(1), 4–24. https://doi.org/10.1177/027614679701700103

Killingsworth, M., Kahneman, D., & Mellers, B. (2023). Income and emotional well-being: A conflict resolved. *Proceedings of the National Academy of Sciences, U.S.A*, *120*(10). https://www.pnas.org/doi/10.1073/pnas.2208661120

Kohlberg, L., Levine, C., & Hewer, A. (1983). *Moral stages: A current formulation and a response to critics*. Karger.

Kreinin, H., Fuchs, D., Mamut, P., Hirth, S., & Lange, S. (2024). Transforming provisioning systems to enable 1.5° lifestyles in Europe? Expert and stakeholder views on overcoming structural barriers. *Sustainability: Science, Practice and Policy*, *20*(1), 2372120. https://doi.org/10.1080/15487733.2024.2372120

Lage, J., Thema, J., Zell-Ziegler, C., Best, B., Cordroch, L., & Wiese, F. (2023). Citizens call for sufficiency and regulation – A comparison of European citizen assemblies and National energy and climate plans. *Energy Research & Social Science*, *104*, 103254. https://doi.org/10.1016/j.erss.2023.103254

Laloux, F. (2014). *Reinventing organizations: A guide to creating organizations inspired by the next stage of human consciousness* (1st ed. (revised)). Nelson Parker.

Lehner, M., Richter, J. L., Kreinin, H., Mamut, P., Vadovics, E., Henman, J., Mont, O., & Fuchs, D. (2024). Living smaller: Acceptance, effects and structural factors in the EU. *Buildings & Cities*, *5*(1). https://doi.org/10.5334/bc.438

Max-Neef, M. (1991). *Human scale development: Conception, application and further reflections*. The Apex Press.

Millward-Hopkins, J., & Fisch-Romito, V. (2025). We have to talk about overconsumption (in three different ways). *Environmental Research Letters*, *20*(3), 031007. https://doi.org/10.1088/1748-9326/adb986

Nielsen, K. S., Nicholas, K. A., Creutzig, F., Dietz, T., & Stern, P. C. (2021). The role of high-socioeconomic-status people in locking in or rapidly reducing energy-driven greenhouse gas emissions. *Nature Energy*, *6*(11), 1011–1016. https://doi.org/10.1038/s41560-021-00900-y

Niessen, L., & Bocken, N. M. P. (2021). How can businesses drive sufficiency? The business for sufficiency framework. *Sustainable Production and Consumption*, *28*, 1090–1103. https://doi.org/10.1016/j.spc.2021.07.030

Niinimäki, K., Peters, G., Dahlbo, H., Perry, P., Rissanen, T., & Gwilt, A. (2020). The environmental price of fast fashion. *Nature Reviews Earth & Environment*, *1*(4), 189–200. https://doi.org/10.1038/s43017-020-0039-9

Nussbaum, M. (2003). Capabilities as fundamental entitlements: Sen and social justice. *Feminist Economics*, *9*(2–3), 33–59. https://doi.org/10.1080/1354570022000077926

Plomteux, A. (2024). Frugal abundance: Conceptualisation for degrowth. *Ecological Economics*, *222*, 108223. https://doi.org/10.1016/j.ecolecon.2024.108223

Princen, T. (2005). *The logic of sufficiency*. MIT Press.

Richter, J. L., Lehner, M., Elfström, A., Henman, J., Vadovics, E., Brizga, J., Plepys, A., & Mont, O. (2024). 1.5° lifestyle changes: Exploring consequences for individuals and households. *Sustainable Production and Consumption*, *50*, 511–525. https://doi.org/10.1016/j.spc.2024.07.018

Robeyns, I. (2024). *Limitarianism: The case against extreme wealth*. Allen Lane.

Schor, J. B. (1999). *The overspent American: Why we want what we don't need* (Nachdr.). HarperPerennial.

Soper, K. (2020). *Post-growth living: For an alternative hedonism*. Verso.

Spengler, L. (2016). Two types of 'enough': Sufficiency as minimum and maximum. *Environmental Politics*, *25*(5), 921–940. https://doi.org/10.1080/09644016.2016.1164355

Stadt Zurich. (2025). *2000-watt society*. Retrieved February 5, 2025, from https://www.stadt-zuerich.ch/de/umwelt-und-energie/klima/klimaschutz/ziele/2000-watt-gesellschaft.html#wo_steht_zuerichaufdemwegzur2000-watt-gesellschaft

Trentmann, F. (2016). *Empire of things: How we became a world of consumers, from the fifteenth century to the twenty-first* (1st U.S. ed.). HarperCollins Publishers.

United Nations Environment Programme. (2024). *Global resources outlook 2024 summary for policymakers: Bend the trend – Pathways to a liveable planet as resource use spikes*. International Resource Panel. https://wedocs.unep.org/20.500.11822/44902

Vadovics, E., Richter, J. L., Tornow, M., Ozcelik, N., Coscieme, L., Lettenmeier, M., Csiki, E., Domröse, L., Cap, S., Puente, L. L., Belousa, I., & Scherer, L. (2024). Preferences, enablers, and barriers for 1.5°C lifestyle options: Findings from citizen thinking labs in five European Union countries. *Sustainability: Science, Practice and Policy*, *20*(1), 2375806. https://doi.org/10.1080/15487733.2024.2375806

PART III

Societal level

10

MYTH 9

Without economic growth, sustainable consumption is impossible

Markus Larsson, Mikael Malmaeus and Göran Finnveden

10.1 The economic-growth-is-necessary myth

The relationship between economic growth and sustainable development has been discussed for a long time (Kallis et al., 2025). Debates over whether and how economic growth can be reconciled with environmental protection played a significant role in the emergence of the concept of sustainable development (Robinson, 2004). Here we will narrow our discussion to a specific aspect and focus on the following statement: '*Without economic growth, sustainable consumption is impossible*'. This is a statement that is often made, implicitly or explicitly, by proponents of green growth, which can be seen as the present major political paradigm for sustainable development.

Economic growth, or sometimes just growth, is often interpreted in a rather unspecified way as an increase in, for example, technological knowledge or welfare. Here, we will give it a more precise meaning as an increase in the Gross Domestic Product (GDP), where GDP is a monetary measure of the market value of all the final goods and services produced and rendered in a specific time period by a country or countries (OECD, n.d.). GDP is measured annually by statistical offices in different countries using standardised procedures. It is calculated as the sum of consumption expenditures (C), Investments (I), governmental spending (G) and net exports (NX, export minus import): C + I + G + NX = GDP (BEA, n.d.).

'Sustainable consumption' can have different meanings depending on the context and backgrounds of the people defining the concept (Svenfelt et al.,

DOI: 10.4324/9781003613718-14

2024). One early definition of Sustainable Consumption and Production was proposed in 1994 at the Oslo Symposium on Sustainable Consumption:

> *[T]he use of services and related products which respond to basic needs and bring a better quality of life while minimizing the use of natural resources and toxic materials as well as the emissions of waste and pollutants over the life cycle of the service or product so as not to jeopardize the needs of future generations.*
>
> *(Oslo Symposium, 1994)*

We will use here a slightly different definition based more directly on the extended version of the classical definition of sustainable development in the so-called Brundtland report (WCED, 1987). We define sustainable consumption as 'consumption that meets today's needs without compromising the ability of future generations to meet their own needs, while giving special consideration to the needs of the world's poor and the limitations of ecosystems'.

In 2015, countries around the world agreed on the 2030 Agenda for Sustainable Development (United Nations, 2015), including the 17 Sustainable Development Goals (SDGs) and associated targets. The agenda, including the goals and targets, can together be seen as a further definition and specification of Sustainable Development. It is also stressed in the document that the goals are integrated and indivisible. Sustainable Consumption can then be defined as consumption that is in line with the Sustainable Development Goals. This implies a consumption that reduces the environmental impacts to sustainable levels while simultaneously achieving social goals such as access to food, healthcare, education, water, energy and housing.

Of special interest here is the SDG 8, which reads 'Promote sustained, inclusive and sustainable economic growth, full and productive employment and decent work for all'. In the short version used for communication, but not included in the 2030 Agenda, SDG 8 reads 'Decent work and economic growth', suggesting that economic growth is one of the SDGs. However, the writing in the 2030 Agenda, which is the document governments agreed on, requires an 'inclusive and sustainable economic growth', which means that any economic growth is not in line with the SDG per se, since it also needs to be inclusive and sustainable. A valid question is then, what is meant by 'sustainable economic growth'? In line with previous definitions, sustainable economic growth can be defined as 'economic growth that meets today's needs without compromising the ability of future generations to meet their own needs, while giving special consideration to the needs of the world's poor and the limitations of ecosystems'. As a further specification it can be defined as 'an economic growth that is in line with the Sustainable Development Goals' (c.f. Finnveden, 2021). It can thus not be an economic growth that, for example, leads to further environmental degradation, increased emissions of greenhouse gases or increased inequalities, as such growth would not be in line with other SDGs.

There is an inherent conflict between economic growth and the ambition of reducing environmental pressure. This is because when the economy grows, more products are produced and consumed, requiring more energy and other resources, also leading to more emissions and other types of environmental impacts. If there are no efficiency improvements, and the mix of production is constant, there will be a direct correlation between increased production and increased environmental pressure. Only if there are efficiency improvements or changes in the production mix, there is a potential for economic growth and at the same time, reduced environmental pressure.

To date, no country has fully achieved sustainable development or sustainable consumption. For richer countries, it is primarily the environmental goals that have not yet been met. For other countries, the social goals may be the primary challenge. In such cases, increased consumption may be necessary. The focus of this chapter is on environmental challenges, although social goals will also be discussed. We start by examining economic growth: what is economic growth, how can it be achieved, and why has it been viewed as the solution to many problems society is facing?

10.2 Origins

Over time, the average income of a citizen in any country has increased. Since 1960, the growth in global GDP has been ninefold (Figure 10.1). This is a remarkable development.

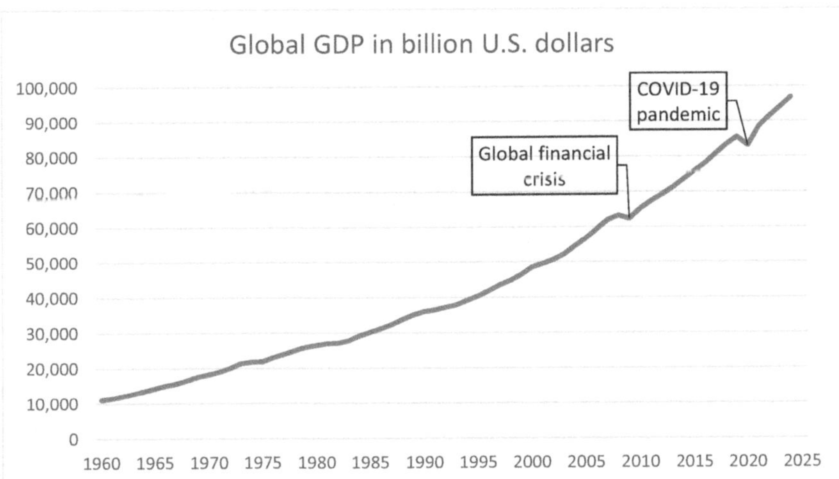

FIGURE 10.1 Global GDP (constant 2015 US$) over time.

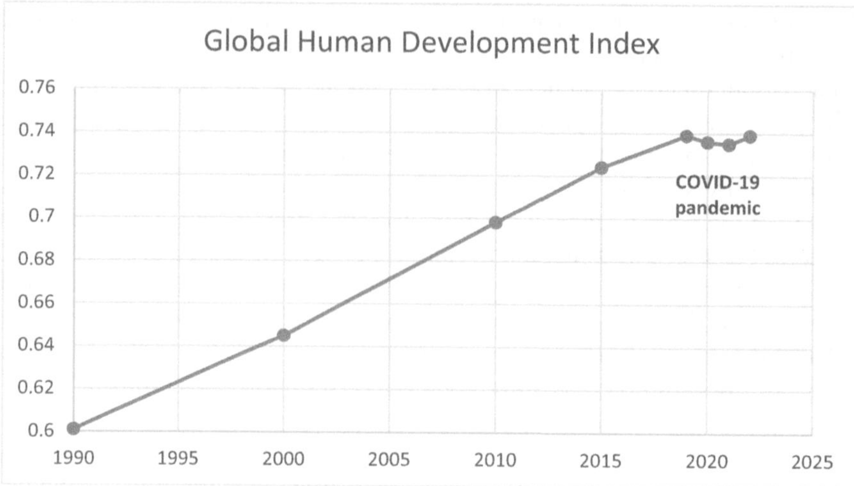

FIGURE 10.2 Global Human Development Index over time. Human Development Report.

There is a well-established narrative that economic growth goes hand in hand with attractive development. One reason why this view is so established could be that historically, increased incomes have been positively correlated with many things we strive for. Perhaps a healthy and long life is the ultimate indicator of this. As income has increased, so has often life expectancy. The populations in rich countries, on average, live longer than those in poor countries, and an average rich individual in a random country lives longer than her poor neighbour (Karolinska Institutet, 2021). In Sweden, this difference in life expectancy between rich and poor has increased over time and is today ten years, according to Hagen et al. (2025). The increase in global GDP since 1985 has been unevenly distributed among the global population. However, most people in most countries have experienced improved living conditions over time (OECD, 2022). Following UNDP's Human Development Index (HDI), where economic, health and educational aspects are given equal weight, life on earth has become better over time, with a minor dip during the COVID-19 pandemic (Figure 10.2). HDI is more or less in tandem with the global GDP over the same period.

Not only do people on average live longer, get better educated, and consume more with higher income, but people also seem to become happier. Contrary to earlier findings suggesting that happiness ceased to increase with income after reaching a plateau (Kahneman & Deaton, 2010), there appears to be a steady association between larger incomes and greater happiness for most people, even at high levels of income (Killingsworth et al., 2023).

Thus, there seems to be a clear connection between economic growth and important aspects of sustainable consumption, including improved health and education. Following this, who would turn down an offer of increased income?

On the other hand, the environmental impacts have increased significantly over time and human activities have now transgressed several environmental limits (Richardson et al., 2023). This is compromising the ability of future generations to meet their own needs and will, for example, lead to significant income losses in the future (Kotz et al., 2024). This is not in line with sustainable consumption. Even so, from an environmental perspective, economic growth has, in the mainstream policy discourse, rarely been seen as problematic and sometimes growth has been presented as a solution to environmental problems.

10.2.1 Neo-classical growth theory

One explanation for the widespread narrative of environmentally friendly growth can be found in neoclassical growth theory. For OECD countries, increased productivity can explain close to 50% of GDP growth in the latter part of the 20th century (Easterly & Levine, 2001). The Swedish equivalent, for the period 1985–2005, amounts to just over 30%. One interpretation of this theory is that efficiency gains and technical innovations can result in economic growth without requiring additional resources (Grafström & Sandström, 2020). Or, according to the so-called Solow model, 'the driving force of growth is the accumulation of knowledge . . . capital accumulation is not central to growth' (Romer, 1996, p. 95, cited in Roine, 2015).

The Solow model can, in its simplest form, be explained by the equation:

$$Y = AK^{\alpha}L^{1-\alpha}.$$

Income, that is, GDP (Y), is dependent on the input of capital (K) and labour (L). Following this equation, economic growth can be achieved through increased input of resources (L, K or both) and increased productivity (A). Thus, theoretically, economic growth can be explained by technical innovation and efficiency gains. Empirical evidence suggests, however, that economic growth consistently requires additional resource inputs (Malmaeus & Hahn, 2022).

To be fair to neo-classical growth theory, economic growth is not a goal in itself, according to many neo-classical economists. 'Economic growth is only desirable insofar as it contributes to increased well-being. The fact that there is compelling evidence that this has been the case so far does not automatically mean that it will continue to be so in the future' (Roine, 2015, p. 51, our translation).

10.2.2 *Green growth: the dominant strategy for a sustainable transition*

When the concept of 'sustainable development' was established with the Brundtland Report (WCED, 1987), criticism of economic growth was virtually absent. In fact, poverty was seen as contributing to environmental degradation, and economic growth was seen as an important tool for addressing both poverty and environmental issues. A couple of years later, Grossman and Krueger (1991) presented a paper with (limited) empirical examples of the correlation between environmental pressures and income. One example is the concentration of $SO_{2,}$ which appeared to increase with GDP/capita up to a certain income level, after which concentrations decreased. This bell-shaped relationship was later coined 'the Environmental Kuznets Curve'.

Neither the relationship between economic growth (increased income) and environmental degradation as presented in the Brundtland Report nor that proposed by the Environmental Kuznets Curve is supported by robust empirical evidence. Some studies suggest that, in certain countries, the Environmental Kuznets Curve may follow an N-shaped pattern (Allard et al., 2018), wherein environmental pressure initially rises alongside income, then declines after reaching a peak, but eventually begins to increase again as economic growth continues. Nonetheless, the notion that economic growth ultimately leads to a reduction in environmental pressure is frequently presented as an unquestioned assumption. Malmaeus and Hahn (2022) studied more than 200 Swedish news articles, books, reports, etc. and identified ten recurring arguments related to economic growth and sustainability. Eight of these argue that growth can be combined with, or is necessary for, environmental sustainability and two argue that this can be problematic. Green growth, as it has been labelled, is today the dominant strategy for transitioning to a sustainable society. This strategy is endorsed by national governments and multinational institutions, including the World Bank (2012), the European Environment Agency (2021) and the OECD (2011) alike. Economic growth is often regarded as a prerequisite for this transition; however, in the green growth paradigm, the economic engine is envisioned as green and decarbonised, with production and consumption increasingly oriented towards services rather than material goods (see Chapter 6 in this book).

One example is the EU's Green Deal, envisioned as a roadmap for transforming the economy into one with no net greenhouse gas emissions by 2050, where economic growth is decoupled from resource consumption and no people or places are left behind. Through innovations and investments in new green technologies, it aims to drive both economic growth and the transition to a climate-neutral and sustainable society.

Thus, a central concept of green growth is the ability to reduce environmental impacts and resource use while simultaneously increase total production.

This requires environmental pressures per unit of GDP to decrease faster than GDP increases. Is this achievable? The answer seems to be yes, at least when focusing on greenhouse gases. For instance, Sweden has reduced emissions within its borders by 38% between 1990 and 2023 (SEPA, 2024a) while its GDP increased. Similarly, emissions caused by Sweden's consumption decreased by 20% between 2008 and 2022 (SEPA, 2024b). Following the Swedish example, decoupling economic growth from greenhouse gas emissions appears to be possible. But as we shall see below, this does not seem to be the case for other important environmental pressures. Equally important, the current rate of emissions reduction remains insufficient to meet the targets set by the Paris Agreement, that is, 'pursuing efforts to limit the temperature increase to 1.5°C above pre-industrial levels' (UNFCCC, 2015, Article 2).

The above discussion assumes that GDP is the metric that should grow in a green growth model. However, this is not always clear when green growth is discussed. In contrast to the definition used here, the concept of economic growth has sometimes (perhaps unintentionally) also been interpreted as referring to the growth of other factors, such as innovations, investments in green technology, or efficiency gains from digitalisation (Malmaeus & Hahn, 2022). If these occur alongside the phasing out of old technologies and production, GDP may not increase at all, while technological progress continues. This interpretation of 'green growth' shifts the discussion entirely. It is therefore crucial to specify what is intended to grow when discussing green or sustainable growth.

A distinction is sometimes made between 'green growth' and 'genuinely green growth' (Stoknes & Rockström, 2018). Green growth typically refers to a decoupling of GDP from environmental impact. Genuinely green growth, however, requires that this decoupling is sufficient to meet scientifically established sustainability targets, including those set by the Paris Agreement and other environmental goals.

10.3 Consequences

By assuming that economic growth is required for sustainable development, environmental and economic policy will continue to be directed towards perpetuating economic growth. There are two main problems associated with this. First, it may be directly counter-productive if there is insufficient decoupling between economic growth and environmental impacts. Second, this myth will prevent alternative strategies that involve a non-growing economy. To evaluate whether there is sufficient decoupling, we need to make a distinction between *relative* and *absolute* decoupling, followed by a discussion of decoupling in a green growth scenario.

Relative decoupling means that the economy grows faster than environmental impact, that is, more economic value is produced per unit of environmental impact or, conversely, that less environmental impact is caused per monetary unit. Energy efficiency improvements, for example, may mean that less energy is required to produce each unit of consumption. However, if we simultaneously increase the overall production and consumption of goods and services, total energy consumption may still rise. In order to achieve reduced environmental impact and reduced resource use, *absolute decoupling* is required. This implies that environmental impacts and resource use must decline sufficiently to offset the effects of continued economic growth.

Let us, for a moment, assume that absolute decoupling between GDP growth and all types of environmental impact, including material footprint, is actually possible to achieve. Let us further hypothetically assume that this decoupling for a certain type of environmental pressure at a given point in time amounts to 5% per year: Put simply, this would mean that if GDP grows by 5%, environmental pressure will remain unchanged. Or if GDP remains unchanged, environmental pressure will decrease by 5%. If we set the condition that GDP must grow, this means that environmental pressure will, by definition, decrease by less than 5% per year. Applied to greenhouse gas emissions, such a rate of decline would be insufficient. To have a reasonable chance of reaching the 1.5°C target, global GHG emissions must decline by 43% from 2019 levels by 2030, and by 84% by 2050 (IPCC, 2022). Yet, as of the time of writing, global emissions have instead increased by 14% since 2010 (IPCC, 2022). This means that achieving the 1.5°C target requires annual emission reductions substantially greater than 5% throughout the current decade.

The left diagram illustrates green growth, where the gains from efficiency (the decoupling) are being used to allow for continued economic growth, rather than to achieve absolute reductions in environmental pressures. The right-hand diagram represents the same focus on efficiency, but instead, the gains from efficiency (the decoupling) are being used to reduce environmental pressures rather than maximising economic growth, leading to a steady-state economy, that is, a stable GDP.

Committing to increased GDP thus means a limitation of the possibilities for reduced environmental impact. But it also prevents more radical thinking regarding economic development. There is much to suggest that the development model that prevailed in the Western world during the 20th century needs to be fundamentally changed. Although it is beyond the scope of this chapter, the myth also prevents radical thinking about societal development in general and blocks initiatives for greater well-being for people and nature that do not involve continued GDP growth. The following section examines economic growth in relation to empirical evidence concerning environmental impacts, economic functioning, technological development and patterns of investment.

10.4 Dispelling the myth

The myth that sustainable consumption is impossible without economic growth can be dismissed on several grounds. First, historical experience shows that growth more often than not leads to an ecologically unsustainable development. Moreover, growth is not a prerequisite for achieving social sustainability. Nor is growth a necessary condition for progress in technology or investment. In fact, due to economic growth, the environmental benefits of technological improvements and efficiency gains are often undermined by rebound effects, where increased efficiency is offset by increased consumption and production. These aspects are further discussed below.

10.4.1 Economic growth is not decoupling fast enough from environmental impact

There are many examples where economic growth has been coupled with increased emissions or resource use. There are also examples where countries have managed to decouple some environmental pressures from growth, but the decoupling is rarely strong enough. In terms of economic growth and emissions of GHG, Sweden is one such example, see above.

For many countries, including the EU and the OECD, the correlation between the material footprint and GDP is very strong. Giljum et al. (2014, p. 328) note that since the year 2000, on global level, 'material consumption increased in parallel to GDP' and that 'not even a relative decoupling was achieved on the global level'. Over a longer period (between 1945 and 2002), the average material use per person in the world increased 0.9% slower than GDP (relative decoupling), but between 2002 and 2015, it instead increased 0.4% faster than GDP (Krausmann et al., 2018). Following this, there are signs of a 're-materialization' of the global economy, which is the opposite of decoupling material use from GDP growth.

As for carbon dioxide emissions, these have actually decreased in a number of countries over the past decades while GDP has also increased. In the United States since the year 2000, consumption-related emissions have decreased by 14%, and in the EU by 23% (Friedlingstein et al., 2023). While this is positive, it is happening at a pace that is nowhere near what is required to reach net-zero emissions by 2050. At the same time, on a global level, there has been no absolute decoupling. Global emissions have increased by close to 70% since 1990. The countries exhibiting absolute decoupling are primarily wealthy, and their emissions are generally high compared to the global average. In contrast to developing nations whose emissions are relatively low, wealthy, high-emitting nations must drastically reduce their emissions within a short timeframe.

Hickel and Kallis (2019) analysed 116 climate and energy scenarios developed by the Intergovernmental Panel on Climate Change (IPCC) and the International Renewable Energy Agency (IRENA) and found that all of them

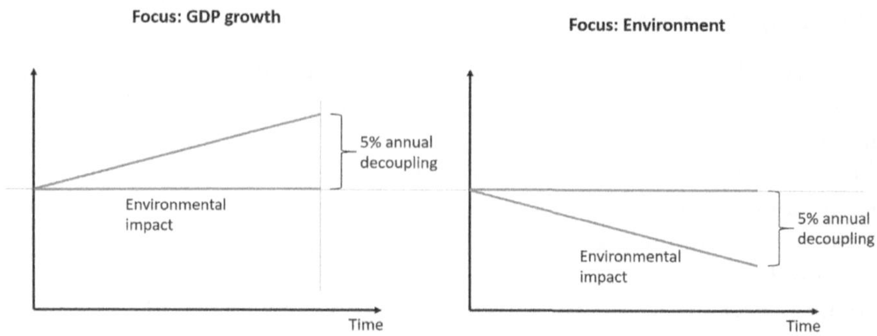

FIGURE 10.3 Directing efficiency efforts towards promoting economic growth (left) or mitigating environmental impacts (right). Modified after Malmaeus and Hahn (2022).

assume continued economic growth. The scenarios that manage to avoid a 2 °C temperature rise compared to pre-industrial levels make strong assumptions about negative emissions involving bioenergy with carbon capture and storage (BECCS) and other technologies that are not yet implemented. These technologies would require extensive use of biofuels, potentially leading to increased land use and biodiversity loss. This illustrates the difficulties in combining economic growth and sustainable development.

None of these rules out the possibility that reduced material footprints and reduced environmental and climate impacts can be achieved while GDP increases. Even so, continued economic growth means that reduced environmental impact must be achieved against a headwind. Although it is possible to sail against the direction of the wind, it is usually slower than sailing in the same direction as the wind (which is illustrated in Figure 10.3).

10.4.2 The economy can function without growth

It is a fairly common belief that our economic system requires growth to function and that without growth, severe problems arise. When GDP in 2020, during the COVID-19 pandemic, dropped to the level of 2015, it was portrayed as a catastrophe, even though 2015 hardly seemed like a catastrophic situation, at least not in high-income countries. If we believe that increasing GDP is absolutely necessary, it is not hard to understand the conviction that growth must be reconcilable with social and ecological sustainability, no matter how difficult it may seem. But what is really behind such a belief?

First of all, we must distinguish the question of what would happen if we had a lower GDP compared to today from the question of what happens to the functioning of the economy if GDP declines. The answer to the first question is trivial: we would produce slightly fewer goods and services compared to today. For example, we would experience the standard of living of 2015 rather than that of 2025. The concern many people have is more related to the second question: Can the macroeconomy remain stable in the absence of continued GDP growth?

In most industrialised countries, the economy has grown continuously for as long as anyone can remember, at least since the Industrial Revolution in the 19th century. Only during severe economic crises has GDP stalled or decreased temporarily. The crises can have various causes, such as rising oil prices, financial irresponsibility or a pandemic (see Figure 10.1). We know that the production of goods and services decreases in such situations, but this is usually a symptom of a crisis rather than an underlying cause of the crisis. Nonetheless, this is a possible explanation for why the absence of growth seems frightening.

Research suggests that the economy may have difficulty adjusting to lower GDP growth in the short term, but that the reason for this mainly relates to expectations (Malmaeus & Alfredsson, 2017). According to a sociological understanding of capitalism, some scholars further argue that growth is necessary to maintain existing power relations within the economy (Driouich & Kallis, 2025).

Since GDP tends to increase year after year, there is an expectation of continued GDP growth built into our planning in various ways – among individuals, businesses and governments. For example, this can involve bank loans and investment decisions made under the assumption that production and consumption in society will increase in the usual way. However, there is little evidence to suggest that the economy could not adjust to lower or zero GDP growth in the long term, provided that we adjust our expectations accordingly (Malmaeus & Alfredsson, 2017). For example, in a recent study comparing a large number of de-growth (and post-growth) models, Lauer et al. (2025) conclude that 'at least in the Global North, further growth is not necessary to achieve well-being while a reduction of the socio-economic metabolism would considerably facilitate the pursuit of ambitious climate goals'. Others argue that degrowth comes with a cost.

D'Alessandro et al. (2020), using a dynamic macrosimulation model, investigate the long-term effects of three scenarios: green growth, policies for social equity and degrowth. They conclude that 'there are no win–win solutions. Each policy mix generates trade-offs' (p. 331). The green growth scenario achieves a significant reduction in greenhouse gas emissions at the cost of increasing income inequality and unemployment. The policies for the social equity scenario result in an environmental performance similar to green growth while improving social conditions at the cost of increasing public deficit. The degrowth scenario achieves a greater reduction in emissions and inequality with a higher public deficit.

Macroeconomic modelling of post-growth scenarios has also been carried out by Peter Victor (Victor, 2008; Jackson & Victor, 2019), who, among other things, concludes that increasing productivity risks leading to structural unemployment unless new demand is continuously created through economic growth. In a literature review, Walker et al. (2021) investigate how welfare systems will cope with a number of challenges in the absence of economic growth. They argue that welfare systems may become difficult to finance without economic growth, but also that (p. 1) 'economic growth is no longer a sustainable solution'. These scholars also propose solutions to these concerns, including work-time reductions and alternative models of welfare. Indeed, working less and shifting systems of production and consumption towards more welfare services rather than material goods may not be entirely negative to human well-being.

These examples show that an economy can function without growth. There will be challenges, just as for societies with growth, and there is thus a need for active policy to mitigate these challenges. Although these conclusions are based on underlying assumptions about the nature of growth stemming from neoclassical growth models, it is a fact that our knowledge of an economy without growth is very limited. These studies highlight important areas for further research regarding how stable macroeconomic systems can be achieved in post-growth economies.

10.4.3 Technology and investments do not necessarily require economic growth

The myth that economic growth is required for sustainable development assumes that green technologies and investments cannot occur without economic growth. This is, however, not necessarily so. It would also be possible to redistribute resources from environmentally damaging activities to the necessary investments in green technologies. While allowing specific green technologies to grow is justifiable, this does not mean that the whole economy (GDP) should grow.

There is also an inherent idea embedded in the neoclassical growth theory that directly associates GDP growth with technical change and innovation. This, however, means reading the theory backwards. The neoclassical growth theory indeed suggests that technological innovation often leads to economic growth, but it does not claim that economic growth itself generates technological development. Endogenous growth theory (Romer, 1990) does argue that technological development occurs within the framework of the economy, but there is nothing specifically stating that innovations cannot occur without economic growth. One could also argue that constraints and crises are the true catalysts of creativity and innovation (e.g. Schumpeter, 1942). Therefore, technology and investments for a green transition do not necessarily require economic growth.

Green innovations have the potential to reduce the environmental impact of the economy. Still, this greening effect may be offset by increasing volumes of production and consumption related to economic growth. This relates to what is often referred to as rebound effects. If the rebound effect is large enough, the increased efficiency can result in increased rather than reduced environmental impact (see Chapter 5 for a discussion on different types of rebound effects). This is sometimes referred to as Jevons' paradox after the economist William Stanley Jevons, who first described the phenomenon. The reason for this is simply that increasing efficiency tends to reduce costs, but it also stimulates increased consumption. In environmental economics, rebound effects are often seen as undesirable, but from a broader societal perspective, they align with the general prioritisation of economic growth (Nørgård & Xue, 2016). As mentioned earlier (see Figure 10.3), efficiency improvements can be used either to reduce emissions or to increase economic growth, but one always comes at the expense of the other.

10.5 Implications

10.5.1 The good news: economic growth is not necessary for a functioning economy

In Section 10.4.2, we discussed that growth is not necessary for a functioning economy. If that is true, it is good news. We can choose to focus on what truly matters – a socially and ecologically sustainable development that maximises well-being without being tied to the assumption that it must be achieved through economic growth.

The narrative of an ever-growing economy is so deeply entrenched in public discourse, including politics, business and academia, that research on how an economy without growth might function until recently hardly existed. Two exceptions include the research projects *Beyond GDP Growth: Scenarios for a Sustainable Built Environment* (Hagbert et al., 2019) and the still ongoing *Pathways towards Post Growth Deals* (European Research Council, 2022), the latter being awarded the largest sum of funding ever for a degrowth research project.

Critics of the growth narrative argue that the growth economy is unsustainable and breaches planetary boundaries. Proponents, on the other hand, point to risks of social and political unrest associated with a shrinking economy.

This dilemma – that current growth is unsustainable but simultaneously seen as necessary to avoid economic collapse – is the starting point of Tim Jackson's Prosperity without Growth? (2009). Jackson highlights the challenge of reducing consumption while maintaining or improving welfare, arguing that this transition will not be straightforward. Political leadership is crucial.

It would be naive to aim for 'negative growth' (GDP reduction) and assume it would automatically improve the environment or human well-being. Reality is more complex. Declining growth risks increasing unemployment and social unrest. However, it is important to understand that the absence of growth does not in itself imply the cessation of all economic activities. A steady-state economy maintains, in principle, the production of goods and services at the current level. In particular, the ecological challenges primarily mean that the harmful production of goods has to decrease, while the production of welfare services does not need to decrease for environmental reasons.

Ecological economist Jeroen van den Bergh advocates for a more relaxed approach to economic growth and GDP. By adopting a neutral stance towards growth, we can focus on the actual goals we wish to achieve, rather than viewing growth as a necessary means to those ends. However, van den Bergh identifies a 'GDP paradox' – 'Despite all theoretically and empirically motivated criticism of GDP as a social welfare and progress indicator, its role in economics, public policy, politics and society continues to be influential' (van den Bergh, 2009, p. 117).

10.5.2 Different measures of welfare

One step towards a more relaxed approach to economic growth could be to complement GDP with other metrics, such as the Human Development Index (HDI), Genuine Progress Indicator (GPI), and Happy Planet Index (HPI) (New Economics Foundation, n.d.). HDI, used by UNDP, combines Gross National Income (GNI) per capita, life expectancy and education into a single index. GPI is a concept developed by ecological economists, adjusting GDP to account for the depletion of natural capital and including social factors. HPI, developed by the UK-based think tank New Economics Foundation, measures life satisfaction in relation to the ecological footprint of different countries. What these metrics generally reveal is that countries with high GDP do not necessarily rank at the top in welfare rankings when factors beyond the production of goods and services are considered (Cox et al., 2025). This is quite logical since GDP is not a measure of welfare but a measure of economic activity (Coyle, 2014).

One of the latest initiatives in this area is the Wellbeing Economy Alliance (WEAll) (n.d.), a global collaboration of nearly 200 organisations working to transform the economic system. This initiative serves as a platform for knowledge sharing and practical efforts, focusing on the welfare of both people and nature. The collaboration also includes the Wellbeing Economy Governments (WEGo) (n.d.) initiative, launched in 2018 as an alternative to the G7. For a number of years New Zealand labelled its official national budget as the 'Wellbeing Budget', where policies 'must be justified by their wellbeing-to-cost ratio'. This budget annually reported on the life satisfaction of various social groups, the population's education, health and, importantly, the state of the environment. Specific government budget items were earmarked to promote a positive development in the well-being of New Zealanders (New Zealand Government, 2019). Recently, however, New Zealand has abandoned the 'Wellbeing Budget'. In other countries, the initiative is still vibrant. Iceland, for example, introduced a framework of 39 well-being indicators in 2019, a balanced set of financial, social and environmental metrics which are considered equally significant measures of the country's success (Icelandic Government, 2019).

A similar initiative is found in Sweden, where the government proposed 15 indicators of prosperity in 2017 to complement GDP, addressing economic, environmental and social dimensions of quality of life (Swedish Government, 2017). As of today, these indicators have not yet translated into real-life policies. According to Birkjær et al. (2021), Sweden, Iceland and New Zealand – at least prior to the latter's abandonment of its 'Wellbeing Budget' – can all be classified as well-being economies. Birkjær et al. (2021) suggest that a well-being economy can function at three levels: (1) passively monitoring people's well-being, (2) actively informing governmental well-being priorities and (3) actively guiding policy decisions to maximise well-being impact. For a country to be considered a well-being economy, it must operate beyond the first level of merely collecting and measuring well-being indicators. Put bluntly, active policy is always needed to ensure that various political goals are achieved. Currently, a lot of active policy is aimed at promoting GDP growth, which could be better redirected towards policies focused on ecological and social sustainability.

10.6 Main message

In this chapter, we have discussed the myth 'Without economic growth, sustainable consumption is impossible'. By referring to research and empirical evidence, we have shown that the statement does not hold and it can therefore be considered a myth. Indeed, the research suggests that sustainable consumption is possible in the absence of economic growth and growth could even hinder consumption from developing in a sustainable direction.

Changing the perception of economic growth as a necessity is an important shift for a sustainable economy. We argue that economic growth is not necessary for sustainable consumption. Advocating continued growth while relying on decoupling environmental impacts lacks empirical support. We conclude that the pursuit of green growth is likely misplaced and that policymakers should turn their attention to alternative approaches. Technological development and efficiency improvements should be used to improve welfare and reduce environmental impacts. Whether this leads to increased or decreased GDP is of secondary importance, and GDP growth should not be the main focus for policymaking. This also has implications for research, which has often assumed that economic growth will happen. It is now also important to direct research towards how improved welfare in a society within ecological limits can be achieved.

Focusing on well-being, equity and environmental health offers a path to a more sustainable and fulfilling future while addressing several severe global risks. Achieving this shift requires rethinking traditional economic metrics and embracing policies and practices that prioritise holistic well-being over continuous material growth.

As of today, economic growth is not green and is very far from being genuinely green. Over time, global income has grown considerably (see Figure 10.1), and so have emissions of GHGs. CO_2 levels in the atmosphere continue to increase, and 2024 was the hottest year on record (World Meteorological Organization, 2025). To hope for economic growth to lead to future reductions in GHG emissions risks being in vain. The best a government can do might be to adopt a neutral stance on economic growth, focusing instead on goals and active policy directly linked to human well-being. Whether policies aimed at better healthcare, sustainable ecological development, or reduced social inequality lead to positive or negative GDP changes should not hinder their implementation. High carbon taxes and phasing out harmful environmental subsidies may be necessary to combat climate threats. If these measures slow economic growth, it should not be a cause for concern. Unfortunately, many experts and politicians remain preoccupied with GDP growth.

As long as policies continue to actively pursue economic growth, critical scrutiny of growth remains essential. However, just as unrestrained growth should not be an objective, neither should negative growth be regarded as a goal in itself. To combine climate goals with other important societal objectives, such as a sustainable economy, we need a more nuanced perspective on growth.

References

Allard, A., Takman, J., Uddin, G. S., & Ahmed, A. (2018). The N-shaped environmental Kuzents curve: An empirical evaluation using a panel quintile regression approach. *Environmental Science and Pollution Research*, *25*, 5848–5861.

BEA (Bureau of Economic Analysis). (n.d.). *GDP-Education-by-BEA.pdf*. https://www.bea.gov/system/files/2020-04/GDP-Education-by-BEA.pdf

Birkjær, M., Gamerdinger, A., & El-Abd, S. (2021). *Towards a Nordic wellbeing economy*. Nordic Council of Ministers. Nord No. 2021:049 Analysis/Nordic Council of Ministers No. 02/2021. https://doi.org/10.6027/nord2021-049

Cox, T., Stafsing, L., Malmaeus, M., Singh, S., Eriksson, F. A., & Schou Bagh, L. (2025). *A beyond-GDP view of Nordic performance* (p. 560). Nordic Council of Ministers, TemaNord 2024. http://dx.doi.org/10.6027/temanord2024-560

Coyle, D. (2014). *GDP – A brief but affectionate history*. Princeton University Press.

D'Alessandro, S., Cieplinski, A., Distefano, T., & Dittmer, K. (2020). Feasible alternatives to green growth. *Nature Sustainability*, *3*(4), 329–335. https://doi.org/10.1038/s41893-020-0484-y

Driouich, R., & Kallis, G. (2025). Sustaining power through economic growth: A régulation theory of growth dependence. *Ecological Economics*, *235*, 108640. https://doi.org/10.1016/j.ecolecon.2025.108640

Easterly, W., & Levine, R. (2001). It's not factor accumulation: Stylized facts and growth models. *The World Bank Economic Review*, *15*(2), 177–219.

European Environment Agency. (2021). *Reflecting on green growth – Creating a resilient economy within environmental limits*. ISBN 978-92-9480-402-0. https://doi.org/10.2800/00936

European Research Council. (2022). *ERC synergy grants 2022 – project highlights*. https://erc.europa.eu/news-events/news/erc-synergy-grants-2022-project-highlights

Finnveden, G. (2021). *Hur definierar vi hållbar ekonomisk utveckling? I Omställningen kräver systemförändringar och mobilisering nu! Slutredovisning av Nationella Samordnaren för Agenda 2030* (pp. 195–208). Statens Offentliga Utredningar.

Friedlingstein, P., O'Sullivan, M., Jones, M. W., Andrew, R. M., Bakker, D. C. E., Hauck, J., Landschützer, P., Le Quéré, C., Luijkx, I. T., Peters, G. P., Peters, W., Pongratz, J., Schwingshackl, C., Sitch, S., Canadell, J. G., Ciais, P., Jackson, R. B., Alin, S. R., Anthoni, P., . . . Zheng, B. (2023). The global carbon budget 2023. *ESSD*, *15*, 5301–5369. https://doi.org/10.5194/essd-15-5301-2023

Giljum, S., Dittrich, M., Lieber, M., & Lutter, S. (2014). Global patterns of material flows and their socio-economic and environmental implications: A MFA study on all countries world-wide from 1980 to 2009. *Resources*, *3*, 319–339. https://doi.org/10.3390/resources3010319

Grafström, J., & Sandström, C. (2020). *Mer för mindre? Tillväxt och hållbarhet i Sverige*. Ratio.

Grossman, G. M., & Krueger, A. B. (1991). *Environmental impacts of a North American Free Trade Agreement*. National Bureau of Economic Research Working Paper 3914. https://doi.org/10.3386/w3914

Hagbert, P., Finnveden, G., Fuehrer, P., Svenfelt, Å., Alfredsson, E., Aretun, Å., Bradley, K., Callmer, Å., Fauré, E., Gunnarsson-Östling, U., Hedberg, M., Hornborg, A., Isaksson, K., Malmaeus, M., Malmqvist, T., Nyblom, Å., Skånberg, K., & Öhlund, E. (2019). *Futures beyond GDP growth. Final report from the research program "beyond GDP growth: Scenarios for sustainable building and planning"*. KTH School of Architecture and the Built Environment.

Hagen, J., Laun, L., Lucke, C., & Palme, M. (2025). The rising income gradient in life expectancy in Sweden over six decades. *Proceedings of the National Academy of Sciences U.S.A.*, *122*(14) e2418145122. https://doi.org/10.1073/pnas.2418145122

Hickel, J., & Kallis, G. (2019). Is green growth possible? *New Political Economy*, *25*(4), 469–486. https://doi.org/10.1080/13563467.2019.1598964

Icelandic Government. (2019). *Indicators for measuring well-being. Government of Iceland*. Prime Minister's Office.

IPCC. (2022). *Climate change 2022: Mitigation of climate change. Contribution of working group III to the sixth assessment report of the intergovernmental panel on climate change*. Cambridge University Press. https://www.ipcc.ch/report/ar6/wg3/

Jackson, T. (2009). *Prosperity without growth: Economics for a finite planet*. Earthscan.

Jackson, T., & Victor, P. (2019). Unraveling the claims for (and against) green growth. *Science*, *366*, 950–951.

Kahneman, D., & Deaton, A. (2010). High income improves evaluation of life but not emotional well-being. *Proceedings of the National Academy of Sciences U.S.A.*, *107*, 16489–16493.

Kallis, G., Hickel, J., O'Neill, D., Jackson, T., Victor, P., Raworth, K., Schor, J., Steinberger, J., & Ürge-Vorsatz, D. (2025). Post-growth: The science of wellbeing within planetary boundaries. *The Lancet Planetary Health*, *9*(1), e62–e78. ISSN 2542–5196. https://doi.org/10.1016/S2542-5196(24)00310–3. https://www.sciencedirect.com/science/article/pii/S2542519624003103

Karolinska Institutet. (2021). *Widening inequalities in old-age life expectancy in Sweden*. https://news.ki.se/widening-inequalities-in-old-age-life-expectancy-in-sweden

Killingsworth, M., Kahneman, D., & Mellers, B. (2023). Income and emotional well-being: A conflict resolved. *Proceedings of the National Academy of Sciences*. https://www.pnas.org/doi/10.1073/pnas.2208661120

Kotz, M., Levermann, A., & Wenz, L. (2024): The economic commitment of climate change. *Nature*, *628*, 551–557.

Krausmann, F., Lauk, C., Haas, W., & Wiedenhofer, D. (2018). From resource extraction to outflows of wastes and emissions: The socioeconomic metabolism of the global economy, 1900–2015. *Global Environmental Change*, *52*, 131–140. https://doi.org/10.1016/j.gloenvcha.2018.07.003

Lauer, A., Capellán-Pérez, I., & Wergles, N. (2025). A comparative review of de- and post-growth modeling studies. *Ecological Economics*, *227*, 108383.

Malmaeus, M., & Alfredsson, E. (2017). Potential consequences on the economy of low or no growth – Short and long term perspectives. *Ecological Economics*, *134*(C), 57–64. Elsevier.

Malmaeus, M., & Hahn, T. (2022). *Tillväxten inför verkligheten*. Cogito. https://assets-global.website-files.com/5defa5994755907e949d9639/622cc8b549ab8537a4734228_Report_2022_MQ.pdf

New Economics Foundation. (n.d.). *Happy planet index*. https://happyplanetindex.org

New Zealand Government. (2019). *The wellbeing budget 2019*. The Treasury. https://budget.govt.nz/budget/2019/wellbeing/

Nørgård, J., & Xue, J. (2016). Between green growth and degrowth: Decoupling, rebound effects and the politics for long-term sustainability. In T. Santarius, H. Walnum, & C. Aall (Eds.), *Rethinking climate and energy policies* (pp. 85–104). Springer.

OECD. (n.d.). *Nominal gross domestic product (GDP)*. https://www.oecd.org/en/data/indicators/nominal-gross-domestic-product-gdp.html

OECD. (2011). *Towards green growth*. OECD Publishing. http://dx.doi.org/10.1787/9789264111318-en

OECD. (2022). *Global outlook on financing for sustainable development 2023: No sustainability without equity*. OECD Publishing. https://doi.org/10.1787/fcbe6ce9-en

Oslo Symposium. (1994). [Oslo Roundtable] *1.2 Defining sustainable consumption*. https://enb.iisd.org/consume/oslo004.html

Richardson, K., Steffen, W., Lucht, W., Bendtsen, J., Cornell, S. E., Donges, J. F., Drüke, M., Fetzer, I., Bala, G., von Bloh, W., Feulner, G., Fiedler, S., Gerten, D., Gleeson, T., Hofmann, M., Huiskamp, W., Kummu, M., Mohan, C., Nogués-Bravo, D., . . . Rockström, J. (2023). Earth beyond six of nine planetary boundaries. *Science Advances*, *9*, eadh2458. https://doi.org/10.1126/sciadv.adh2458

Robinson, J. (2004). Squaring the circle? Some thoughts on the idea of sustainable development. *Ecological Economics*, *48*(3), 369–384.

Roine, J. (2015). Vad är ekonomisk tillväxt? In U. Stavlöt (Ed.), *Nationalekonomi för miljöintresserade* (pp. 103–121). Fores/Ivrig.

Romer, P. M. (1990). Endogenous technological change. Journal of Political Economy, 98(5), S71–S102.

Romer, D. (1996). *Advanced macroeconomics*. McGraw-Hill.

Schumpeter, J. (1942). *Capitalism, socialism, and democracy*. Harper & Brothers.

SEPA. (2024a). *Sveriges utsläpp av växthusgaser*. Swedish Environmental Protection Agency.

SEPA. (2024b). *Tre sätt att beräkna klimatpåverkande utsläpp*. Swedish Environmental Protection Agency.

Stoknes, P. E., & Rockström, J. (2018). Redefining green growth within planetary boundaries. *Energy Research & Social Science*, *44*, 41–49.

Svenfelt, Å., Wadha, N. B., & Parekh, V. (2024). Sustainable consumption futures: According to whom? *Sustainability: Science, Practice and Policy*, *20*(1), 2341495. https://doi.org/10.1080/15487733.2024.2341495

Swedish Government. (2017). *Prop. 2016/17:100; 2017-ars-ekonomiska-varproposition-prop. 201617100.*

UNDP. (2024). *Human development report*. https://ourworldindata.org/grapher/human-development-index

UNFCCC (United Nations Framework Convention for Climate Change). (2015). *Paris Agreement*. Quote from Article 2. https://unfccc.int/sites/default/files/english_paris_agreement.pdf

United Nations. (2015). Resolution adopted by the General Assembly on 25 September 2015. A/RES/70/1. *Transforming our world: The 2030 agenda for sustainable development*. https://docs.un.org/en/A/RES/70/1

van den Bergh, J. (2009). The GDP paradox. *Journal of Economic Psychology*, *30*(2), 117–135. https://doi.org/10.1016/j.joep.2008.12.001

Victor, P. (2008). *Managing without growth: Slower by design, not disaster*. Edward Elgar Publishing. https://doi.org/10.4337/9781848442993

Walker, C. C., Druckman, A., & Jackson, T. (2021). Welfare systems without economic growth: A review of the challenges and next steps for the field. *Ecological Economics*, *186*, 107066. https://doi.org/10.1016/j.ecolecon.2021.107066

WCED (World Commission on Environment and Development). (1987). *Report of the world commission on environment and development: Our common future (The Brundtland Report)*.

Wellbeing Economy Alliance (WEAll). (n.d.). *About WEAll*. https://weall.org

Wellbeing Economy Governments (WEGo). (n.d.). *About WEGo*. https://wellbeingeconomygovs.org

World Bank. (2012). *Inclusive green growth. The pathway to sustainable development*. World Bank.

World Meteorological Organization. (2025). *WMO confirms 2024 as warmest year on record at about 1.55°C above pre-industrial level*. https://wmo.int/news/media-centre/wmo-confirms-2024-warmest-year-record-about-155degc-above-pre-industrial-level

11

MYTH 10

Economic progress will naturally lead to more free time

Matthias Lehner

11.1 The leisure time myth

Economic progress will naturally lead to more free time.

It is often assumed that as societies grow wealthier and productivity increases, people will naturally reduce their working hours and enjoy more leisure. Yet, since the 1980s, this vision has not materialised for many people in high-income societies.

Long working hours increase income, which often fuels consumption – not only raising environmental pressure but also exacerbating inequality. Understanding this dynamic is crucial for rethinking sustainability, well-being and societal priorities. The question of why work hours have stagnated – and even increased for some – despite economic progress is important to challenging unsustainable consumption patterns and imagining new work-time models aligned with human flourishing and ecological limits.

11.2 Origins

The assumption that rising economic prosperity would lead to reduced working hours and greater leisure is rooted in both historical developments and enduring cultural ideologies. In pre-industrial societies, time was commonly structured around tasks and natural rhythms, with labour understood primarily as a means to meet subsistence needs. The emergence of Protestantism, however, introduced a powerful cultural transformation. Max Weber (1905) argued that the Protestant work ethic, particularly within Calvinist traditions, imbued work with intrinsic moral value. Diligence, discipline and

DOI: 10.4324/9781003613718-15

frugality became signs of spiritual virtue, while idleness was condemned. This ethic played a formative role in the development of capitalist economies, in which economic productivity and personal morality became increasingly intertwined.

With the onset of the Industrial Revolution, time began to be measured, regulated and commodified. Rather than a flexible and task-oriented activity, work became organised around the clock and defined by measurable outputs. As Wajcman (2016) notes, this transformation led to the institutionalisation of long, rigid working hours, which were often physically demanding and poorly compensated. However, organised labour movements began to resist these conditions, eventually securing significant gains such as the eight-hour workday and the five-day workweek (Pencavel, 2018). These victories reinforced the perception that economic and technological progress could and would lead to shorter working hours over time.

This belief was articulated by John Maynard Keynes, who in his essay *Economic Possibilities for Our Grandchildren* predicted that by the beginning of the 21st century, people in industrialised nations would work as little as 15 hours per week (Keynes, 2010 [1930]).

> *For many ages to come the old Adam will be so strong in us that everybody will need to do some work if he is to be contented. We shall do more things for ourselves than is usual with the rich today, only too glad to have small duties and tasks and routines. But beyond this, we shall endeavour to spread the bread thin on the butter – to make what work there is still to be done to be as widely shared as possible. Three-hour shifts or a fifteen-hour week may put off the problem for a great while. For three hours a day is quite enough to satisfy the old Adam in most of us!*
>
> *(Keynes, 2010 [1930], pp. 328–329)*

Keynes assumed that as productivity and material wealth increased, individuals would choose to value leisure more highly, using their affluence to reduce their working time. This assumption reflected the dominant logic of the early to mid-20th century: that the primary challenge of the future would not be scarcity, but the responsible distribution of abundance. (A belief that rings true again today in many's predictions for Artificial Intelligence.)

The Swedish researcher Christer Sanne (1992) calculated over 30 years ago that, assuming no drastic changes to the global economic system, by the year 2000, a 30-hour workweek would suffice to uphold steady increases in material well-being. Sanne's calculations thus confirm the validity of Keynes' claim, assuming a constant value distribution between time and material wealth. However, this trend towards reduced working hours has lost strength since the late 20th century. Indeed, in their book *How Much is Enough?*, Skidelsky and Skidelsky (2012) wonder why it is that people in wealthy nations are on average four to five times better off than in the 1930s, but work hours have only fallen by a fifth since then. This indicates that Keynes and others were missing factors that determine how much society values income over time.

Thus, the idea that economic progress naturally results in increased free time reflects a specific cultural moment that no longer holds. What once seemed like an inevitable trajectory – from productivity gains to leisure – no longer holds true, with several undesirable consequences.

11.3 Consequences

11.3.1 Inequality and labour market polarisation

The continued belief in a natural progression from economic growth to increased leisure obscures deepening inequalities in the distribution of time and income. Labour markets in many high-income countries have become increasingly polarised: while some individuals – often in managerial or professional roles – work excessively long hours, others face underemployment or precarious part-time work (Bick et al., 2018). This divergence is further intensified by income inequality. Kuhn and Lozano (2005) show that since the early 1980s, the top-earning 20% of US workers have become significantly more likely to work long hours than those at the bottom of the wage distribution, reversing earlier trends. This polarisation is also gendered. Women continue to perform the bulk of unpaid domestic and care labour, even as their participation in the formal labour market has increased. The resulting dual burden leads to heightened levels of time poverty, especially for working mothers (Wajcman, 2016). On the contrary, Larsson and Björk (2017) find that, in Sweden, many fathers express a desire to reduce work hours to increase childcare involvement but are constrained by social norms and structural expectations of full-time male breadwinning.

11.3.2 Erosion of work–life balance and well-being

Rather than experiencing an increase in leisure time, many individuals report escalating levels of stress, fatigue and time scarcity. This deterioration in work–life balance is not only due to the number of hours worked but also due to the qualitative shift in work patterns. Digital technologies have transformed how work is organised and experienced, enabling greater flexibility while simultaneously eroding boundaries between work and personal life (Xu et al., 2023). Schor (2011) vividly describes the contemporary lifestyle in affluent countries as one of acceleration. In an article for YES! Magazine from 2011 entitled 'Work Less, Live More', she writes, '*[Americans] work too much, eat too quickly, socialize too little, drive and sit in traffic for too many hours, don't get enough sleep, and feel harried too much of the time*'.

This intensification of daily life is increasingly associated with declines in psychological and physical well-being. The widespread valorisation of busyness, compounded by performance-based assessments and expectations of constant availability, contributes to a culture of overwork that is detrimental to health. Reduced work hours, Wajcman (2016) claims, would go a long way to ease this pressure.

11.3.3 Erosion of civic participation

Time scarcity can undermine democratic engagement and participation in civic life by eroding the temporal resources necessary for such activities. Time is a fundamental prerequisite for involvement in democratic processes, such as voting, attending community meetings, engaging in political discourse or participating in volunteerism and local governance. Putnam (2000) famously argued in *Bowling Alone* that the decline in social capital in the United States was partially attributable to time pressures from work and commuting, which reduce opportunities for building and maintaining community networks. Schor (2005) similarly highlights that overwork diminishes the capacity for 'time affluence', which is essential not only for individual well-being but also for collective engagement. Empirical studies confirm that individuals working long hours are less likely to participate in political activities and volunteer work (Verba et al., 1995). This civic disengagement can have broader societal implications, including diminished democratic accountability and weaker community resilience. As such, the proliferation of long work hours contributes to a feedback loop in which individuals are both overburdened and increasingly isolated from the social and institutional mechanisms that enable collective problem-solving and political voice.

Rising income inequality is partly driven by differences in work hours, as the highest earners work more hours and earn more for each hour worked, while the lowest paid have fewer work hours (cf. Piketty, 2014). This growing gap weakens democratic values, social cohesion and trust in institutions. According to Wilkinson and Pickett (2009), this results in a negative feedback loop. Schor (2010) calls it a 'squirrel cage', where increasing wealth inequality in turn leads to increasing need people feel to compare and compete with others in their environment, resulting in the even stronger desire for high income and wealth to secure one's societal status.

11.3.4 Environmental degradation

The myth that wealthier societies naturally reduce working time also neglects the environmental consequences of overwork. Bunting (2005), for example, makes the direct connection between being overworked and (unnecessary) overconsumption. Longer working hours are positively correlated with higher levels of income and consumption, which in turn lead to greater ecological degradation. In a study from 2007, Rosnick and Weisbrot (2007) show that if Americans chose to use some of their productivity gains by shortening their workweek to the EU-15 average, the United States would consume about 20% less energy. If, on the other hand, Europeans worked as much as Americans did, the continent's energy consumption would increase by 25%. This connection between work hours and environmental impact causes Gerold et al. (2023, p. 1) to call work '*a biophysically intense, consumption-causing, heteronomous institution with ambivalent health impacts that stabilises societies in environmentally and socially unsustainable ways*'. They, as well as others (e.g. Schor, 2005), argue that a reduction in working hours is necessary to achieve environmental sustainability. Schor (2005) believes that, in the Global North, only a reduction in work hours will achieve the needed stabilisation of consumption to avoid ecological catastrophe.

These consequences reveal that the myth of economic progress translating automatically into more free time is not only inaccurate but also socially and ecologically harmful. The valorisation of overwork sustains and reproduces inequality, undermines individual well-being and civic engagement, and accelerates environmental degradation. Dispelling this myth is therefore essential to envisioning more equitable and sustainable modes of living.

11.4 Dispelling the myth

In the following, four aspects will be discussed that all qualify and undermine the myth that increased wealth, by definition, leads to fewer work hours. This discussion also adds understanding to what, in fact, defines possible future working hour trends.

11.4.1 Productivity gains do not automatically lead to more leisure

One of the central tenets of the myth is that increasing productivity will naturally result in a reduction of working hours. This assumption was most famously articulated by John Maynard Keynes (2010 [1930]). Although productivity has steadily increased in most high-income countries, this has not translated into proportional reductions in work time. In fact, working hours have plateaued or even increased in several contexts (Giattino et al., 2024). It is estimated that, in 1870, an American worker worked 3,096 hours annually, a German 3,284 hours and a Swede 3,436 hours. By 1980, an American worked 1,801 hours annually, a German 1,756 hours and a Swede only 1,517 hours (Giattino et al., 2024). Thus, a dramatic reduction in working hours occurred. While Keynes' prediction held true during much of the 20th century, the pattern began to shift in the 1980s. Although working hours had steadily declined in most capitalist economies from the 19th century onward, that trend has largely stagnated in countries such as the United States and Sweden. By 2017, Americans worked 1,757 hours annually, and Swedes worked 1,609 hours annually (Giattino et al., 2024). This plateauing has occurred despite continuous increases in productivity and per capita income (Roser et al., 2023). For instance, between 1980 and 2017, GDP per capita in the United States and Sweden roughly doubled, yet average annual working hours remained essentially the same (Roser et al., 2023).

This disjuncture suggests that productivity gains are not inherently tied to reductions in work hours; rather, how these gains are distributed depends on broader institutional and political frameworks. When productivity improvements are channelled into increased profits or consumption rather than leisure, the assumed link between progress and time affluence breaks down (Schor, 2005).

11.4.2 Policy decisions, not progress, shape work hours

Work-time reduction is not an automatic outcome of economic growth but is highly contingent on political and institutional choices. For example, while – as described earlier – countries such as the United States and Sweden have seen stagnation or increases in work hours since the 1980s, Germany and France have seen a continued reduction in work hours (1,756 to 1,354 hours in Germany and 1,779 to 1,514 hours in France) (Giattino et al., 2024). These differences correlate with variations in labour policies, union strength and collective bargaining systems. Labour market deregulation, weakened unions and declining worker protections have contributed to the erosion of bargaining power and made it more difficult to advocate for shorter workweeks (Pencavel, 2018). Comparative research shows that where governments have implemented work-time reduction policies, such as caps on weekly hours or incentives for part-time work, reductions have been achieved without sacrificing productivity (Rosnick & Weisbrot, 2007). In France, for example, the government of Lionel Jospin passed legislation in 1998 and 2000 (the 'Aubry laws') that reduced the legal standard workweek from 39 to 35 hours per week for full-time employees. This was partly done with the intention to share work more equally and reduce unemployment and also to improve work–life balance.

The latter appears to have been achieved to some degree, with surveys showing that workers used the additional time off work to rest, spend time with their children and leisure activities such as going to restaurants and cinemas. Interestingly, in the context of environmental sustainability, tourism did not seem to grow because of reduced weekly work time. While some of the initial legislation has since been softened, leading to increased work time again among certain sectors of the economy, overall, the policy has significantly contributed to reduced work hours in France since the 1980s

(Askenazy, 2013). In Germany, unions in particular have played a strong role and were able to negotiate gradual work time reductions. Legislatively, to prevent rising unemployment in times of economic downturns, Germany has adopted a policy tool called 'Kurzarbeit' (work-sharing), where firms reduce hours instead of letting go of staff members, with the government partially compensating workers for lost wages. Furthermore, in 2001, the Part-Time and Fixed-Term Employment Act was put into force, which gave workers the legal right to request part-time work, facilitating labour market participation for parents and older workers (cf. Absenger et al., 2014). The cases of both Germany and France confirm that institutional design, rather than economic logic alone, determines whether societies move towards more leisure, or not.

11.4.3 Overwork as a status symbol: cultural and symbolic drivers

Another barrier to work-time reduction is the cultural valorisation of overwork. In contrast to Veblen's (1899) depiction of the leisure class, who once displayed social status by disengaging from labour, today's elites often signal prestige through constant busyness and work intensity. Bourdieu's (1984) theory of social distinction helps explain this inversion: dominant groups continuously redefine high-status behaviours to preserve symbolic distance from others. In contemporary professional culture, busyness has become a mark of dedication, ambition, and indispensability (Bellezza et al., 2017; Wajcman, 2016). Empirical research supports this shift. Bellezza et al. (2017) find that individuals associate overwork with high status in the United States, particularly when it is seen as a choice rather than a necessity. Lupu and Empson (2015) similarly describe how professionals in high-status fields internalise overwork as a game worth playing, reinforcing the illusion that long hours signify value. According to Schor (2010), high-income individuals often conflate income with identity and success. The desire to maintain or display one's social position drives longer working hours and higher consumption, reinforcing the work-and-spend cycle (Bunting, 2005). In particular, in highly unequal societies, the pressure to 'keep up' through visible markers of success exacerbates this cycle, making leisure appear both less attainable and less valuable (Wilkinson & Pickett, 2009). This has resulted in top earners becoming significantly more time-poor (Kuhn & Lozano, 2005). Once, excessive work hours were characteristic of low-paying professions, such as agriculture or manufacturing. While still the case in developing countries, in the richest countries, it is now more common for prestigious, high-paying jobs to result in the longest hours. Workweeks of 60 hours or more are not uncommon among managers, medical professionals or financial workers in the United States, the United Kingdom or Japan. 'Overwork' (defined as workweeks exceeding 48 hours of work) is still most common in developing countries such as Turkey or Mexico (where as much as 30% of the working population overwork). However, in these contexts, overwork is typically associated with low-paid sectors, such as agriculture, retail or transport. Although even in rich countries there are low-paying jobs that commonly result in overwork, notably in the service sector, most often, overwork is associated with high-paying and high-status work (ILO, 2022).

11.4.4 Capitalism's growth imperative resists time affluence

At a structural level, capitalism's dependence on continuous growth undermines incentives to reduce working time. As Schumpeter (1942) argued, capitalist economies are driven by the principle of *creative destruction* – constant innovation, expansion and reinvestment. This dynamic creates pressure to reinvest productivity gains into further economic activity rather than translating them into leisure (Gerold et al., 2023). The logic of growth is also embedded in political institutions and corporate strategies. Businesses may strive to increase efficiency, but they rarely share these gains as additional free time for workers. Instead, they often demand greater output or responsiveness. Consequently, shorter working hours are seen as a threat to competitiveness, even though numerous case studies show that reduced workweeks can maintain or improve productivity (Schor, 2010; Gerold et al., 2023). Between 2015 and 2019, for example, Iceland conducted a large-scale trial of a 35-hour workweek among public sector workers. The results were equal or better productivity, workers reporting a better work–life balance, and no noticeable deterioration of public services (Haraldsson & Kellam, 2021). In the United Kingdom, in 2022/23, a six-month-long trial took place with 61 companies to introduce a four-day workweek. After the trial, 92% of companies continued the policy, productivity was maintained, and employee turnover and sick days declined (Lewis et al., 2023).

11.5 Implications

Dispelling the myth that economic progress naturally leads to increased leisure time necessitates a comprehensive re-evaluation of how societies conceptualise work, time and well-being. Recognising that working time is shaped by institutional arrangements, cultural norms and policy choices – rather than by individual preferences or economic laws – opens new avenues for reform. These implications extend across political, organisational and individual domains.

11.5.1 Implications for policymakers

For governments and public institutions, the key implication is that working time is not merely an economic variable but a matter of political will and normative orientation. Countries that have continued to reduce working hours in recent decades, such as Germany and France, have done so not because of inevitable economic trends but because of deliberate policy design and institutional commitment to shared prosperity and well-being. Their experiences demonstrate that shorter workweeks not only are possible but can also be economically viable and socially beneficial when embedded in strong collective bargaining systems and comprehensive welfare frameworks (Rosnick & Weisbrot, 2007).

Policy mechanisms to support such outcomes may include introducing or strengthening legislative caps on weekly working hours, as seen in France's implementation of the 35-hour workweek. In addition, fiscal reforms can make part-time and flexible work more attractive and sustainable, particularly when benefits such as pensions and social insurance are not disproportionately tied to full-time employment. Investing in publicly funded childcare and eldercare services also plays a crucial role, as these reduce the time burdens disproportionately carried by women and allow for more equal participation in both paid and unpaid spheres of life (European Commission, 2023).

Moreover, public narratives must shift away from equating full-time work with social legitimacy. In many political discourses, reduced work hours are associated with laziness or lack of ambition, and part-time work is seen as a second-best option. Reframing shorter work hours as a strategy for improving public health, supporting families, and reducing ecological pressures could help change the cultural tide and pave the way for structural reform.

11.5.2 Implications for business

The implications for business might appear less obvious, though they are equally significant. While conventional wisdom holds that shorter workweeks might reduce productivity, a growing body of evidence suggests otherwise. Experiments with four-day workweeks in countries such as Iceland and the United Kingdom have shown that employee performance does not suffer – and often improves – when working hours are reduced. Workers report higher levels of satisfaction, reduced stress, and improved focus, which in turn benefit employers through reduced turnover and absenteeism (Lewis et al., 2023; Haraldsson & Kellam, 2021). In practice, this may involve piloting reduced-hour schemes such as job sharing or condensed workweeks, particularly in roles that require high levels of cognitive or emotional labour.

Promoting employee well-being as a core organisational value is another critical step. Too often, workplace well-being is addressed through individual-level interventions, such as mindfulness apps or gym memberships, which do little to challenge the structural pressures of overwork. A more effective strategy involves reshaping the very organisation of work by giving employees more control over their schedules, recognising rest as productive, and supporting a workplace culture that values balance over burnout.

There are also reputational and competitive advantages for businesses that lead in this domain. With younger generations increasingly prioritising flexibility, purpose and mental health over traditional career progression, businesses that adopt sustainable work practices may find it easier to attract and retain top talent. In this sense, reducing working time is not merely a social responsibility but also a strategic investment (World Economic Forum, 2022).

11.5.3 Implications for individuals

While structural and institutional change is essential, individuals also have a role to play in reshaping how time is valued and used. Numerous studies indicate that, when given the choice, many people express a preference for reduced working hours, especially if this does not entail a significant loss of income or benefits (Sanne, 1998; Persson et al., 2022). However, these preferences are often suppressed by societal expectations, financial insecurity and organisational norms that equate long hours with commitment and success.

Individual action can contribute to change in several ways. Employees can initiate conversations within their organisations about the feasibility of flexible work arrangements or voluntary reductions in hours, especially when framed in terms of health, family life or productivity. Joining or supporting collective efforts – whether through trade unions, advocacy groups or workplace campaigns – can also help shift the norm from isolated requests to collective demands for better work–life balance.

Beyond the workplace, individuals may also explore alternative lifestyles that prioritise time over consumption. The voluntary simplicity movement, for example, encourages people to reduce material needs in favour of meaningful experiences, community involvement and environmental stewardship. These choices challenge the dominant narrative that equates happiness with income and consumption and instead promote a vision of well-being grounded in time affluence, autonomy and relational richness (Alexander & Ussher, 2012; Elgin, 2010).

Ultimately, while individuals cannot dismantle systemic drivers of overwork on their own, their choices and voices are vital in creating the social pressure and cultural legitimacy needed to enable broader reforms. When people organise around shared values, rather than adapt in isolation, the potential for meaningful transformation increases.

11.6 Main message

This chapter has shown that the belief that economic growth will automatically lead to more free time is not supported by evidence. Instead, this expectation reflects historically contingent assumptions and policy decisions that have favoured material accumulation over time affluence. It is a socially constructed myth that can be actively dismantled. Reclaiming time is not only possible but also essential for creating societies that value well-being, equity and ecological sustainability. Moving beyond the work-and-spend cycle invites us to imagine new norms and structures in which economic progress is measured not only in monetary terms but also in time – time for rest, care, creativity and connection.

This chapter challenges the persistent belief that economic progress and rising productivity will naturally lead to more leisure time. While historical trends and thinkers like Keynes fostered optimism that affluence would enable shorter working hours, contemporary developments reveal a very different reality. Since the 1980s, work hours in many high-income countries have stagnated or even increased, particularly among the most affluent, despite sustained productivity gains. Rather than reflecting personal preferences for more income over time, this shift must be understood as the outcome of institutional decisions, cultural norms and political choices. Deregulated labour markets, declining collective bargaining power and the cultural valorisation of busyness have redirected the benefits of productivity into higher consumption rather than increased time affluence. At the same time, this dynamic has exacerbated income inequality, eroded work–life balance and intensified environmental degradation – effects that are unsustainable both socially and ecologically.

It is worthwhile to also touch upon the latest development in what pertains to be an innovation to spur productivity growth: Artificial Intelligence. Looking forward, AI looks certain to enhance efficiency. AI evangelists such as Elon Musk have, remarkably like John Maynard Keynes 100 years ago, predicted that these rapid productivity gains will make work optional, more like a hobby for those who, to paraphrase Keynes, cannot shake off the 'old Adam'. If the past teaches us anything, this is as unlikely a prediction as it turned out to be 100 years ago, unless structures are put into place to make it so. In today's system, AI risks intensifying work through algorithmic management, constant monitoring, and raised productivity expectations. Without intentional policy interventions, AI is thus unlikely to reduce work hours; it may instead reinforce overwork and increase job demands, particularly for knowledge workers in high-pressure (and high-salary) environments (Gerold et al., 2023). In the end, AI's effects will depend heavily on governance, design and labour regulation. Without democratic oversight and worker-centred design, AI is more likely to entrench overwork than to liberate time. Conversely, if guided by social priorities, it could enable significant reductions in working hours and greater flexibility. Interestingly, another – probably *the* – AI evangelist, Sam Altman of OpenAI, acknowledges as much publicly when he calls for universal basic income as a way to redistribute the increased prosperity from AI deployment.

References

Absenger, N., Ahlers, E. Bispinck, R., Kleinknecht, A. H., & Klenner, C. (2014). *Arbeitszeiten in Deutschland: Entwcilungstendenzen und Herausforderungen für eine modern Arbeitszeitpolitik*. WSI Report, No. 19, Hans-Böckler-Stifung, Wirtschafts- und Sozialwissenschaftliches Institut (WSI), Düsseldorf, https://nbn-resolving.de/urn:nbn:de:101:1–201602176083

Alexander, S., & Ussher, S. (2012). The voluntary simplicity movement: A multinational survey analysis in theoretical context. *Journal of Consumer Culture*, *12*(1), 66–86. https://doi.org/10.1177/1469540512444019

Askenazy, P. (2013). Working time regulation in France from 1996 to 2012. *Cambridge Journal of Economics*, *37*(2), 323–347. https://doi.org/10.1093/cje/bes084

Bellezza, S., Paharia, N., & Keinan, A. (2017). Conspicuous consumption of time: When busyness and lack of leisure time become a status symbol. *Journal of Consumer Research*, *44*(1), 118–138. https://doi.org/10.1093/jcr/ucw076

Bick, A., Fuchs-Schündeln, N., & Lagakos, D. (2018). How do hours worked vary with income? Cross-country evidence and implications. *American Economic Review*, *108*(1), 170–199. https://doi.org/10.1257/aer.20151720

Bourdieu, P. (1984). *Distinction: A social critique of the judgement of taste*. Harvard University Press.

Bunting, M. (2005). *Willing slaves: How the overwork culture is ruling our lives*. Harper Perennial.

Elgin, D. (2010). *Voluntary simplicity: Toward a way of life that is outwardly simple, inwardly rich*. Harper.

European Commission. (2023). *Working time reduction in the EU: Recent patterns and main drivers*. https://op.europa.eu/webpub/empl/lmwd-annual-review-report-2023/chapter3/working-time-reduction-intro.html

Gerold, S., Hoffmann, M., & Aigner, E. (2023). Towards a critical understanding of work in ecological economics: A postwork perspective. *Ecological Economics*, *212*, 107935. https://doi.org/10.1016/j.ecolecon.2023.107935

Giattino, C., Ortiz-Ospina, E., & Roser, M. (2024). Are we working more than ever? *Our World in Data*. https://ourworldindata.org/working-more-than-ever

Haraldsson, G. D., & Kellam, J. (2021). *Going public: Iceland's journey to a shorter working week*. Autonomy Research Ltd & Alda Association for Democracy and Sustainability. https://autonomy.work/wp-content/uploads/2021/06/ICELAND_4DW.pdf

ILO – International Labour Office. (2022). *Working time and work-life balance around the world*. ILO, ISBN 978-92-2-037941-7.

Keynes, J. M. (2010). *Essays in persuasion*. Palgrave Macmillan UK. https://doi.org/10.1007/978-1-349-59072-8

Kuhn, P., & Lozano, F. (2005). *The expanding workweek? Understanding trends in long work hours among U.S. men, 1979–2004 (Working Paper 11895)*. National Bureau of Economic Research. https://doi.org/10.3386/w11895

Larsson, J., & Björk, S. (2017). Swedish fathers choosing part-time work. *Community, Work & Family*, *20*(2), 142–161. https://doi.org/10.1080/13668803.2015.1089839

Lewis, K., Stronge, W., Kellam, J., & Harper, A. (2023). *The results are in: The UK's four-day week pilot*. Autonomy Research Ltd. https://autonomy.work/wp-content/uploads/2023/02/The-results-are-in-The-UKs-four-day-week-pilot.pdf

Lupu, I., & Empson, L. (2015). Illusio and overwork: Playing the game in the accounting field. *Accounting, Auditing & Accountability Journal*, *28*(8), 1310–1340. https://doi.org/10.1108/AAAJ-02-2015-1984
Pencavel, J. H. (2018). A brief history of working hours. In J. H. Pencavel (Ed.), *Diminishing returns at work: The consequences of long working hours* (Chapter 2). Oxford University Press. https://doi.org/10.1093/oso/9780190876166.003.0002
Persson, O., Larsson, J., & Nässén, J. (2022). Working less by choice: What are the benefits and hardships? *Sustainability: Science, Practice and Policy*, *18*(1), 81–96. https://doi.org/10.1080/15487733.2021.2023292
Piketty, T. (2014). *Capital in the twenty-first century*. Belknap Press.
Putnam, R. D. (2000). *Bowling alone: The collapse and revival of American community*. Simon & Schuster.
Roser, M., Arriagada, P., Hasell, J., Ritchie, H., & Ortiz-Ospina, E. (2023). Economic growth. *Our world in data*. https://ourworldindata.org/economic-growth
Rosnick, D., & Weisbrot, M. (2007). Are shorter work hours good for the environment? A comparison of U.S. and European energy consumption. *International Journal of Health Services*, *37*(3), 405–417. https://doi.org/10.2190/D842-1505-1K86-9882
Sanne, C. (1992). How much work?. *Futures*, *24*(7), 743–752. https://doi.org/10.1016/0016-3287(92)90045-H
Sanne, C. (1998). The working hours issue in Sweden. *Transfer: European Review of LabourandResearch*,4(4),715–728.https://doi.org/10.1177/102425899800400410
Schor, J. (2010). *Plenitude: The new economics of true wealth*. Penguin Press.
Schor, J. (2011, September 2). Work less, live more. *YES! Magazine*. https://www.yesmagazine.org/issue/jobs/2011/09/02/less-work-more-living
Schor, J. B. (2005). Sustainable consumption and worktime reduction. *Journal of Industrial Ecology*, *9*(1–2), 37–50. https://doi.org/10.1162/1088198054084581
Schumpeter, J. A. (1942). *Capitalism, socialism and democracy*. Harper & Brothers.
Skidelsky, E., & Skidelsky, R. (2012). *How much is enough?: Money and the good life*. Penguin. https://books.google.com/books?hl=en&lr=&id=1uErhhSnRN0C&oi=fnd&pg=PT10&dq=How+Much+is+Enough%3F,+Skidelsky+%26+Skidelsky+(2013)+&ots=k0CzRCvPQi&sig=sT6bjsO-lCPFMrUz0ve_aYjlj4c
Veblen, T. (1899). *The theory of the leisure class*. Macmillan.
Verba, S., Schlozman, K. L., & Brady, H. E. (1995). *Voice and equality: Civic voluntarism in American politics*. Harvard University Press.
Wajcman, J. (2016). *Pressed for time: The acceleration of life in digital capitalism*. University of Chicago Press.
Weber, M. (1905). *The protestant ethic and the spirit of capitalism*. Routledge.
Wilkinson, R., & Pickett, K. (2009). *The spirit level: Why greater equality makes societies stronger*. Bloomsbury.
World Economic Forum. (2022). *This is what the 4-day workweek means for equal rights, productivity and climate change*. https://www.weforum.org/stories/2022/02/what-the-four-day-workweek-means-for-the-future-of-employment/#:~:text=Working%20four%20days%20a%20week,the%20environment%2C%20and%20the%20economy. (Retrieved 2025-04-24)
Xu, C., Yao, Z., & Xiong, Z. (2023). The impact of work-related use of information and communication technologies after hours on time theft. *Journal of Business Ethics*, *187*(1), 185–198. https://doi.org/10.1007/s10551-022-05167-1

12

MYTH 11

Transition to sustainable consumption is primarily driven by consumer demand

Oksana Mont and Åsa Svenfelt

12.1 The consumer demand myth as driver of sustainability transformation

The belief that sustainable consumption transformations are mainly driven by consumer demand portrays individual purchasing choices as the key influencing force, with all other societal actors seen as secondary.

This myth is built on three interconnected assumptions: '*driven by – consumer – demand*'. First, the 'driven by' assumption implies that consumers have disproportionate influence over markets, portraying businesses and governments as passive entities that merely respond to consumer preferences rather than actively shaping sustainability outcomes. Second, emphasising 'consumers' reduces individuals to their role as buyers, overlooking the many roles they play in everyday life, such as parents, partners, workers, voters or activists. This also frames their sustainability preferences as something only expressed through market choices. Third, the focus on 'demand' presumes that sustainable consumption can be achieved if people make deliberate and informed purchasing decisions, signalling demand that triggers businesses and policymakers to act.

The significance of the myth for the shift to sustainable consumption lies in its effect on how responsibility for initiating, implementing and maintaining change is perceived and allocated. Treating sustainable consumption mainly as consumer-driven overlooks the complex interaction between individual choices and structural conditions, a dynamic explained by Giddens' structuration theory (Giddens, 1984). Structuration theory highlights the interdependent relationship between individual agency and societal structures, emphasising that structures both shape and are shaped by human action.

DOI: 10.4324/9781003613718-16

Likewise, everyday decisions made by individuals are embedded in a broader context influenced by policies, market forces, social norms and infrastructure. Instead of placing an undue burden on consumers alone, this perspective encourages us to see sustainable consumption as an ongoing dialogue between individuals and institutions. It emphasises the need to align individual lifestyle changes with systemic transformations. Therefore, although consumer preferences can indeed signal demand for sustainability, structural actors, including businesses and governments, must also actively create conditions that promote and support sustainable choices. As Norgaard (2018) aptly states:

> *The focus on individuals is more than a theoretical choice, it has the political function of leaving government and corporations unaccountable.*
>
> *(Norgaard, 2018, p. 174)*

This approach shifts from simple consumer power narratives to a richer view of shared responsibilities (Mamut et al., 2025). It urges reconsideration of policy and infrastructure design, promoting strategies that empower consumers and make sustainable living accessible and attractive. Sustainable consumption is not just about individual choices; it is about shaping an environment where such decisions become default – naturally sustainable, feasible and desirable for all.

12.2 Origins

The idea that consumer demand drives markets took shape in the late 19th century, when economics began paying greater attention to individual choice as a force shaping markets. William Stanley Jevons argued that value derives from subjective utility rather than labour, positioning consumer satisfaction as the key measure of worth. Around the same time, Carl Menger emphasised that individuals assign value based on perceived usefulness, presenting markets as fluid and shaped by preferences. In the mid-20th century, Paul Samuelson advanced this reasoning by suggesting that rational consumers maximise utility and thereby generate efficient markets. And finally, by the 1940s, W. H. Hutt introduced the notion of 'consumer sovereignty', asserting that production should respond to consumer choices. Together, these developments established the foundation for treating consumers as the driving force in markets.

In the 1970s, environmental concerns introduced a moral dimension to economic logic, depicting consumers as both economic agents and morally responsible actors driving environmental change. Campaigns urging people to 'vote with their wallets' framed consumption as a pathway for achieving systemic transformation, reinterpreting concepts like consumer sovereignty (e.g. Green America, 2024). Environmental responsibility became personalised, with consumers regarded as crucial in addressing planetary crises through their purchasing decisions.

Over time, this framing spread throughout corporate and policy narratives. Companies frequently describe their role as providing 'sustainable' choices while depending on consumers to create enough demand for them (Parekh & Svenfelt, 2022). In doing so, attention shifts away from the structural causes of unsustainability, such as extractive global supply chains, carbon-intensive production, policies driven by corporate interests and inadequate infrastructure, which remain mostly unchallenged (Hirth et al., 2023). Gabriel and Lang (2006) highlight the tension in this narrative, portraying the consumer as both 'god-like' in power and yet subject to marketing, manipulation, and limited freedom of choice:

> *The consumer is now a god-like figure, before whom markets and politicians alike bow. Everywhere it seems, the consumer is triumphant. Consumers are said to dictate production; to fuel innovation; to be creating new service sectors in advanced economies; to be driving modern politics; to have it in their power to save the environment and protect the future of the planet.*

Governments and international bodies adopt behavioural framings, viewing consumer choice as vital for sustainability, assuming better-informed consumers can fix market failures. The European Commission's New Consumer Agenda (2020–2025) aims to equip consumers with information on product sustainability and combat practices like greenwashing (EC, 2020). It presumes consumers can and should identify deception and hold firms accountable via their buying choices. Meanwhile, the role of businesses is described as voluntary and supportive: 'The green transition cannot happen without companies – the Commission is determined to work with economic operators to encourage their pledges in support of sustainable consumption, beyond what is required by law' (EC, 2020). Instead of regulation to reshape markets and remove harmful practices, responsibility lies with consumers, managed through soft commitments. This governance model promotes the myth that consumer demand alone can drive deep sustainability changes, concealing the need for systemic, institutional and structural reforms.

12.3 Consequences

Framing consumers as the key change agents has significant consequences. It shifts responsibility away from businesses and policymakers, placing the burden of failure on individuals who cannot or do not choose sustainable options (Evans, 2011). Sustainability becomes a question of personal ethics or informed choice, depicting those who fall short as unwilling, unaware or morally deficient (Mayer & Kohl, 2024). However, sustainability transformations require structural interventions, such as regulation, infrastructure and changes in production and distribution, that go well beyond individual consumption (Cap et al., 2024). By primarily placing responsibility and blaming consumers, governments and businesses avoid creating the systemic conditions that would make sustainable practices the default rather than an individual struggle (Mont, 2008).

Another consequence of this consumer-centric framing is its persistence in research and policy. Structural changes are more difficult to measure, model and communicate than behavioural outcomes, which leads policymakers and researchers to focus on quantifiable indicators like energy use or product adoption that can be associated with individuals. Fuchs et al. (2025) emphasise how this bias towards behavioural metrics reinforces the misconception that individual choices are the main drivers of change. Consequently, structural levers, such as legal, economic and material factors, remain insufficiently examined, despite their importance for sustainable consumption.

This reliance on consumer choice also has practical implications for policy design. It assumes that market forces like demand, prices and competition will steer businesses towards sustainability. However, without regulation, infrastructure and public investment, these forces have rarely achieved the necessary scale and speed of change (Dubois et al., 2019). Instead of adopting ambitious measures to phase out harmful products or hold producers accountable, many governments focus on consumer campaigns, behavioural nudges and voluntary agreements. For example, in the food sector, policymakers promote dietary changes through information and labelling but are reluctant to introduce measures such as taxing high-carbon foods, restricting fossil fuel marketing or subsidising plant-based options. Research indicates that behavioural change alone is unlikely to alter consumption without structural interventions (Röös et al., 2021). The EU's reluctance to impose a meat tax illustrates this hesitance despite evidence that even modest rates could reduce emissions (Engström et al., 2024). Likewise, although marketing restrictions on unhealthy and unsustainable foods are recognised as effective, most remain weak or voluntary, allowing industry practices to continue largely unchanged (Dalhammar et al., 2022).

Stronger instruments, such as bans on unsustainable products or ecodesign standards, are often criticised as too prescriptive or costly. Nevertheless, evidence shows that regulatory measures can significantly reduce impacts, as with the European Ecodesign Directive, which has improved the efficiency of household appliances (Dalhammar, 2023). Efforts to expand such standards, however, face industry resistance and policymaker reluctance. A similar dynamic affects right-to-repair legislation: France introduced pioneering laws against planned obsolescence in 2015 and 2020, but wider EU adoption has been slow. Even when the sustainability benefits are clear, policymakers tend to rely on consumer demand to steer markets rather than challenge business models directly.

This hesitation also affects extended producer responsibility (EPR) schemes, particularly in electronics. Most programmes remain limited in scope, offering weak incentives for durability, repairability and material recovery (Dalhammar et al., 2022). EU EPR policies, for example, mainly focus on recycling rather than promoting longer product lifespans, which allows manufacturers to continue producing short-lived gadgets for frequent replacement. Expanding EPR policies to include ecodesign, extended warranties and take-back schemes could create stronger incentives for a circular economy (Dalhammar, 2023). However, such policies face opposition from industries that depend on high sales and rapid turnover.

The same pattern appears in infrastructure and planning. Policies encouraging consumers to switch to electric vehicles, for example, often neglect the parallel need for charging networks, renewable energy expansion, and improved public transport (Morfeldt et al., 2023). Similarly, advancing sustainable food systems requires investment in regional supply networks and agricultural subsidies, rather than relying solely on consumer demand for organic or plant-based products (Engström et al., 2024). Without these systemic supports, structural barriers continue to undermine individual action.

Finally, focusing on consumer-led change can slow down stronger governance. Policymakers often argue that consumers are either unprepared or not demanding enough, which causes delays in implementing ambitious reforms – a cycle known as 'responsibility ping-pong' (Mamut et al., 2025). Corporate lobbying contributes to this pattern, especially in high-emission sectors like aviation. For example, although aviation makes up about 25% of household emissions, only 1.2% of consumer-facing sustainability policies address it (Elofsson, 2019; Dubois et al., 2019), while regulatory frameworks are progressing, improvements are inconsistent and reliance on consumer responsibility continues to limit the speed and extent of systemic change.

12.4 Dispelling

The idea that consumer demand alone drives sustainability transformations greatly oversimplifies how markets function and misrepresents the dynamics of change. While individual choices generate market signals, businesses actively shape demand through product design, marketing, pricing, and control of infrastructure and supply chains. Surveys show public support for climate action, but actual implementation remains limited. A global survey conducted across 125 countries, involving 130,000 respondents, demonstrates that '69% of the global population expresses a willingness to contribute 1% of their personal income, 86% endorse pro-climate social norms, and 89% demand intensified political action' (Rinkinen et al., 2021). Another survey of 73,000 individuals from 77 countries, representing 87% of the global population, found that 80% want their countries to do more about climate change and 72% support a rapid shift away from fossil fuels (UNDP, 2024). Recognising the disconnect between public willingness and policy action is essential because, while individual choices matter, they must be supported and reinforced by structural and policy changes (Dubois et al., 2019). Below, we explore four key arguments that challenge the core assumptions of this myth and show why consumer demand alone cannot drive sustainability transformations.

12.4.1 Marketing and choice architecture shape consumption

One of the biggest challenges to the idea of consumer-led change is how marketing and choice architecture influence, rather than merely follow, consumer preferences. What appears to be independent consumer demand often results from targeted advertising, behavioural nudges and the strategic design of retail and digital spaces. In fact, global advertising revenue is expected to exceed $1 trillion by 2025, with digital marketing recognised as the fastest-growing sector (Graham, 2024). Companies now allocate about 9% of their revenue to marketing (Statista, 2025). However, these techniques do more than promote products. They generate desires, normalise unsustainable behaviours and limit the scope for conscious choice, driven more by external influences than internal needs and preferences.

The mid-20th century marked a pivotal point in the evolution of marketing. Agencies such as Ogilvy & Mather, located on Madison Avenue in New York City, pioneered sophisticated advertising strategies that actively influenced consumer choices. As advertising theorist James Twitchell (1996) observed, this era redefined marketing as an active force in shaping consumer behaviour, creating the illusion that markets are driven by consumer preferences when, in fact, they are influenced by corporate interests.

Edward Bernays, often regarded as the 'father of public relations', played a key role in demonstrating how psychological insights could be exploited to influence public opinion. Building on his uncle Sigmund Freud's theories, Bernays devised campaigns that created new consumer cravings. One of his most well-known examples was a 1920s campaign to normalise smoking among women, portraying cigarettes as symbols of freedom and sophistication (Bernays, 1928). This approach did not merely reflect existing preferences; it established a market for women smokers where none had previously existed.

Another notable example of demand creation is how diamonds have become a cultural symbol of love and marriage. The De Beers campaign, 'A diamond is forever', launched in 1948, successfully associated diamonds with romance, marriage and lifelong commitment (Bergenstock & Maskulka, 2001). Before this campaign, diamonds were not typically linked to engagement rings. By promoting this connection through extensive advertising, De Beers generated a market demand that still influences consumer behaviour today. The bottled water industry also illustrates how marketing creates demand. Despite safe tap water being common in many developed countries, bottled water remains highly profitable. Campaigns emphasising purity, health and convenience have convinced consumers to pay for a product they can access for free (Brei & Tadajewski, 2015).

These examples show how demand is generated through marketing. Today, this process is more subtle and manipulative, such as fast-food chains offering toys with children's meals. Originally intended to attract families, this marketing tactic influences preferences, makes unhealthy food more tempting, and increases consumption, contributing to childhood obesity (Longacre et al., 2016). These products are often criticised for being environmentally wasteful and culturally outdated, emphasising a mismatch between marketing strategies and consumer interests in health and sustainability. It also demonstrates a tendency towards low-cost, high-volume market models.

Increasingly, companies rely on advanced tools such as neuromarketing, which uses brain imaging, eye-tracking and physiological monitoring to identify emotional triggers that influence purchases (Lindstrom, 2010). Marketers leverage these insights to refine designs and adverts that appeal to subconscious processes. These are often combined with 'dark patterns', that is, interface designs that manipulate users into making choices that bypass rational decision-making (Narayanan et al., 2020). These tactics include pre-selected options, countdown clocks, or hidden costs, exploiting cognitive biases rather than supporting informed choices (Mathur et al., 2019). Critics warn that these methods may be exploitative (see Chapter 3, Retail therapy).

Beyond advertising, businesses influence consumption through physical choice architecture – how products, services and environments are designed to sway decisions. Studies show that consumer choices are heavily influenced by context (Lehner et al., 2016). Supermarkets, for example, position items to boost sales, with candy and unhealthy foods near checkout and essentials like milk at the back, prompting impulse purchases.

Sensory marketing, used in retail and real estate (Krishna, 2011), involves placing fragrances near entrances or lighting scented candles like coffee or cinnamon buns to create inviting environments that attract shoppers and evoke a homely atmosphere. These cues influence purchasing decisions by shaping behaviour. Expecting consumers to lead sustainability efforts without addressing these environmental influences seems unrealistic.

12.4.2 Sociotechnical systems constrain consumer autonomy

Another key flaw in the belief that consumers drive sustainability transformation is the assumption that individual behaviour is mainly determined by personal choice, preference or values. In reality, consumption occurs within sociotechnical systems that shape what people can and cannot do. These systems consist of interconnected infrastructures, technologies, institutions, and routines developed over time. Transition theory emphasises the importance of these systemic structures, noting that resource-intensive consumption patterns are not merely personal decisions but stem from how societies organise the provision of essential services such as housing, mobility, energy and food (Geels et al., 2015).

Infrastructure design influences consumption by making certain options more convenient, affordable or unavoidable. Jelsma and Knot (2002) suggest that sociotechnical contexts shape consumers into engaging in environmentally harmful behaviours. Products and systems carry 'scripts' guiding actions and embedding routines. For instance, supermarkets and restaurants not offering vegetarian, local, or organic food limit dietary shifts and reinforce unsustainable norms (Bauer et al., 2022). Urban environments that prioritise private cars over public transport trap people into high-emission mobility. Cities built around motorways with urban sprawl and limited public transport make switching to low-carbon options difficult. Similarly, in energy systems, countries with fossil fuel-dominated grids make renewable energy adoption challenging even for motivated consumers (IPCC, 2022).

These constraints are not just about what infrastructure provides but also about what it fails to offer. When waste management systems are limited or poorly designed, individuals face structural barriers to sorting and reducing waste. Conversely, South Korea's strict food waste separation policies and digital tracking systems have led to notable reductions in food waste, demonstrating that consumer behaviour changes when systemic conditions make sustainable options accessible and easy to use (Lee et al., 2024). A similar dynamic applies to sharing and repair. The absence of infrastructures such as libraries of things, tool-sharing schemes or community repair hubs significantly hampers those wanting to reduce consumption through reuse or borrowing. In such cases, even if people are motivated to cut back, they are often pushed into buying new products due to the lack of alternative ways to satisfy their needs (Mont, 2025).

Infrastructures are not neutral enablers of consumer agency but rather deeply embedded structures that influence, restrict and normalise specific forms of behaviour. Their material and institutional aspects – from urban design and zoning laws to energy grids, logistics networks and retail architectures – often leave consumers with limited opportunities to manoeuvre or opt out of dominant systems altogether (Solér et al., 2020). These systems are also dynamic. The concepts of 'path dependency' and 'technological lock-in' describe how infrastructures and institutions develop together, generating strong momentum behind certain ways of organising consumption. Once established, infrastructure such as motorways, energy grids or single-purpose urban layouts influences behaviour not only in the present but also for decades, limiting possibilities for future alternatives. For example, the '15-minute city' concept has gained interest during and after COVID-19, emphasising proximity, accessibility and reduced car use (Abdelfattah et al., 2022). However, implementing this within existing car-centric, single-use zones is challenging (Lu & Diab, 2025).

Ultimately, individuals cannot easily escape the infrastructures and institutions shaped by planners, authorities and providers. These actors define available mobility, housing and energy options, and, as the next section demonstrates, similar dynamics are at work in markets, where the design and supply of goods often take precedence over consumer preferences and promote unsustainable consumption.

12.4.3 The market floods consumers with unwanted and unsustainable products

The gap between consumer preferences and market supply is clear in the rise of unsustainable and often damaging products over sustainable ones, frustrating those seeking long-lasting, ethical options. For instance, many products in the market have short lifespans due to poor quality or planned obsolescence, leading to frequent replacements and waste (McVeigh et al., 2019). The fast fashion industry, with brands like Zara, Temy and Shein, produces low-quality garments that quickly wear out and encourages consumers to buy frequently and discard perfectly functioning items. Consumer frustration with short-lived products is evident in the growing popularity of repair cafés and the 'right to repair' movement, which advocates for extending product lifespans (Bradley & Persson, 2022). However, these grassroots efforts are often undermined by companies that produce hard-to-repair disposable goods. From electronics with unreplaceable batteries to household appliances with inaccessible parts, businesses often design products that make repair difficult, forcing consumers into overconsumption and waste even when they are willing to buy differently.

Markets continue to supply products with serious environmental, social and ethical impacts, despite rising public concern. Products, such as so-called blood diamonds, sourced through violent or exploitative labour practices like child labour and slavery (Schulte & Paris, 2020), or foie gras, now widely criticised for its link to animal cruelty (DeSoucey, 2016), remain available on the market. This persistence reflects both the weakness of existing regulatory frameworks and the resistance of entrenched corporate interests to reform.

Over time, some once-accepted products and services have become stigmatised due to ethical or environmental concerns. Air travel faces scrutiny from 'flight shame' debates over its high carbon footprint (Becken et al., 2021), and palm oil is criticised for causing deforestation, biodiversity loss and human rights issues (Meijaard et al., 2020). Recently, products with microplastics, like glitter, exfoliants and synthetic textiles, have sparked consumer concern and calls for regulation.

Yet, despite growing awareness, such products remain dominant across various sectors due to structural and commercial factors that limit consumer agency. In the fast fashion industry, for instance, exploitative labour practices persist (Gunawan et al., 2023), even though many consumers favour ethically produced clothing. Therefore, these market structures are rarely driven by demand alone. Instead, they reflect business decisions that prioritise profit, cost-efficiency, speed and convenience over environmental and social responsibility. As a result, unsustainable products and practices remain prevalent in many markets.

12.4.4 Active citizen engagement challenges the myth

Considering the above, the idea that consumers can 'vote with their wallets' to promote sustainability becomes increasingly implausible, as limited and unsustainable options, infrastructures and commercial pressures often restrict people.

One response to this disconnect is *political consumerism*, defined as the 'use of the market as an arena for politics in order to change institutional or market practices found to be ethically, environmentally, or politically objectionable' (Stolle & Micheletti, 2013, p. 39). It includes boycotts, refusing to buy from unethical or environmentally unsustainable companies, and buycotts, supporting and rewarding more responsible market actors. *Anti-consumption campaigns* are an example of boycott activism. Annual events like Buy Nothing Day and White Monday challenge the culture of excess by promoting simply not buying. Participants in the 'No Spend Year' campaign go even further, abstaining from non-essential purchases for an entire year and instead promoting creative ways of reusing, sharing and repurposing existing items or doing without (McGagh, 2017).

During COVID-19, many communities turned to sharing-based solutions as public and retail services strained. Sharing economy groups and mutual aid mobilised to provide food, medicine, and essentials via community fridges, informal delivery and online exchanges (Mont et al., 2021). These efforts reconfigured provision systems when public and commercial services failed.

Beyond political consumerism, there is a shift from passive consumption to prosumerism, where individuals and communities actively produce, maintain and share resources. This approach aims to step outside market logic (Lehner, 2019). For example, energy prosumers install solar panels and join wind power cooperatives, reducing reliance on fossil fuels. Food prosumers dedicate time to community-supported agriculture, enhancing food sovereignty and reconnecting people with their sources of consumption. Citizens create alternatives to the market, not just signal preferences. The growth of repair cafés and freecycling networks also reflects the cultural importance of prosumer activities. Instead of buying new products, people repair, upcycle, learn new skills, build community and cut waste. These efforts emphasise use value, community and repair, providing a radically different provisioning model.

However, they remain marginal in a dominant, consumer-driven economy, yet their existence challenges the myth that sustainability is primarily achieved through consumer demand. Emerging not because of market conditions but often despite them, these practices reveal the extent to which individuals must resist, reshape or withdraw from unsustainable provision systems. Sharing and prosumer initiatives often face structural barriers such as spatial constraints, inadequate funding, limited policy support and prevailing social norms (Mont, 2025). Nevertheless, they endure and grow, showing that meaningful change does not have to depend on choosing the better option within existing systems, but on collectively imagining and co-creating new, more democratic and sustainable ways of provisioning and consuming.

12.5 Implications

Recognising barriers such as limited agency, power and institutional lock-ins has vital implications for policymakers, businesses and society. While the discussion concentrates on societal actors, the ability to influence consumption is not limited to individuals or institutions. It is distributed among people, organisations, technologies and social contexts, requiring coordinated action across these systems. This includes addressing structural barriers, aligning institutions, and making sustainable options accessible, affordable, desirable and easy to adopt.

12.5.1 Implications for policymaking

Recognising consumer limits, policymakers must take the lead in designing systems that support sustainable consumption (Heiskanen & Laakso, 2019). Policies need to intervene across multiple levels – regulatory, infrastructural, fiscal and symbolic (Mont et al., 2022). The Netherlands' urban planning demonstrates that long-term policy can influence behaviour: cycling is widespread because of both preference and city design. In Germany, rooftop solar expanded through feed-in tariffs and subsidies before consumer demand increased. Effective policies should go beyond education and nudges to establish structural boundaries. France's ban on short-haul flights where trains are available exemplifies a regulation that removes high-impact options (Åkerman et al., 2021). Reducing price and convenience differences between rail and air travel through better ticketing, night trains and reinvestment of aviation taxes can substantially affect mobility choices (Curtale et al., 2023).

To enable systemic change, policy must also address the cultural narratives that influence consumption. Instead of relying on 'smooth' framings that focus on individual choice, adopting 'rough' framings, such as emphasising institutional constraints, power dynamics and global inequalities, can support more ambitious and coherent sustainability policies (Klintman, 2025). For example, Chile's restrictions on advertising unhealthy foods to children redefine what is socially acceptable and desirable, reducing corporate influence on preferences and significantly cutting back on sugar-sweetened beverages (Taillie et al., 2020).

Finally, instead of expecting consumers to lead the sustainability transformation, engaging citizens in participatory processes can help co-design necessary policies and increase legitimacy and public support (Lage et al., 2023). Citizens' assemblies have become a powerful policy tool to reshape values and broaden what is recognised as relevant knowledge and public interest in sustainability-related work. Their participatory and deliberative format encourages more inclusive understandings of sustainability and supports the co-design of socially accepted, politically feasible and more ambitious sustainability policies (Schmid et al., 2024). Assemblies have proven their ability to include underrepresented voices, navigate complex trade-offs and build legitimacy and public trust, especially when linked to decision-making processes and widely communicated to the public (Reuchamps et al., 2023). They can thus contribute to better policies and a cultural shift in how sustainable consumption is understood and governed.

12.5.2 Implications for businesses

Businesses also play a crucial role in shaping the systems, products and narratives that underpin unsustainable consumption. Dispelling the myth that consumers alone can drive sustainability highlights the importance for companies to redesign their business models and take greater responsibility for supporting low-impact lifestyles. Some leaders are shifting away from volume-driven, linear models towards strategies that reduce material throughput and extend product lifespans. Examples include Fairphone, which manufactures modular and repairable smartphones, and Interface, which integrates regenerative principles into its operations. Similarly, subscription-based services like VIGGA in Denmark offer children's clothing through circular business models, helping garments last longer.

Beyond redesigning products and services, businesses influence how lifestyles are conceived and practised. For instance, IKEA's Live Lagom programme assists households in adopting lower-impact routines through financial incentives, product trials and peer engagement (Elf et al., 2021).

Instead of focusing solely on transactions, such initiatives position companies as partners in promoting more sustainable daily habits. This shift requires new success measures centred on service, well-being and value – not just sales volume. Extending this idea, the concept of the Lifestyle Change Support System (LCSS) presents businesses as long-term facilitators of sustainable lifestyles (Mont et al., 2025). An LCSS involves ongoing collaboration with customers and communities, contributions to enabling infrastructures, and support for practices that facilitate sustainable living. Rather than nudging isolated choices, it fosters deeper behavioural and societal transformations.

To expand such approaches, companies should collaborate with municipalities and civil society to invest in infrastructure for sharing, repairing and access-based services. Instead of simply responding to demand, they can proactively shape markets and practices that facilitate sustainable living. Those dedicated to transformation must also back ambitious regulation to create conditions where alternative business models can prosper.

12.5.3 Implications for individuals

Dispelling the myth that consumers are the main drivers of sustainability changes frees people from unrealistic expectations and allows them to act more effectively beyond simply making market choices. Instead of focusing too much on 'buying better', people can engage in advocacy, collective actions, and cultural shifts that help establish new norms, values and systems of provision.

One way individuals can contribute is by *challenging the dominant idea of consumerism* and promoting alternatives such as sharing, circularity and sufficiency. The success of the 'Right to Repair' movement, which has led to legislative changes in the EU and the United States, demonstrates how individuals, when organised collectively, can pressure businesses and governments to change unsustainable systems. Similarly, '1.5° Lifestyle Challenges' question the consumerist logic that drives overproduction and waste and engage individuals in promoting more sustainable lifestyles (1.5° Lifestyles, 2025). Legal activism is another avenue. The Urgenda Foundation's successful lawsuit against the Dutch government set a precedent for holding states accountable for missing climate targets (Urgenda Foundation v. Netherlands, 2015). It was the first time a government was legally compelled to reduce its greenhouse gas emissions.

Moving beyond the myth opens space for more active civic participation and collective change. In Barcelona, participatory budgeting allows citizens to decide how to spend municipal funds on local sustainability projects. Urban food-sharing platforms and citizen-managed zero-waste grocery co-operatives show how individuals can act independently of market forces.

12.6 Main message

The shift to sustainable consumption cannot rely on consumers alone. While individual choices are important, they are influenced and limited by systemic factors such as policies, market structures and corporate practices. Real progress requires collective action and an integrated approach that emphasises regulatory reforms, business accountability and infrastructure supporting sustainable living. Policymakers must tackle structural barriers, businesses must incorporate sustainability into core operations and individuals must engage beyond market solutions. Recognising consumer demand limitations enables a move towards genuine transformation to sustainability.

References

1.5° Lifestyles. (n.d.). *EU 1.5° lifestyles challenges*. Retrieved May 18, 2025, from https://onepointfivelifestyles.eu/EU1_5-degree-challenges

Abdelfattah, L., Deponte, D., & Fossa, G. (2022). The 15-minute city: Interpreting the model to bring out urban resiliencies. In M. Tira & G. Maternini (Eds.), *Transportation research procedia* (Vol. 60, pp. 330–337). Elsevier B.V.; Scopus.

Åkerman, J., Kamb, A., Larsson, J., & Nässén, J. (2021). Low-carbon scenarios for long-distance travel 2060. *Transportation Research Part D: Transport and Environment*, *99*. Scopus.

Bauer, J. M., Aarestrup, S. C., Hansen, P. G., & Reisch, L. A. (2022). Nudging more sustainable grocery purchases: Behavioural innovations in a supermarket setting. *Technological Forecasting and Social Change*, *179*, 121605.

Becken, S., Friedl, H., Stantic, B., Connolly, R. M., & Chen, J. (2021). Climate crisis and flying: Social media analysis traces the rise of "flightshame." *Journal of Sustainable Tourism*, *29*(9), 1450–1469.

Bergenstock, D. J., & Maskulka, J. M. (2001). The de beers story: Are diamonds forever? *Business Horizons*, *44*(3), 37–44.

Bernays, E. L. (1928). *Propaganda*. Ig publishing.

Bradley, K., & Persson, O. (2022). Community repair in the circular economy – fixing more than stuff. *Local Environment*, *27*(10–11), 1321–1337.

Brei, V., & Tadajewski, M. (2015). Crafting the market for bottled water: A social praxeology approach. *European Journal of Marketing*, *49*(3/4), 327–349.

Cap, S., de Koning, A., Tukker, A., & Scherer, L. (2024). (In)Sufficiency of industrial decarbonization to reduce household carbon footprints to 1.5°C-compatible levels. *Sustainable Production and Consumption*, *45*, 216–227.

Curtale, R., Larsson, J., & Nässén, J. (2023). Understanding preferences for night trains and their potential to replace flights in Europe. The case of Sweden. *Tourism Management Perspectives*, *47*, 101115.

Dalhammar, C. (2023). Making sustainable products the norm on the internal market: An assessment of the proposal for a new ecodesign regulation. *Europarättslig Tidskrift*, *2023*(1). https://www.ert.se/Authors/Author/3335

Dalhammar, C., Mont, O., & Lehner, M. (2022). *Politik och styrning för hållbar konsumtion* (p. 118). Formas. https://formas.se/analys-och-resultat/rapporter/2022-06-10-politik-och-styrning-for-hallbar-konsumtion.html

DeSoucey, M. (2016). *Contested tastes: Foie gras and the politics of food*. https://www.torrossa.com/gs/resourceProxy?an=5560366&publisher=FZO137

Dubois, G., Sovacool, B., Aall, C., Nilsson, M., Barbier, C., Herrmann, A., Bruyère, S., Andersson, C., Skold, B., Nadaud, F., Dorner, F., Moberg, K. R., Ceron, J. P., Fischer, H., Amelung, D., Baltruszewicz, M., Fischer, J., Benevise, F., Louis, V. R., & Sauerborn, R. (2019). It starts at home? Climate policies targeting household consumption and behavioral decisions are key to low-carbon futures. *Energy Research & Social Science*, *52*, 144–158.

EC. (2020, November 13). *New consumer agenda: European Commission to empower consumers to become the driver of transition* [Text]. European Commission – European Commission. https://ec.europa.eu/commission/presscorner/detail/en/ip_20_2069

Elf, P., Isham, A., & Gatersleben, B. (2021). Above and beyond? How businesses can drive sustainable development by promoting lasting pro-environmental behaviour change: An examination of the IKEA Live Lagom project. *Business Strategy and the Environment*, *30*(2), 1037–1050.

Elofsson, A. (2019). *Climate policy for aviation. Analyses of measures at multiple levels*. Chalmers University of Technology. https://core.ac.uk/download/pdf/270108704.pdf

Engström, E., Larsson, M., Bradley, K., Dotterud Leiren, M., Ejelöv, E., Finnveden, G., Haugs Langvik, K., Heinonen, J., Larsson, J., & Thøgersen, J. (2024). *Policy options for reducing consumption-based emissions: A Nordic survey*. Nordisk Ministerråd. https://www.diva-portal.org/smash/record.jsf?pid=diva2:1905550

Evans, D. (2011). Blaming the consumer – once again: The social and material contexts of everyday food waste practices in some English households. *Critical Public Health*, *21*(4), 429–440.

Fuchs, D., Debourdeau, A., Dütschke, E., Fahy, F., Garzon, G., Kirchler, B., Klöckner, C. A., & Sahakian, M. (2025). Assessing the impact of structural change in sustainable consumption and lifestyles research. *Consumption and Society*, *4*(1), 122–140.

Gabriel, Y., & Lang, T. (2006). *The unmanageable consumer: Contemporary consumption and its fragmentations* (1st ed., 1995). Sage Publications.

Geels, F. W., McMeekin, A., Mylan, J., & Southerton, D. (2015). A critical appraisal of sustainable consumption and production research: The reformist, revolutionary and reconfiguration positions. *Global Environmental Change*, *34*, 1–12.

Giddens, A. (1984). *The constitution of society. Outline of a theory of structuration*. Polity Press.

Graham, M. (2024, June 10). Global ad revenue will hit $1 trillion faster than expected, GroupM forecast says. *Wall Street Journal*.

Green America. (2024). *What does it mean to vote with your dollar?* [Green America]. https://www.greenamerica.org/show-ga-blog?nid=5570

Gunawan, Y., Matahariza, A., & Putri, W. K. (2023). The dark side of fast fashion: Examining the exploitation of garment workers in Bangladesh. *Jurnal Hukum Dan Peradilan*, *12*(3), 441–468.

Heiskanen, E., & Laakso, S. (2019). Editing out unsustainability from consumption: From information provision to nudging and social practice theory. In O. Mont (Ed.), *A research agenda for sustainable consumption governance*. Edward Elgar Publishing Ltd.

Hirth, S., Kreinin, H., Fuchs, D., Blossey, N., Mamut, P., Philipp, J., Radovan, I., Consortium, T. E. 5°Lifestyles, Antal, O., Belousa, I., Bösch, M., Brizga, J., Bronstering, G., Dumitru, A., Langner, S., Laksevics, K., Leutermann, C., Klosterberg, C., Kramer, N., . . . Zsemberovszky, L. (2023). Barriers and enablers of 1.5° lifestyles: Shallow and deep structural factors shaping the potential for sustainable consumption. *Frontiers in Sustainability*, *4*.

Hutt, W. H. (1940). The concept of consumers' sovereignty. *The Economic Journal*, *50*(197), 66.

IPCC. (2022). *Climate change 2022. Mitigation of climate change* (p. 2913). IPCC. https://doi.org/10.1017/9781009157926.001

Jelsma, J., & Knot, M. (2002). Designing environmentally efficient services; a 'script' approach. *The Journal of Sustainable Product Design*, *2*(3), 119–130.

Jevons, W. S. (1871). *The theory of political economy* (3rd ed., 1888). Macmillan and Co.

Klintman, M. (2025). Framing: The social art of influence. In *Framing*. Manchester University Press. https://www.manchesterhive.com/display/9781526170422/9781526170422.xml

Krishna, A. (2011). *Sensory marketing: Research on the sensuality of products*. Routledge.

Lage, J., Thema, J., Zell-Ziegler, C., Best, B., Cordroch, L., & Wiese, F. (2023). Citizens call for sufficiency and regulation – A comparison of European citizen assemblies and national energy and climate plans. *Energy Research & Social Science*, *104*, 103254.

Lee, E., Shurson, G., Oh, S.-H., & Jang, J.-C. (2024). The management of food waste recycling for a sustainable future: A case study on South Korea. *Sustainability*, *16*(2), 854.

Lehner, M. (2019). An exploration of the significance of prosumption for sustainable consumption, and its implications for sustainable consumption governance. In O. Mont (Ed.), *A research agenda for sustainable consumption governance* (pp. 105–120). Edward Elgar Publishing Ltd.

Lehner, M., Mont, O., & Heiskanen, E. (2016). Nudging – A promising tool for sustainable consumption behaviour? *Journal of Cleaner Production*, *134*, 166–177.

Lindstrom, M. (2010). *Buyology: Truth and lies about why we buy*. Crown Currency.

Longacre, M. R., Drake, K. M., Titus, L. J., Cleveland, L. P., Langeloh, G., Hendricks, K., & Dalton, M. A. (2016). A toy story: Association between young children's knowledge of fast food toy premiums and their fast food consumption. *Appetite*, *96*, 473–480.

Lu, M., & Diab, E. (2025). Developing a 15-minute city policy? Understanding differences between policies and physical barriers. *Transportation Research Part A: Policy and Practice*, *191*, 104307.

Mamut, P., Fuchs, D., Becker, L., Laksevics, K., Kreinin, H., & Brizga, J. (2025). From responsibility ping-pong to shared responsibility for 1.5° lifestyles? Examining European stakeholder perspectives. *Consumption and Society*, *4*(1), 33–54.

Mathur, A., Acar, G., Friedman, M. J., Lucherini, E., Mayer, J., Chetty, M., & Narayanan, A. (2019). Dark patterns at scale: Findings from a crawl of 11K shopping websites. *Proceedings of the ACM on Human-Computer Interaction*, *3*(CSCW), 1–32.

Mayer, M., & Kohl, P. (2024). Playing the blame game: How attribution of responsibility impacts consumer attitudes toward plastic waste. *Frontiers in Communication*, *9*, 1337332.

McGagh, M. (2017). *The no spend year: How i spent less and lived more*. Hodder & Stoughton.

McVeigh, M. K., Dalhammar, C., & Richter, J. L. (2019). *Planned obsolescence: Build not to last*. European Liberal Forum.

Meijaard, E., Brooks, T. M., Carlson, K. M., Slade, E. M., Garcia-Ulloa, J., Gaveau, D. L., Lee, J. S. H., Santika, T., Juffe-Bignoli, D., & Struebig, M. J. (2020). The environmental impacts of palm oil in context. *Nature Plants*, *6*(12), 1418–1426.

Mont, O. (2008). The role of households in SCP agenda: A one-actor show or concerted action? *Journal of Innovation and Sustainable Development*, *2*(2), 201–214.

Mont, O. (Ed.). (2025). *Understanding the urban sharing economy: Sustainability and institutionalisation*. Edwar Elgar Publishing Limited.

Mont, O., Curtis, S., & Voytenko Palgan, Y. (2021). Organisational response strategies in the sharing economy to COVID-19. *Sustainable Production and Consumption, October*, 52–70.

Mont, O., Elf, P., & Isham, A. (2025). Marketing sustainable lifestyles. In K. Peattie, R. De Angelis, N. Koenig-Lewis, & C. Strong (Eds.), *The Routledge companion to marketing and sustainability* (Vol. 2025). Routledge, Taylor & Francis Group.

Mont, O., Lehner, M., & Dalhammar, C. (2022). Sustainable consumption through policy intervention – A review of research themes. *Frontiers in Sustainability*, *3*.

Morfeldt, J., Larsson, J., Andersson, D., Johansson, D. J. A., Rootzén, J., Hult, C., & Karlsson, I. (2023). Emission pathways and mitigation options for achieving consumption-based climate targets in Sweden. *Communications Earth & Environment*, *4*(1), Article 1.

Narayanan, A., Mathur, A., Chetty, M., & Kshirsagar, M. (2020). Dark patterns: Past, present, and future. *Queue*, *18*(2), 67–92.

Norgaard, K. M. (2018). The sociological imagination in a time of climate change. *Global and Planetary Change*, *163*, 171–176.

Parekh, V., & Svenfelt, Å. (2022). Taking sustainable eating practices from niche to mainstream: The perspectives of Swedish food-provisioning actors on barriers and potentials. *Sustainability: Science, Practice and Policy*, *18*(1), 292–308.

Reuchamps, M., Vrydagh, J., & Welp, Y. (2023). *De Gruyter handbook of citizens' assemblies*. de Gruyter. https://library.oapen.org/handle/20.500.12657/63773

Rinkinen, J., Shove, E., & Marsden, G. (2021). *Conceptualising demand. A distinctive approach to consumption and practice* (Vol. 2021). Routledge.

Samuelson, P. (1947). *Foundations of economic analysis*. Harvard University Press.

Schmid, P., Lamotte, L., Curran, M., & Bieri, S. (2024). Creating pathways to just and sustainable food systems with citizen assemblies. *Innovation: The European Journal of Social Science Research*, *37*(3), 832–850.

Schulte, M., & Paris, C. M. (2020). Blood diamonds: An analysis of the state of affairs and the effectiveness of the Kimberley Process. *International Journal of Sustainable Society*, *12*(1), 51–75.

Solér, C., Koroschetz, B., & Salminen, E. (2020). An infrastructural perspective on sustainable consumption – Activating and obligating sustainable consumption through infrastructures. *Journal of Cleaner Production*, *243*, 118601.

Statista. (2025, January 14). *Advertising and marketing*. Statista. https://www.statista.com/markets/479/advertising-marketing/

Stolle, D., & Micheletti, M. (2013). *Political consumerism: Global responsibility in action*. Cambridge University Press.

Taillie, L. S., Reyes, M., Colchero, M. A., Popkin, B., & Corvalán, C. (2020). An evaluation of Chile's law of food labeling and Advertising on sugar-sweetened beverage purchases from 2015 to 2017: A before-and-after study. *PLoS Medicine*, *17*(2), e1003015.

Twitchell, J. B. (1996). *Adcult USA: The triumph of advertising in American culture*. Columbia University Press.

UNDP. (2024). *Peoples' climate vote 2024* (p. 179) [UNDP Peoples' Climate Vote]. UNDP. https://peoplesclimate.vote/document/Peoples_Climate_Vote_Report_2024.pdf

Urgenda Foundation v. State of the Netherlands, [2015] HAZA C/09/00456689, Climate Change Litigation. (2015). https://climatecasechart.com/non-us-case/urgenda-foundation-v-kingdom-of-the-netherlands/

13

MYTH 12

Strong sustainable consumption governance means sacrificing freedom and well-being

Lea Melissa Becker, Paula Berendt and Doris Fuchs

13.1 Myth that strong sustainable consumption governance means sacrificing freedom and well-being

> *Strong sustainable consumption policies endanger freedom and well-being and will therefore never be accepted by people.*

Strong sustainable consumption (SSC) policies, addressing levels and fundamental patterns of resource use, are often framed and perceived as interfering with quality of life, freedom and well-being. It is the unshakable belief in this myth that makes policymakers shy away from SSC policies. Instead, they opt for weak sustainable consumption (WSC) policies focusing on improvements in energy efficiency, micro-targets, and efforts to convince consumers to buy allegedly 'more sustainable' products and services (Fuchs & Lorek, 2005).

Why is this problematic? SSC policies have several fundamental characteristics that make them a necessity in our times of concurrent social and ecological crises. First, they create the basis for protecting and – where necessary – restoring the environmental foundations of societal well-being. While such a governance focus might seem obvious as well as highly acceptable, it is, in fact, not evident at all in a system that is structured first and foremost around the pursuit of economic growth. Second, SSC governance addresses this very system with its structural barriers and deep intertwinement with the transgression of planetary and social boundaries. It thus offers an alternative to *business as usual*. Third, empirical evidence has shown that reductions in energy use enabled by improvements in energy efficiency tend to be more than eaten up by simultaneous increases in consumption levels, due

DOI: 10.4324/9781003613718-17

to so-called *rebound effects*. Thus, efficiency gains are insufficient for a sustainability transformation and, for example, for reaching the 1.5° goal of the Paris Climate Agreement (Cap et al., 2024; Fuchs et al., 2021; Spangenberg & Lorek, 2019). Given this fundamental shortcoming, SSC policies focus instead on levels and quality of consumption, oriented towards human needs and the pursuit of a good life for all.

And yet, SSC policies are perceived as harming 'quality of life' because they supposedly restrict freedom of choice. Due to the dominance of this framing in public discourse, political decision-makers may well consider SSC policies too controversial. Countering this perspective, this chapter argues that SSC policies are indispensable for protecting freedom as well as enabling a good life for all.

13.2 Origins

Our current social and economic system is reigned by deeply unequal power relations. As economic growth is the overriding imperative, those actors most aligned with the pursuit of profit and perpetuating the growth paradigm, such as big businesses with vested interests, wield unparalleled and highly disproportionate political power. These power relations are ingrained in societal, political, economic and technological structures (Brand & Wissen, 2021; Fuchs et al., 2016). *Weak* sustainable consumption policies maintain these very structures through the idea that natural resources can be replaced by human and physical capital. For advocates of this form of sustainability, a system is sustainable as long as the total capital (consisting of natural resources, human and physical capital) remains the same or grows. A decline in natural capital, that is, the extraction of raw materials or the decline of natural habitats, is still sustainable if it is offset by increasing capital in the other areas. This increase in artificial capital particularly refers to the idea of technical progress, in which many green growth advocates place their hopes (see Chapter 5). In this system, the preservation of the environmental and societal foundations of well-being is not the main focus, but rather the maintenance and increase of economic growth, which benefits powerful elites that became powerful through the exact treadmills of growth. *Strong* sustainable consumption governance on the contrary, does not accept the idea that natural resources can easily be substituted or replaced by human or real capital (Ott & Döring, 2004). Accordingly, it rejects the idea that technological progress alone will solve complex sustainability problems, especially in light of rebound effects. Set around the objectives of freedom and just societies, SSC governance therefore challenges the undifferentiated prioritisation of growth and underlying power relations. Instead, it calls for the establishment of new and different structures that can genuinely protect the ecological foundations for life on Earth. What keeps the myth that SSC policies endanger freedom and well-being alive, however, is the will of powerful actors to maintain current power relations. Hence, they uphold the perception that SSC policies are inacceptable.

But what does power have to do with consumption? Power is fundamental to consumption governance because it shapes who makes decisions about systems of production and consumption, how these decisions are made and whose interests are prioritised (Fuchs et al., 2016; Stör, 2017): Who sets the agenda, who defines the rules, and who controls the narratives around (sustainable) consumption and lifestyles? Mostly, this power lies in the hands of corporate actors who control production, and the investors owning these corporations. In an economy dominated by mass production of cheap goods, producing and selling as much as possible is the basis for making profit and thus the primary interest of these actors. Accordingly, they need individuals to (over-)consume. Less consumption would equate to less growth. To maintain and continuously increase consumption levels, actors with non-sustainable vested interests thus create narratives around the connection of well-being and material consumption and push for WSC policies.

This already shows that limiting consumption would contradict its economic functions in growth-oriented societies. However, consumption also has a social function, best captured in the concepts of conspicuous and compensatory consumption. Understanding this social function is also crucial to understanding the powerful bases of the myth addressed in this chapter.

Conspicuous consumption is an idea coined by the American economist and sociologist Thorstein Veblen in his widely known book *The Theory of the Leisure Class* (1899) that refers to the purchase of goods or services for the specific purpose of displaying one's wealth and social status. Often these are easily recognisable as expensive items, such as the latest technology, high-end cars and luxury accessories. If consumption was limited, those consuming most excessively as part of their lifestyle would be affected the most as they would lose a means to show off their affluence. The fact that this dynamic already existed in 1899, when Veblen developed the concept, illustrates how deeply rooted it is. Strong sustainability would precisely imply tackling inequities in resources, resource use and power. The benefits of growth have been distributed extremely unevenly, with material benefits of growth accruing mostly to those with existing wealth and high levels of overconsumption, and many of the poorest members of global societies becoming effectively poorer. However, powerful, affluent actors naturally try to maintain their powerful position and continue consuming conspicuously. For less affluent parts of society, this excessive consumption is perceived as desirable to signal success in increasing social competition. This dynamic contributed to the creation of the myth by promoting the idea that limiting consumption inherently threatens social mobility and the demonstration of status.

Compensatory consumption is another function in growth-oriented societies. In a system where the growth imperative is inscribed not only in the profit margins of companies but also in narratives of continuous self-improvement, performance and personal growth in every area of life, consumption serves as a means to achieving these. This link helps explain why reducing consumption is perceived as a threat to well-being, thereby contributing to the myth. But why does consumption lead to perceived self-fulfilment? As working hours and demands are ever-increasing and ever-flexible, they co-opt more and more of our time, leaving less time and energy for other non-consumptive activities that would contribute to personal well-being (Schor, 1991). In this system, consumption is a fast reward – treat yourself! On the other hand, limiting consumption in the social and economic system we currently live in is therefore likely to expose people to the negative psychological impacts of unsatisfactory conditions, alienated relationships and the ever-increasing demands in growth societies.

These functions of consumption are coupled with a specific interpretation of freedom that is just as well strongly connected to the logics of a growth- and efficiency-oriented system. The idea of freedom as unlimited consumption choices and volumes forms an important part of the dominant narrative of what makes a good life. Freedom forms a central value in neo-liberal, growth-oriented democracies. Neo-liberalism in particular is characterised by the focus on individual freedoms to shape one's life according to one's own preferences (Wissenburg, 2001). While the autonomy of the individual is emphasised, neo-liberalism interprets social, state, intellectual or political rules and regulations as coercion. Even limiting one's own preferences for the sake of the environment is understood as coercion. This is because the neo-liberal mainstream defines freedom as the absence of physically coercive interventions or intrusions into the privacy and personal property of individuals (Dierksmeier, 2019) – a definition that is characterised above all by non-interference. For the idea of a good life, this would accordingly imply an infinity of one's own freedom and choices. The connection of the myth with this idea of freedom, in particular, is often what makes people argue that SSC policies are too controversial.

Assessing limits on behavioural options as an encroachment on personal freedom is consistent with the impression that boundlessness seems to characterise our society. The mantra 'further, faster, higher, bigger' shows how we are in the throes of a growth addiction. On an individual level, this manifests itself in the constant growth of the goods we own and the pursuit of a steady wealth accumulation. In social and economic terms, it is reflected in the commitment of states worldwide to the goal of GDP growth, seen as a central indicator of the well-being of society. Yet, GDP disregards important – even economic – components such as the distribution of inequality, while at the same time, it is rising due to the industrial destruction of the environment.

The existence of such narratives around consumption and associated definitions of freedom, the influence of vested interests, which maintain these narratives for the sake of their own power, the inscription of the economic growth paradigm in social relations, political priorities, and everyday life, all these deep barriers reinforce each other and lock in the myth that SSC policies endanger freedom and well-being (Hirth et al., 2023). The opportunities and potentials of SSC policies for an economy that foregrounds societal well-being are neglected as it challenges existing power relations. The idea of individual well-being that results from these barriers strongly opposes visions of sufficiency, on which SSC policies would be built. Hence, such policies are perceived and framed as unacceptable even though they would lead to a higher quality of life for all and reduced social inequality.

13.3 Consequences

The maintenance of this powerful myth has major consequences on consumption and provisioning systems. Most importantly, relying on WSC policies and shying away from SSC governance manifests the systemic lock-in that drives current ecological crises and the widening of social gaps. *Holistic provisioning systems* would sustainably mediate how resources are extracted and transformed into the material and cultural things that contribute to needs satisfaction (O'Neill et al., 2018). Instead, what we see is *appropriating systems* that focus on rent-seeking (Kreinin et al., 2024a). The food system could for example be set up in a way that ensures everybody is provided the alimentation they need to thrive. Instead, it is driven by profit-seeking: from the total global food system supply chain, only 19% of the aggregate profits are captured by producers and traders, while food manufacturers and distributors capture more than half of the total profits (54%). It is therefore not surprising that the very workers who provide much of our food, particularly from the Global South, are the most food insecure and malnourished (Planet Tracker, 2023). In the following, we will break down the consequences of the myth with regard to policymakers, economic actors and citizens respectively.

For policymakers, the myth causes reluctance to implement or even suggest SSC policies. The consequence is a lack of stringent, holistic, predictable, consistent policies. Very few SSC policies are actually in place. Instead, policymakers keep prolonging policies, which are curing emerging problems superficially, but hindering strategic developments for systemic change, which would necessarily address socio-economic power relations.

The mobility transition provides an example of this. In many countries, particularly in Germany, where the car lobby is especially powerful, a fundamental transition was largely prevented and instead left to industry, resulting in far too large electric cars with an undersupply of charging technology. Still, the promotion of (large) electric cars is framed as sustainable, while in fact neither the policy approach is consistent regarding the increased needs for provision of charging technology nor does it actually have a positive environmental impact (Font et al., 2021). At the same time, investments in internal combustion engine vehicles are prolonged while rethinking and reorganising mobility, for example, by investing in public transport and bike infrastructure, is hardly considered.

This illustrates that while sustainability seems to be everywhere – in every policy justification, on every packaging, and in every e-SUV – only weak sustainability that focuses on enhancing efficiency instead of reducing the sheer amount of consumption is considered by policymakers. The Circular Economy Action Plan provides another example of this. It was developed by the European Commission in 2020 with the aim of increasing recycling rates, promoting product longevity and reducing waste. However, while recycling rates have improved, absolute material consumption continues to rise as rebound effects stimulate more consumption and production. This underlines the inadequacy of approaches that only focus on technological change, yet overlook and neglect the need for behaviour change enabled by reshaping the structural context of practices.

Still, such policies are framed as being 'sustainable'. Sustainability governance has thus become ubiquitous. This paradox is also referred to as *sustained unsustainability* (Blühdorn, 2016): a high level of sustainability-related activity is secured through politics that actually sustain unsustainability without challenging socio-economic structures and power relations. Hausknost (2017) suggests that this association of political legitimacy with economic growth and material well-being of those with the most powerful voices forms a *glass ceiling* to truly deep socio-ecological transformation. The glass ceiling describes the dilemma that, on the one hand, state action is seen as essential for socio-environmental transformation, but, on the other hand, for more transformative state action to be possible, it is first necessary to gain broader democratic legitimacy for a sustainability imperative over the growth imperative. This is difficult, however, because consumption-oriented lifestyles are currently perceived as non-negotiable imperatives for democratic legitimacy and state stability (Kreinin et al., 2024b). The myth that SSC policies threaten well-being, which makes them unacceptable, is both a symptom of, and reinforces, sustained unsustainability and the glass ceiling – a vicious cycle that deeply curtails the room for manoeuvre for actual strong sustainability governance.

For the market economy and economic actors, the myth and its interaction with the paradigm of sustained unsustainability, creates a paradoxical position. On the one hand, it is precisely this market economy of growth that has swallowed sustainability: WSC policies follow the capitalist market logics of consumerism, profit-orientation and efficiency. In line with these logics, sustainable consumption is individualised, privatised and de-politicised. On the other hand, economic actors tend to evade their immense responsibility for unsustainability. Instead of rethinking ways of production in order to enable needs-oriented provisioning systems, they participate in a *responsibility ping-pong* with other actors (Mamut et al., 2025). Instead of using their power to change unsustainable structures, economic actors primarily ascribe responsibility to others than themselves, which leads to the diffusion of responsibility and collective failure with regard to the sustainability transformation.

These dynamics seem even more paradoxical with regard to the logical dependence of capitalist actors on environmental and social resources that are continuously depleted through unsustainable practices. While most business models critically depend on stable ecosystems and societal support, their practices contribute to global warming, pollution, and social unrest – ultimately undermining the very foundations of long-term economic stability and human well-being (Fraser, 2022). This strongly underlines the fact that WSC policies, following the growth- and profit-orientation that is built into capitalism, do in fact endanger well-being.

For citizens and consumers, government inaction, faith in technological solutions and growth-oriented narratives around the good life and individual freedom cause confusion and scepticism regarding the necessity of SSC governance (Lorenzoni et al., 2007). In reality though, weak sustainability puts most pressure on individual consumers. The fragmentation and avoidance of responsibility perpetuate and deepen socio-ecological injustices: It superficially holds consumers responsible for systemic outcomes over which they, as individuals, have only very limited control, while differentiated responsibilities for the climate catastrophe, as well as differences in the power of actors, are relegated to the background (Fuchs et al., 2021).

In addition, despite the fact that societies over-produce and over-consume almost all goods on the market to such an extent that we are confronted with the consequences of human activity on the environment and the limits of finite resources (Richardson et al., 2023; Sanye Mengual & Sala, 2023), many people still grapple with a lack of access to necessary resources. Today, 8.5% of the world's population lives in extreme poverty (less than $2.15 per person per day) and, at a poverty line more relevant to upper-middle-income countries (less than $6.85 per person per day), 44% of the world's population lives in poverty (World Bank, 2024). This is a crucial problem of weak sustainability that is not in line with sustainable provisioning but with growth-orientation. While on the one hand in the current system, most consumers are expected to spend as much money as possible on consumption, on the other hand, it is not even guaranteed that all people will have access to the necessary services and products to meet their needs at all. Social inequities are increasingly reinforced, with many people struggling to satisfy their most basic needs and suffering from the negative effects of environmental degradation – for example, people living in low-income communities or near coastlines being more vulnerable to flooding, severe storms, and sea level rise – while a few, particularly the affluent and powerful, are responsible for the vast majority of emissions, resource depletion and ecological crises (Dorninger et al., 2021). Paradoxically, given that WSC policies often are about adjusting pricing mechanisms, which put a special burden on the poorest, most vulnerable parts of population, this enforces the myth that well-being is necessarily curtailed because of sustainability governance. Besides, the overemphasis on material over-consumption entirely neglects other aspects of well-being, such as community, engagement with nature and a sense of purpose. As a result, instead of enabling well-being, WSC policies push the good life for all further and further away.

13.4 Dispelling the myth

As we have shown, the origins and consequences of the myth that SSC policies endanger well-being and would therefore not be accepted are in close interaction, mutually reinforcing themselves. This implies that, in the current system – within the deeply ingrained structures, the current power relations and the prevailing ideas of well-being – there *is* some truth at the heart of the myth. The question therefore is not only how to dispel the myth but also how to transform the very system that produces it.

13.4.1 Quality of life depends on the satisfaction of human needs

Quality of life, first and foremost, depends on the satisfaction of human needs. While many factors may influence life satisfaction, such as comparison to other people, life events, subjective and wishes. '[N]eeds are absolute demands for human functioning that do not adjust to any and all conditions; in fact, they mark the limits of human adaptability' (Veenhoven, 1996, p. 23). As argued in Chapter 8, we can identify needs – access to material necessities for life, a sense of belonging to some form of community, bodily health, etc. – that are universal to every human being across cultures and historical periods.

What does this mean for the myth that SSC policies endanger well-being and will therefore never be accepted? It shows very clearly that focusing on human needs is, in fact, decisive for sustainability policies to support well-being. Subjective preferences do play an important role in individual well-being. Still, not every want actually enhances well-being, nor is their satisfaction compatible with the satisfaction of others' needs. Therefore, governance should be directed in such a way that it enhances societal well-being and, thereby, also individual well-being. This requires a universal point of reference: the needs we share as humans. In a world with limited resources, this shines a light on the conditions that allow for the satisfaction of universal needs for everyone, bringing the principle of sufficiency into focus.

Contrary to the myth, SSC governance that focuses on these conditions, which are the basis for individual as well as societal well-being, is exactly what is needed in order to support well-being. Policies promoting free or subsidised plant-based meals in public institutions, as for example the 'Barcelona + Sustainable Food' strategy, reduce environmental impact, which benefits future generations and secures their well-being, while promoting health and aligning with the basic need for nutritious and sufficient food for present generations. Beyond providing sustainable meals, the strategy ensures food security by making healthy food accessible to all, supports local farmers and sustainable agriculture and fosters food literacy. By addressing health, equity and ecological sustainability, it demonstrates how SSC policies can meet universal human needs while countering the myth that they threaten well-being.

13.4.2 Freedom results from agency

Despite what the neo-liberal, growth-oriented mainstream would have us believe, freedom cannot be understood solely as non-interference, nor does it necessarily result from unrestrained overconsumption. As we have seen, the latter can rather be described as a symptom of the growth-dependent system we live in. Instead of relying solely on quantitative and non-interference approaches to freedom, it can also be understood through a qualitative lens that focuses on agency instead of the sheer availability of options.

Dierksmeier (2019) contrasts quantitative freedom with 'qualitative freedom', which focuses on the nature of options, while Pettit (2003) uses the term 'agency freedom', which is determined by the recognised, protected status of a person in relation to their fellow citizens. These conceptions show that in addition to the number of options, criteria such as human dignity, rationality, universality and autonomy must also be considered in connection with freedom. Moreover, these conceptions introduce the idea that a distinction can be made between meaningful freedoms, such as democratic freedom of expression, and less meaningful freedoms, such as driving without speed limits. Non-restrictive overconsumption might, therefore, be less meaningful and less critical for well-being than, for example, the freedom to participate in democratic practices. Moreover, these notions show that freedom is never a purely individual matter. Unless you live on a desert island, you always articulate yourself interacting with other people. This is why well-being, as well as freedom, must always be seen as societal issues – an important acknowledgement that the myth lacks. Lastly, Dierksmeier and Pettit underline that decision-making power for – or against – certain actions is the highest expression of freedom. In this context, Cheryl Hall (2010) argues that 'sacrifice' in the sense of voluntarily restricting one's own quantitative freedom, that is, deliberate acts of renunciation, also represents an act of freedom. A sacrifice means giving up something important to us for something else that is even more important. However, we only sacrifice something voluntarily, which in turn underlines the connection to agency (Gumbert & Bohn, 2021).

Progressive Energy Pricing, such as California's Tiered Electricity Rates, provides an example of a policy that balances freedom and strong sustainability. What 'progressive' means in this context is that electricity prices increase as consumption rises. This policy discourages excessive energy use while ensuring basic needs remain affordable. Another example is Paris' Vélib' System, a heavily subsidised bike-sharing program. Such subsidies, combined with investments in cycling infrastructure, encourage sustainable mobility while preserving individual freedom of transport choice. Citizens are enabled to voluntarily reduce or give up car use, which, in turn, increases their health, improves air quality and reduces energy consumption, while preserving freedom.

The point is not to deny the legitimacy of quantitative aspects of freedom per se. However, limiting oneself to this perspective is insufficient, as is often the case regarding the prevalent narrative around individual freedom. The complexity of the social world requires a perspective on freedom that combines quantitative and qualitative elements. Such an interpretation of freedom, which can grasp its different forms in different situations, seems much more compatible with a good life for all than the concept of boundlessness described before. Freedom is a cornerstone of democracy, as liberalism rightly emphasises, but the question arises about *what kind of* freedom (Becker & Fuchs, 2023). A reduction of freedom to the sheer number of options available ignores essential aspects of human interaction and interdependencies with our non-human environment. Freedom mainly results from agency, not from non-restrictive overconsumption, which is why the myth around SSC policies endangering individual freedom falls short. Active participation in discourses and practices concerning sustainable policies or local projects, such as local greening, community-supported farming or local deliberative citizen assemblies, on the other hand, perfectly correspond to the idea of agency-freedom: They involve utilising personal freedom to exert democratic influence and help shape society in the interests of the common good.

13.4.3 Sustainable welfare increases quality of life while decreasing environmental pressure

An important aspect of an SSC governance approach resides in the design of welfare systems. Especially from a holistic provisioning perspective, welfare plays a crucial role, both for staying within planetary boundaries and for increasing societal and individual well-being. In fact, the powerful role of deep structural barriers, as pointed out in the 'Origins' section, becomes particularly visible with regard to welfare systems. They are designed to depend on and reinforce economic growth by stimulating consumption (Laksevics et al., 2025). Their transformation towards the satisfaction of basic needs is, therefore, crucial. This is particularly the case with regard to justice aspects. On the one hand, the gap between the rich and the poor leads to worsening environmental degradation and ecological crises that affect every member of a community, while on the other hand, the negative impact of ecological crises is most pronounced for the most disadvantaged parts of society and, therefore, increases inequalities. Historically, social and environmental goals have often been treated as separate, sometimes conflicting, objectives – a dichotomy that is largely mirrored within current polarisation and harsh discussions around sustainability. However, well-designed ecosocial welfare policies following the notion of strong sustainability and devoted to enabling a good life for all, such as income ceilings or universal basic services, can, in fact, reduce inequality and increase quality of life while decreasing emissions (Kallis et al., 2025).

Implementing universal basic services (UBS), such as healthcare, education and housing, often comes up as a promising measure to address the unequal distribution of such basic services, with more affluent parts of the population over-exploiting resources, while others have inadequate access to them. UBS can thus be regarded as an essential measure that prevents increasing inequalities. Providing citizens with a wide range of public services to meet their basic needs also reduces the need for individuals to purchase these services from private, often more resource-intensive providers, and lessens their reliance on employment for accessing basic necessities (Gough, 2019). The positive ecological effects are particularly evident with regard to free public transport, which is generally seen as part of UBS. If people are generally provided with the universal opportunity to access public transport, the reliance on private vehicles shrinks drastically (Holmgren, 2020).

Income ceilings and wealth taxes are examples of complementary policies that tackle socio-ecological inequalities by directly targeting the wealthiest. Such measures can reduce excessive consumption and limit the carbon footprint of the wealthiest individuals who often engage in – particularly conspicuous as well as polluting – luxury consumption while also promoting a fairer distribution of resources (Buch-Hansen & Koch, 2019).

Further measures that could be implemented in order to create a sustainable, needs-oriented welfare state through SSC governance could be work time reduction, job guarantee, and renovation programs for the least energy-efficient buildings (Laksevics et al., 2025). All of these policies aim to foster societal well-being and decrease environmental harm in an ecosocial manner. They necessarily form an important part of any strong sustainability governance approach which clearly shows the deficiencies of the myth around SSC policies.

13.4.4 *Addressing specific barriers can increase the acceptability of strong sustainable consumption policies*

While SSC policies do interfere with neo-liberal narratives around governance as well as well-being and, therefore, undoubtedly do challenge what citizens are used to in terms of politics, research shows that the acceptability of such policies can be increased if specific conditions for acceptance are acknowledged.

As pointed out in Chapter 8, policy acceptability can be increased through the discussion of sustainable lifestyles with other people. Participants tended to shift from lower to higher acceptance rates as their reservations were challenged through collective dialogue and deliberation.

Moreover, specific conditions for acceptance of sustainable lifestyle options can be identified. The most critical barriers to adoption – and, reciprocally, factors for acceptance – are (1) costs, (2) convenience and accessibility, (3) cultural attachments and societal norms, (4) lack of awareness and misinformation and (5) consumption in field-specific conditions such as health concerns (Vadovics et al., 2024).

While these factors currently often form barriers that hinder people from adopting sustainable lifestyle options, an SSC governance approach would reflect on and put into place the necessary infrastructures and implement adequate supporting policies. At the same time, it would consider these barriers and turn them into factors for acceptance. Meat substitutes, electric vehicles, housing and energy improvements like installing heat pumps or solar panels would be guaranteed to be affordable. Public transport would be made no less convenient than car use. Educational campaigns, promoting new norms and narratives around the good life and providing transparent information would be developed. This would share positive experiences of plant-based diets and raise awareness of the environmental impact of air travel. Concerns about insufficient nutrition connected to diet change or on technical performance for electric vehicles would be addressed constructively. Acceptability hinges on such specific conditions, which can and must be addressed. If this is the case, then governance with a focus on well-being is indeed likely to be highly acceptable.

What is more, in a different system where scientific knowledge on environmental issues is widely accessible, and environmental education and first-hand interactions with nature are part of everyday life, acceptance of policies that reduce absolute consumption levels would likely be much higher. Over time, as communities and shared values take centre stage, such policies might eventually become unnecessary. The strength of a strong sustainability governance approach is that bringing about the transformation to such a system is inherently built into it as it is aimed at societal well-being on a large scale.

13.4.5 *Effective societal deliberation is needed for the implementation of strong sustainable consumption governance*

It is often argued that SSC policies are too controversial to be taken up. In fact, it is true that strong sustainability governance is controversial. It challenges power relations, prevailing practices and dominant narratives about individual freedom and well-being, which necessarily makes it controversial. Anything with a transformative scope is bound to be controversial. We would not need transformation if such policies could be easily agreed upon. It is precisely because of this that we argue that societal conflict and controversy are essential for disruptive politics.

As Amanda Machin (2023: 849) argues, '[D]isagreement in environmental politics allows alternative futures to be imagined, articulated, negotiated, and demanded, and it prevents the foreclosure of political questions around climate change'. How should we be able to come to new ideas about what society looks like if we do not have controversial discussions that bring out the different ideas people have about a just and socio-ecological future? The literature on agonal (conflictual) democracy has widely highlighted the value and relevance of conflict and dissent in pluralistic societies if the emancipatory potential of democracy is to be realised (Mouffe, 1995). Even political thinkers who do not start from the assumption that politics is necessarily about conflict, as agonal democrats do, have emphasised the need to provide space for 'reasonable disagreement' (Bohn & Fuchs, 2019). Too narrow an orientation towards consensus might conceal existing conflicts and suppress marginalised ideas, interests or identities (Young, 1996).

So, should we instead think of conflict than of dialogue, communication and deliberation? What it rather means is that the successful implementation of SSC policies requires exactly the combination of both. Driving truly deep transformation is possible through collective action systems engaging in systemic, society-wide deliberation that consciously addresses political disagreement rather than hiding it behind superficial consensus. Overcoming deep-seated barriers to transformation and addressing power imbalances requires highly engaging forms of deliberation. Harnessing both dialogue and contestation to create a more inclusive and resilient political process can provide a way forward for this.

Apart from accommodating conflictual elements into discussions and deliberations on sustainability, the good life and societal well-being, acknowledging the need for disagreement for change also implies supporting practices that challenge the unsustainable status quo, such as social movements, strategic climate litigation and civil disobedience. Only the combination of different democratic practices can enable a deep-cutting change that prioritises societal well-being over economic growth. This is sure to lead to controversial discussions, but that is exactly what is needed for an effective transformation to take place.

13.5 Implications

So, what to do? The previous chapters have offered a range of suggestions for new practices, solutions that can and should be implemented as we move towards a world that prioritises societal well-being and inspiration from examples around the world that show how change is already happening. Given the broad focus of this chapter, many of these hopeful implications could be repeated and underlined here. Instead, focusing on the *how* of the transformation, we want to point out three crucial strategies that are essential for bringing about these changes and for debunking myths around sustainable consumption.

First, policymakers, businesses and individual citizens and consumers should begin looking at the transformation ahead in terms of shared responsibility. This represents a balanced approach that recognises the intertwined roles of multiple actors and acknowledges that those with greater capabilities bear special responsibilities (Young, 2011). Looking forward, we must embrace a more holistic, interconnected understanding of responsibility that fosters transformative change through multi-level collaboration and recognises current power imbalances (Mamut et al., 2025). Encouragingly, we already see examples of this emerging – such as European cities implementing participatory climate budgeting, where citizens have a direct role in shaping local sustainability policies. These initiatives demonstrate that shared responsibility is not an abstract ideal but an evolving reality. As outlined before, this particularly demands a combination of agonistic (conflictual) and deliberative (communicative) elements in the public sphere. A starting point for this lies in critically scrutinising any narrative that puts all responsibility on individual consumers – a narrative that should be dispelled once and for all.

Second, a deep integration of social justice and ecological sustainability is needed. Far too often, social and environmental policies have been regarded as separate, even conflicting sectors. The solution cannot lie in playing out different policy sectors against one another. As we have shown, SSC governance that holistically reflects on resources and needs for a good life for all is necessarily socio-ecological. Initiatives such as the Wellbeing Economy Governments (WEGo) partnership – comprising Scotland, New Zealand, Finland and others – show that governments can shift policy priorities beyond GDP growth towards holistic societal well-being. These efforts demonstrate that integrating social and ecological concerns is not just possible but already happening. For any stakeholder engaging in discussions and actions around sustainability and sustainable consumption, this implies questioning exclusive framings that only include either ecological or social aspects. Often, these two go hand in hand, and if they do not, then the idea in question should be re-evaluated from a holistic standpoint.

Third, while SSC governance clearly demands a responsible democratic state that addresses barriers to transformation, prioritises societal well-being over economic growth and creates structures that enable sustainable consumption and provisioning, change does not only come from this level. Throughout the different chapters, multiple successful examples from local practices have been introduced. For instance, experiments with reduced working hours in Sweden and Iceland have not only improved worker well-being but also contributed to sustainability by reducing energy use and consumption. Similarly, city-level policies in Paris and Amsterdam that reduce car dependency through expanded cycling infrastructure and pedestrian-friendly planning provide scalable models for rethinking urban mobility. While it will certainly take many consistent and interlinked actions to change entrenched social structures, practical experimental spaces that take the first steps in this direction can provide valuable insights while preparing the ground on a small scale for more comprehensive change. Moreover, local action can also foster trust and increase acceptability for larger scale SSC governance. Hence, any policymaker, business and individual can think of their realm of action and try to implement sustainable practices within the scope that seems feasible to them. The welfare states of Northern Europe already offer broader systemic examples of how strong state capacity, public infrastructure and redistribution mechanisms can support sustainable lifestyles in ways that are both just and effective. While they are not without contradictions, these models illustrate that prioritising collective well-being through policy design is not utopian but achievable. Social change comes from all directions.

By drawing attention to these real-world examples, we underscore that SSC governance is not just a theoretical aspiration but also a tangible, evolving process. While challenges remain, emerging practices show that transformation is already underway and can be expanded, adapted and institutionalised.

13.6 Main message

This chapter has shown that current power relations and the profit interests those with power pursue foster only WSC governance and perpetuate a system that moves further and further away from the potential for an effective sustainability transformation and a good life for all. SSC policies, on the contrary, can enhance societal and individual well-being by moving societies towards a more inclusive and resilient quality of life. Doing so, such an approach necessarily challenges hegemonic paradigms as it confronts limitless consumption and signifiers of 'status' as the essence of quality of life, related definitions of 'freedom', as well as entrenched narratives of growth. Rather, it focuses on alternative ideas of freedom and well-being that underline the role of agency as well as a good life for all, living now and in the future. Especially if given attention to affordability, convenience and accessibility, the focus of SSC policies on well-being and qualitative freedom is precisely what makes this governance approach acceptable. Nevertheless, our discussion has also shown the deeply ingrained sources of the myth that strong sustainable consumption policies endanger freedom and well-being and will therefore never be accepted by people. Challenging it successfully thus requires an effective and inclusive political and societal debate as a force for creating an understanding for what is necessary and feasible in the pursuit of a world worth living for all of us, now and in the future.

Acknowledgements

Funding for this work benefited from the European Union's Horizon 2020 research and innovation programme in the context of the *EU 1.5° Lifestyles* project. The sole responsibility for the content of this article lies with the authors. We would like to thank the *EU 1.5° Lifestyles* consortium and its advisory board for their expertise, ideas and contributions to the project.

References

Becker, L., & Fuchs, D. (2023). Freiheit, ja – aber welche? Zum Verhältnis zwischen Freiheit, Gerechtigkeit und einem guten Leben. *AMOS International*, *17*(3), 14–20.

Blühdorn, I. (2016). Sustainability – Post-sustainability – Unsustainability. In T. Gabrielson (Ed.), *The Oxford handbook of environmental political theory* (pp. 259–273). Oxford University Press.

Bohn, C., & Fuchs, D. (2019). Partizipative transformation? – Die zentrale Rolle politischer Urteilsbildung für nachhaltigkeitsorientierte Partizipation in liberalen (Post-) Demokratien. In C. Bohn, D. Fuchs, A. Kerkhoff, & C. Müller (Eds.), *Gegenwart und Zukunft sozialökologischer Transformation* (pp. 77–100). Nomos.

Brand, U., & Wissen, M. (2021). *The imperial mode of living. Everyday life and the ecological crisis of capitalism*. Verso.

Buch-Hansen, H., & Koch, M. (2019). Degrowth through income and wealth caps? *Ecological Economics*, *160*, 264–271. https://doi.org/10.1016/j.ecolecon.2019.03.001

Cap, S., de Koning, A., Tukker, A., & Scherer, L. (2024). (In)Sufficiency of industrial decarbonization to reduce household carbon footprints to 1.5°C-compatible levels. *Sustainable Production and Consumption*, *45*, 216–227. https://doi.org/10.1016/j.spc.2023.12.031

Dierksmeier, C. (2019). *Qualitative freedom – Autonomy in cosmopolitan responsibility*. Springer. https://link.springer.com/book/10.1007/978-3-030-04723-8

Dorninger, C., Hornborg, A., Abson, D. J., Von Wehrden, H., Schaffartzik, A., Giljum, S., Engler, J.-O., Feller, R. L., Hubacek, K., & Wieland, H. (2021). Global patterns of ecologically unequal exchange: Implications for sustainability in the 21st century. *Ecological Economics*, *179*, 106824. https://doi.org/10.1016/j.ecolecon.2020.106824

Font Vivanco, D., Nechifor, V., Freire-González, J., & Calzadilla, A. (2021). Economy-wide rebound makes UK's electric car subsidy fall short of expectations. *Applied Energy*, *297*, 117138. https://doi.org/10.1016/j.apenergy.2021.117138

Fraser, N. (2022). *Cannibal capitalism: How our system is devouring democracy, care, and the planet – and what we can do about it*. Verso Books.

Fuchs, D., Di Giulio, A., Glaab, K., Lorek, S., Maniates, M., Princen, T., & Røpke, I. (2016). Power: The missing element in sustainable consumption and absolute

reductions research and action. *Journal of Cleaner Production*, *132*, 298–307. https://doi.org/10.1016/j.jclepro.2015.02.006
Fuchs, D., & Lorek, S. (2005). Sustainable consumption governance: A history of promises and failures. *Journal of Consumer Policy*, *28*(3), 261–288. https://doi.org/10.1007/s10603-005-8490-z
Fuchs, D., Steinberger, J., Pirgmaier, E., Lamb, W., Brand-Correa, L., Mattioli, G., & Cullen, J. (2021). A corridors and power-oriented perspective on energy-service demand and needs satisfaction. *Sustainability: Science, Practice and Policy*, *17*(1), 162–172. https://doi.org/10.1080/15487733.2021.1912907
Gough, I. (2019). Universal basic services: A theoretical and moral framework. *The Political Quarterly*, *90*(3), 534–542. https://doi.org/10.1111/1467-923X.12706
Gumbert, T., & Bohn, C. (2021). Are liberal objections to consumption corridors justified? On the relation of freedom and limits in green liberal thought. *Sustainability: Science, Practice and Policy*, *17*(1), 90–101. https://doi.org/10.1080/15487733.2021.1878733
Hall, C. (2010). Freedom, values, and sacrifice: Overcoming obstacles to environmentally sustainable behavior. In M. Maniates & J. Meyer (Eds.), *The environmental politics of sacrifice* (pp. 61–86). MIT Press.
Hausknost, D. (2017). Greening the Juggernaut? The modern state and the 'glass ceiling' of environmental transformation. In M. Domazet (Ed.), *Ecology and justice: Contributions from the margins* (pp. 49–76). Institute for Political Ecology.
Hirth, S., Kreinin, H., Fuchs, D., Blossey, N., Mamut, P., Philipp, J., Radovan, I., The EU 1.5° Lifestyles Consortium, Antal, O., Belousa, I., Bösch, M., Brizga, J., Bronstering, G., Dumitru, A., Langner, S., Laksevics, K., Leutermann, C., Klosterberg, C., Kramer, N., . . . Zsemberovszky, L. (2023). Barriers and enablers of 1.5° lifestyles: Shallow and deep structural factors shaping the potential for sustainable consumption. *Frontiers in Sustainability*, *4*. https://doi.org/10.3389/frsus.2023.1014662
Holmgren, J. (2020). The effect of public transport quality on car ownership – A source of wider benefits?. *Research in Transportation Economics*, *83*, 100957. https://doi.org/10.1016/j.retrec.2020.100957
Kallis, G., Hickel, J., O'Neill, D., Jackson, T., Victor, P., Raworth, K. Schor, J., Steinberger, J., & Ürge-Vorsatz, D. (2025). Post-growth: The science of wellbeing within planetary boundaries. *The Lancet Planetary Health*, *9*(1), e62–e78.
Kreinin, H., Fuchs, D., Mamut, P., Hirth, S., & Lange, S. (2024a). Transforming provisioning systems to enable 1.5° lifestyles in Europe? Expert and stakeholder views on overcoming structural barriers. *Sustainability: Science, Practice and Policy*, *20*(1), 2372120. https://doi.org/10.1080/15487733.2024.2372120
Kreinin, H., Mamut, P., & Fuchs, D. (2024b). The 'glass ceiling' of Germany's socio-ecological transformation: Citizen, expert, and local stakeholder perspectives on responsibility for change. *Zeitschrift für Politikwissenschaft*, *34*, 273–293. https://doi.org/10.1007/s41358-024-00383-9
Laksevics, K., Brizga, J., Mamut, P., Kreinin, H., Fuchs, D., & Belousa, I. (2025). An eco-social policy mix for 1.5°C lifestyles: A multi-country policy Delphi analysis. *Regulation & Governance*. https://doi.org/10.1111/rego.12655
Lorenzoni, I., Nicholson-Cole, S., & Whitmarsh, L. (2007). Barriers perceived to engaging with climate change among the UK public and their policy implications. *Global Environmental Change*, *17*(3), 445–459. https://doi.org/10.1016/j.gloenvcha.2007.01.004
Machin, A. (2023). Democracy, agony, and rupture: A critique of climate citizens' assemblies. *Politische Vierteljahresschrift*, *64*(4), 845–864. https://doi.org/10.1007/s11615-023-00455-5

Mamut, P., Fuchs, D., Becker, L., Laksevics, K., Kreinin, H., & Brizga, J. (2025). From responsibility ping-pong to shared responsibility for 1.5° lifestyles? Examining European stakeholder perspectives. *Consumption and Society*, *4*(1), 33–54. https://doi.org/10.1332/27528499Y2024D000000039

Mouffe, C. (1995). Democracy and pluralism: A critique of the rationalist approach. *Cardozo Law Review*, *16*(5), 1533–1546.

O'Neill, D. W., Fanning, A. L., Lamb, W. F., & Steinberger, J. K. (2018). A good life for all within planetary boundaries. *Nature Sustainability*, *1*(2), 88–95. https://doi.org/10.1038/s41893-018-0021-4

Ott, K., & Döring, R. (2004). *Theorie und Praxis starker Nachhaltigkeit*. Metropolis. https://www.econbiz.de/Record/theorie-und-praxis-starker-nachhaltigkeit-ott-konrad/10002161032

Pettit, P. (2003). Agency-freedom and option-freedom. *Journal of Theoretical Politics*, *15*(4), 387–403.

Planet Tracker. (2023). *Financial markets roadmap for transforming the global food system*. https://planet-tracker.org/wp-content/uploads/2023/03/Financial-Markets-Roadmap-for-transforming-the-Global-Food-System.pdf

Richardson, K., Steffen, W., Lucht, W., Bendtsen, J., Cornell, S. E., Donges, J. F., Drüke, M., Fetzer, I., Bala, G., Von Bloh, W., Feulner, G., Fiedler, S., Gerten, D., Gleeson, T., Hofmann, M., Huiskamp, W., Kummu, M., Mohan, C., Nogués-Bravo, D., . . . Rockström, J. (2023). Earth beyond six of nine planetary boundaries. *Science Advances*, *9*(37), eadh2458. https://doi.org/10.1126/sciadv.adh2458

Sanye Mengual, E., & Sala, S. (2023). Consumption footprint and domestic footprint: Assessing the environmental impacts of EU consumption and production: Life cycle assessment to support the European Green Deal. *Publications Office of the European Union*. https://data.europa.eu/doi/10.2760/218540

Schor, J. B. (1991). *The overworked American: The unexpected decline of leisure*. Basic Books.

Spangenberg, J. H., & Lorek, S. (2019): Sufficiency and consumer behaviour: From theory to policy. *Energy Policy*, *129*, 1070–1079. https://doi.org/10.1016/j.enpol.2019.03.013

Stör, L. (2017). Theories of power. In *Routledge handbook of ecological economics*. Routledge.

Vadovics, E., Richter, J. L., Tornow, M., Ozcelik, N., Coscieme, L., Lettenmeier, M., Csiki, E., Domröse, L., Cap, S., Puente, L. L., Belousa, I., & Scherer, L. (2024). Preferences, enablers, and barriers for 1.5°C lifestyle options: Findings from citizen thinking labs in five European Union countries. *Sustainability: Science, Practice and Policy*, *20*(1), 2375806. https://doi.org/10.1080/15487733.2024.2375806

Veblen, T. (1899). *The theory of the leisure class*. Macmillan.

Veenhoven, R. (1996). The study of life satisfaction. In W. E. Saris, R. Veenhoven, A. C. Scherpenzeel, & B. Bunting (Eds.), *A comparative study of satisfaction with life in Europe* (pp. 11–48). Eötvös University Press.

Wissenburg, M. (2001). Sustainability and the Limits of Liberalism. In J. Barry & M. Wissenburg (Eds.), *Sustaining liberal democracy: Ecological challenges and opportunities*. Palgrave. https://link.springer.com/chapter/10.1057/9781403900791_12

World Bank. (2024). *Poverty, prosperity, and planet report 2024: Pathways out of the polycrisis*. https://openknowledge.worldbank.org/server/api/core/bitstreams/ed189cbd-46e7–4c9f-ab78-a68d50df5e67/content

Young, I. M. (1996). Communication and the other: Beyond deliberative democracy. In S. Benhabib (Ed.), *Democracy and difference: Contesting the boundaries of the political* (pp. 120–136). Princeton University Press.

Young, I. M. (2011). *Inclusion and democracy*. Oxford University Press.

PART IV

Pathways beyond myths

14

FROM MYTHS TO TRANSFORMATION

Oksana Mont

14.1 Breaking the spell

This book started with a simple question: why do everyday lives constantly demand more from the Earth than it can provide, despite growing awareness of ecological and social crises? Part of the answer lies in the stories that shape how problems are viewed, how their root causes are explained and where solutions are sought. We refer to these stories as myths – narratives that influence everyday thinking and behaviour. Unlike traditional tales, they seldom arise from collective storytelling; instead, they are formed through powerful interests in politics, business and media that benefit from propagating them. Their impact increases as they resonate in policy speeches, boardrooms and news outlets, where they come to be seen as common sense.

In this book, we aim to identify and systematically examine myths that hinder sustainable consumption. Each chapter addresses a specific myth, exploring its origins, analysing the consequences of accepting it at face value, considering counterarguments and discussing implications for governments, businesses and individuals. While each myth, when viewed in isolation, points to a single source of inertia, together they form a web of stories that support the unsustainable status quo. Comparing across chapters helps us understand the mechanisms behind the endurance of myths (while the emergence of myths was discussed in Chapter 1) and why they spread so readily across politics, business and everyday life.

Seen in this light, the unique contribution of a myth perspective becomes clearer when compared with other methods of analysing inertia. Lock-in, path dependency and political economy are well-established frameworks for explaining why unsustainable practices persist (Koch & Mont, 2016).

DOI: 10.4324/9781003613718-19

They focus on infrastructures, procedures and power relations that maintain existing systems. However, they do not fully account for the cultural narratives that make these systems appear legitimate and natural. Here, the concept of myth provides an additional viewpoint, one that not only exposes the limits of certain stories but also encourages critical reflection. It prompts us to ask: What is missing from this story? Who benefits from it? What might change if we ceased to believe it? This reflexive attitude is central to this book's aim: not merely to list myths but to enhance the capacity for critical questioning and to imagine alternative options.

In the next section, we turn from understanding the initial appeal of myths to the mechanisms that allow them to endure over time.

14.2 Why myths persist

The insights in this section draw on a cross-chapter analysis of the myths explored throughout the book. While each chapter highlighted the specific origins and persistence mechanisms of a particular myth, together they reveal broader, recurring patterns. What follows is an overview of interconnected mechanisms across culture, practices, institutions, psychology and politics that sustain and reproduce myths over time.

Cultural reinforcement. As discussed in Chapter 1, myths initially gain traction by resonating with commonly held values. Once established, myths are propagated through education, advertising, political speeches, and business communication. Cultural industries, from film and literature to social media, do not merely reflect existing myths but act as powerful vehicles for disseminating them widely, circulating and embedding them in the cultural imagination until they are experienced as self-evident (Barthes, 1957/2009). Advertising, influencer culture and corporate storytelling popularise myths of sustainable consumption by linking them to images of desirable lifestyles and aspirations. Then, broad ideals are reduced to simple, easily transferable proxies: 'status' becomes associated with high-paced, long-hours' work, and 'security' is equated with the consumption of surveillance products rather than safer communities. Well-being, for instance, is often narrowed to material comfort, conflating flourishing with quantitative measures – more options and more consumption – while overlooking qualitative aspects such as time, relationships, dignity, resilience and autonomy (Becker et al., in this volume). These proxies then embed into institutions, becoming part of routines, metrics and designs, which makes recognising and supporting alternative ways of realising these ideals more difficult. The connection to treasured values makes it challenging to oppose the myths, as critique can be seen as attacking the values themselves. Questioning such narratives often triggers defensive reactions designed to protect the myth from scrutiny.

Anchoring in everyday practices and material artefacts. According to the social practice theory, practices stabilise when meanings, skills and materials align, making them resilient to change (Shove et al., 2012). Myths endure because they become woven into these configurations and are enacted in the routines of everyday life. For example, the myth that 'services will dematerialise consumption' persists through infrastructures such as data centres, delivery fleets and platform technologies, combined with cultural meanings that portray the 'cloud' as immaterial and competencies of on-demand streaming and ride-hailing that normalise frequent use. Similarly, 'retail therapy' is reproduced not simply by individual preference but through shopping practices shaped by materials like frictionless checkouts and 'buy-now-pay-later' systems, meanings of self-care and comfort, and skills such as scrolling, unboxing and returning goods. The myth that 'more choice equals more freedom' is anchored in the practice of shopping itself, sustained by material environments like endless aisles or personalised digital platforms, by cultural meanings equating autonomy with options and by skills of constant searching and comparison. Finally, 'new beats repair' is reinforced by materials, such as sealed devices and proprietary fasteners that make repair physically difficult or impossible without specialised tools. At the same time, cultural meanings elevate novelty as a marker of modernity and social status, while competencies in repair have declined as once widespread skills, such as sewing, mending or repairing basic electronics, are no longer routinely taught or passed down. Through these alignments, myths become embedded in practices that are collectively reproduced, making them durable and resistant to critique. These examples highlight why myths are not just ideas but are enacted through social routines and infrastructures that generate real environmental consequences.

Institutional embedding. Myths are also perpetuated through established systems of governance, education and business practice. Innovation policies and funding regimes reward novelty, fostering credibility for techno-optimism and neophilia. GDP-focused policymaking solidifies growth as the main measure of success, making it difficult to envision or experiment with steady-state and post-growth ideas (Jackson, 2011). Discourses of consumer sovereignty circulate within business strategies and regulatory frameworks, reinforcing the notion that consumer demand drives sustainability transformation. Education systems often prioritise the transmission of information over knowledge co-creation, problem-solving, lifelong learning or critical reflection, thereby sustaining the belief that more information alone will change behaviour. In each of these ways, myths are enacted through institutional structures and routines: whenever a growth target is set, a curriculum is delivered, or a product is marketed, these narratives are reinforced and reproduced. Furthermore, myths gain further strength when institutionalised in organisational structures and policies. Meyer and Rowan (1977) described how organisations adopt 'myths and ceremonies' to maintain legitimacy, even where substantive change is limited. In sustainability, voluntary codes, corporate social responsibility reports and incremental efficiency standards often embody myths by signalling action without altering the underlying drivers of overconsumption. The idea that 'growth is good at any cost' is repeated in budget targets and news reports; the emphasis on individual responsibility for climate change is taught in schools and echoed in corporate and NGO campaigns.

Psychological appeal. Myths endure because they meet emotional needs and provide comfort by promising relief or control during stressful times: shopping can be seen as therapy, more choices as freedom, and visions of future leisure as hope despite current pressures. They also protect people from anxiety, shielding them from guilt or paralysis when faced with overwhelming sustainability crises (Norgaard, 2011). Simultaneously, myths simplify complexity. In a world overloaded with information and conflicting demands, myths act as mental shortcuts, saving effort by offering ready-made scripts rather than requiring constant reflection (Thaler & Sunstein, 2008). Through slogans and catchphrases, they distil complicated matters into memorable and emotionally reassuring claims. This dependence on intuitive, emotionally charged judgments over careful reasoning is well supported by research on cognitive biases (Kahneman, 2011). Lastly, myths endure because they lessen resistance. When new information challenges identity, stability or belonging, it is often ignored or reinterpreted, as evidence from studies on knowledge resistance shows (Klintman, 2021). Overall, these factors explain why claims like 'growth will deliver sustainability' or 'small green purchases make a difference' stay relevant: they maintain consistency with people's worldviews and ease discomfort.

Political function. Myths are not only passively reproduced but also actively mobilised in political struggles. They serve actors who benefit from the status quo by displacing responsibility and narrowing the spectrum of feasible options. A clear example is the idea that 'if everyone does a little, we will achieve a lot' (Mont et al., 2013). This message endures because it enables policymakers to appear proactive without addressing politically sensitive issues and offers citizens reassurance of involvement without requiring significant lifestyle changes. Yet research consistently shows that small, symbolic actions like turning off lights or recycling paper provide only minor benefits compared to the much greater impacts of diet, housing, mobility, and leisure travel (Cap et al., 2024). The myth essentially sustains inertia by presenting 'easy wins' as the main path to sustainability: it shifts focus away from systemic interventions and justifies procrastination. The claim that 'consumers must drive the transition' illustrates what Maniates (2001) called the 'individualisation of responsibility', a strategy that reframes systemic issues as matters of personal choice. Similarly, the promise of green growth sustains dependence on GDP while creating the illusion of compatibility with ecological limits (Jackson, 2011). In these cases, myths provide discursive cover that shields governments and companies from deeper reforms. As Hirth et al. (2023) show, such narratives focus debate on shallow interventions like consumer choice or efficiency, while leaving deeper structural drivers of unsustainability unchallenged. Mamut (2023) further demonstrates how counter-discourses such as sufficiency can be co-opted and reframed within consumerist logics, neutralising their transformative potential. In this way, myths protect existing business models and weaken alternatives that might threaten growth-dependent institutions.

These mechanisms demonstrate that myths persist because they are culturally meaningful, embedded in everyday practices, reproduced by institutions, psychologically attractive, and politically useful. This also implies that addressing them requires more than just fact-checking or raising awareness. To diminish their influence, one must engage with the values they evoke, reshape the everyday practices they are anchored in, transform the institutions that uphold them, offer alternative sources of psychological comfort, and contest the interests that promote them. The endurance of myths is therefore both a sign of unsustainable systems and a force that sustains them.

14.3 Myths as barriers to transformation

This section explores how persistent myths hinder societal progress by defining what is considered possible and desirable in sustainability transitions. A cross-chapter analysis identified five main barriers that were most prominent across the examined myths. Four of these, that is, techno-optimism, shifting responsibility to individuals, growth dependency and consumption as therapy, were previously discussed as individual myths in earlier chapters. Importantly, all four also appeared across other chapters as overarching constraints, as summarised in Table 14.1. The fifth, short-termism, was not addressed as a separate chapter but was a recurring structural constraint throughout the volume.

Overreliance on technology. Many myths depict technology as the default path to sustainability. The idea of *'In tech we trust'* (Myth 5) and *Neophilia* (Myth 7) promote innovation and efficiency as the main solutions, while '*Services will save us*' (Myth 6) suggests that digitalisation, servitisation and sharing will automatically decrease consumption and decouple impacts. Together, these stories create a barrier by fostering confidence in technical fixes while overlooking well-documented issues: direct and indirect rebound effects; the material and energy requirements of digital infrastructure; new forms of induced demand and the tendency for service models to shift resource use rather than eliminate it. The problem is not technology itself but the assumption that innovation alone will achieve sustainability, making sufficiency, governance reform, and changes in provisioning systems seem less important or unnecessary. In policy, this barrier appears as a preference for 'smart' solutions, pilots, gadgets and incremental efficiency standards instead of measures that could reshape demand, infrastructure, or business models. This dependence is further reinforced by other myths that dismiss structural interventions as less legitimate. The *strong governance myth* (Myth 12) supports this view: by portraying comprehensive regulation as limiting freedom, it biases policy towards technical fixes that are presented as neutral and unobtrusive, yet often have limited effectiveness at the system level.

Shifting responsibility to individuals. A second barrier occurs when responsibility for systemic change is mainly placed on consumers. *Little Me* (Myth 1) burdens individuals with moral responsibility despite their limited agency; *Infophilia* (Myth 2) suggests that providing more information and labels will be enough; while *consumer demand drives sustainability* (Myth 11) attributes system-level change to aggregate purchasing decisions. This setup normalises 'light-touch' tools, such as information campaigns, voluntary pledges, ecolabels, carbon calculators and 'nudges', while allowing powerful actors avoid structural reforms that could alter infrastructures, rules, and incentives. The *strong governance myth* (Myth 12) depicts ambitious, binding measures as threats to freedom, undermines regulation and shifts policy towards voluntary, consumer-facing methods. The barrier, therefore, is a policy framework that personalises systemic issues and normalises weak instruments. Its effects are paradoxical: citizens feel burdened, anxious and constrained, while collective and infrastructural levers remain underused.

Growth dependency. A third obstacle is the deep-rooted belief that economic growth is the main measure of prosperity and the default justification for policy. The growth paradigm reinforces the *Sufficiency* myth (Myth 8). The *economic growth* myth (Myth 9) claims that sustainability depends on ongoing GDP increase; *economic progress brings more leisure* (Myth 10), promising that growth will lead to future leisure, while elements of Myth 12 stabilise GDP-focused policy defaults by portraying meaningful sufficiency measures as unrealistic or overly restrictive. This obstacle limits what is viewed as achievable: post-growth, sufficiency-focused and degrowth strategies are seen as politically unacceptable or harmful, even when evidence shows they are essential to respect ecological limits and ensure equitable needs. Dependence on growth keeps business models focused on expansion and financial extraction, biases fiscal and welfare policies and suppresses alternative indicators of prosperity, such as need satisfaction, fairness and ecological stability.

Consumption as a form of identity and therapy. A fourth obstacle is the cultural association between consumption, identity, recognition and emotional comfort. *Retail therapy* (Myth 3) encourages shopping as a dependable way to reduce stress and achieve happiness; *More choice = freedom* (Myth 4) links personal liberty with greater consumer options; *Neophilia* (Myth 7) ties status and self-esteem to novelty and ongoing upgrading; *Sufficiency = deprivation* (Myth 8) portrays restraint as backwards and joyless. Collectively, these narratives normalise excess, glorify acquisition and make sufficiency seem unappealing. They also foster psychological resistance: suggestions to reduce consumption may be viewed as threats to autonomy, status or well-being. From a social practice perspective, this barrier is reproduced through routines (shopping as leisure), meanings conveyed in marketing messages (self-care through purchase), materials and infrastructures (fast-fashion outlets, seamless checkout, 'buy-now-pay-later' services), and skills (scrolling, unboxing, managing constant choices). These patterns sustain high-consumption behaviours and embed myths into everyday life. As long as these associations persist, cultural norms will reinforce rather than challenge high-impact consumption habits, making demand-side transformation more difficult to recognise and sustain.

Short-termism. Finally, a common obstacle is the dominance of short-term decision-making in politics and business. Although not dedicated to a separate chapter, short-termism appears throughout the myths. *In tech we trust* (Myth 5) emphasises visible, near-term efficiency gains; the *economic growth* (Myth 9) and *Sufficiency = deprivation* (Myth 8) frame the immediate 'losses' of restraint without recognising long-term gains in resilience, health and equity. This obstacle manifests through electoral cycles, quarterly reporting, discounting practices and risk aversion towards measures whose benefits develop over longer periods. It prioritises quick wins and incremental steps over precautionary and intergenerational responsibilities. Essentially, policies and corporate strategies are driven by what yields immediate returns, even if that undermines the feasibility of fundamental transitions, whose benefits are lasting but delayed.

These five barriers reinforce one another. Overreliance on technology encourages short-term thinking by offering quick, visible solutions; shifting responsibility interacts with consumption as a form of identity or therapy by attributing change to individual coping and self-expression; growth dependency normalises weak or GDP-compatible instruments, thereby reinforcing both techno-optimism and short-termism. The clear implication is that addressing only one barrier risks displacement or rebound effects through the others. Consequently, transformation strategies should be designed as mutually reinforcing packages, such as pairing demand-side and sufficiency policies with strong social guarantees; combining regulatory measures with innovation policies that emphasise absolute reductions (not just efficiency) and reframing prosperity and freedom in qualitative terms. Table 14.1 provides a map linking each barrier to the myths that sustain it. It can serve as a diagnostic tool to identify where interventions should be bundled rather than isolated.

TABLE 14.1 Structural barriers to sustainable consumption and related myths.

Barrier	*Definition*	*Reinforcing myths*
Overreliance on technology	Reliance on efficiency and innovation distracts from sufficiency and structural change. Efficiency gains are undermined by rebound effects, and digitalisation or new services carry hidden material impacts.	Myth 5 *In tech we trust*; Myth 6 *Services will save us*; Myth 7 *Neophilia*; Myth 12 *The strong governance myth*
Shifting responsibility to individuals	Responsibility is shifted onto consumers through appeals to information, awareness or consumer sovereignty. This obscures structural and institutional drivers and legitimises weak, voluntary policy measures.	Myth 1 *Little me*; Myth 2 *Infophilia*; Myth 11 *Consumer demand drives transition*; Myth 12 *The strong governance myth*
Growth dependency	GDP is treated as a key prerequisite for well-being and sustainability, constraining exploration of post-growth strategies and sufficiency-oriented governance.	Myth 8 *Sufficiency*; Myth 9 *Without economic growth . . .*; Myth 10 Economic progress results in free time; Myth 12 *The strong governance myth*
Consumption as identity and therapy	Freedom, happiness and status are equated with acquisition. Consumption is normalised as emotional relief, identity-building and a marker of progress.	Myth 3 *Retail therapy*; Myth 4 *More choice = freedom*; Myth 7 *Neophilia*; Myth 8 *Sufficiency = deprivation*
Short-termism	Decision-making privileges immediate returns and visible wins while neglecting long-term ecological stability, justice and well-being. Companies reject long-term sustainability because of slow payoffs, and policymakers favour policies that deliver results within election cycles.	Myth 5 *In tech we trust*; Myth 8 *Sufficiency = deprivation*; Myth 9 *Without economic growth . . .*; Myth 10 Economic progress results in free time

14.4 Implications for change agents

Building on Section 14.3, which illustrated how myths solidify into barriers to change, this section explores the implications of debunking them. It emphasises three key actors whose decisions influence the conditions for transition: policymakers, businesses and individuals (including civil society). The aim is to demonstrate how their actions can be reoriented so that governance, market strategies and everyday practices support each other rather than undermine one another. The synthesis draws on a comparative review of implications across chapters, with recommendations presented in two formats: common pathways for change that address multiple myths, and specific proposals linked to individual myths.

14.4.1 Policymakers

The chapters convey a consistent message to policymakers and governments: voluntarism and soft instruments alone are insufficient on a large scale. While appeals to information and individual choice can support change, structural interventions are necessary to change default unsustainable conditions. This involves using standards, bans, fiscal reforms and public investments to eliminate unsustainable options and make sustainable consumption appealing and accessible. Innovation policy remains important, but it must be combined with exnovation, meaning the deliberate phase-out of unsustainable products, technologies, business models, and infrastructure. Sufficiency should be integrated through binding targets for emissions and resource use, along with indicators that prioritise well-being, equity and ecological stability over gross domestic product. As robust measures are politically difficult, legitimacy must be established through transparent communication, inclusive deliberation (including citizens' assemblies) and fairness-focused design, such as compensation and just transition mechanisms.

The chapters also introduce a range of distinct policy strategies. The myth of technological salvation highlights the need for exnovation roadmaps: sunset clauses, 'no new assets' rules and conditional funding, ensuring that innovation is linked to absolute reductions in environmental impact and resource use rather than merely efficiency. The idea that services and digitalisation will save us calls for safeguards to guarantee genuine dematerialisation, such as clear rules that prevent digital models from increasing material and energy demand, including resource-based taxation on data and throughput, low-data defaults in public services, explicit criteria for access-based schemes, and location and impact conditions for data centres, such as clean power, limited water use, and transparent reporting. The critique of neophilia supports establishing a legal framework for repair, such as a statutory right-to-repair, repairability indices, reduced value-added tax on repairs, repair vouchers and investment in repair skills as part of public infrastructure.

Where 'more choice equals freedom' has overshadowed quality, governments can implement choice editing in high-impact sectors, standardise components and interfaces and curb manipulative advertising, including ultra-fast fashion and fossil fuel promotion. The argument that growth is essential for sustainability advocates for post-growth policies: well-being budgets, resource caps and green tax shifts. City-level, reversible pilots could be developed and assessed using well-being, equity and ecological indicators instead of GDP. These might be supported by fiscal rules that do not presuppose growth, such as multi-year expenditure limits in real terms, a 'golden rule' permitting borrowing for investment but not for daily spending, and tax shifts from labour to resource use and pollution. Finally, in response to the claim that strong governance is illiberal, legitimacy frameworks can be integrated into policy design: engaging in deliberation prior to regulation and crafting narratives that link rules to tangible improvements in health, time and security.

14.4.2 Businesses

For companies, dispelling myths starts with a rethinking of purpose. Strategies centred on throughput growth, constant novelty and ever-expanding assortments often produce unsustainable demand. The common advice is to shift from volume to value-in-use: compete on durability, repairability and extended service lives; design offerings that enable people to live well with less; and support the rules that make such models sustainable. This rethinking requires honesty about hidden materiality, especially in digital and access-based services where induced use can rise rapidly. Instead of lobbying against fair rules, businesses are encouraged to help establish them, such as minimum lifetimes, robust warranties, repairability requirements and open access to parts and repair information, ensuring that models aligned with sufficiency do not face systematic disadvantages.

Beyond this broad reorientation, the chapters provide specific recommendations. The critique of neophilia translates into making repairability a core skill: modular product designs, long-term spare parts supplies, open manuals and reverse logistics for repair and refurbishment. Where services and platforms are central, sufficiency should become standard in contracts and system design through fair-use caps, extended replacement cycles, pricing that discourages over-consumption and transparent material and energy footprints for digital services. The myth of a technological fix highlights the importance of exnovation portfolios by streamlining product ranges through discontinuing the most impact-heavy items and removing design features that promote extra consumption, such as features that increase the frequency, duration or speed of use. Against the idea that 'more choice' equals freedom, companies can simplify ranges in high-impact categories, end 'free returns' models that encourage excess and adopt advertising standards that avoid status-driven upselling and 'therapy' framing. When the 'consumer-demand' narrative dominates, efforts should shift from expecting individuals to drive change by 'voting with their wallets'. Instead, focus should be on upstream measures like supplier standards, regulatory limits and absolute-reduction targets, with political consumerism serving as a complement rather than the main driver of change. Lastly, the myth that economic progress will eventually free up time points to innovations in working hours: pilots of shorter workweeks and compressed hours can cut high-impact commuting and consumption patterns while boosting well-being.

14.4.3 Individuals and civil society

A recurring recommendation for individuals is to resist reducing people's roles solely to that of the 'consumer'. Viewing oneself only through purchasing weakens agency and burdens the structural levers that are necessary. Throughout the chapters, the most common advice is to act across roles as citizens, workers and community members, so that daily practices align with and support institutional change. For instance, challenging the myth that individual behaviour change alone is sufficient requires not only adopting low-impact practices at home but also supporting sufficiency-oriented policies as citizens and advocating for sustainability strategies in workplaces. Focus should be on high-impact areas such as mobility, housing, food and leisure travel, while embracing sufficiency not as a sacrifice but as a path to quality: comfort, time, health and fairness. Civil society organisations play a key role in linking personal action to collective capacity through dialogue, organising and mutual aid.

More specific suggestions advance this approach further. Challenging the 'Little me' narrative, individuals are encouraged to become co-producers of change by establishing or joining repair cafés, Buy-Nothing groups, sharing networks and community energy or food initiatives, as well as participating in mini-publics and local planning processes. The critique of retail therapy advocates for cultivating non-market sources of meaning and support, such as community, nature, culture and care. The notion that sufficiency equals deprivation can be contested through deliberate 'choice editing' in one's life, which involves avoiding ultra-fast fashion and the most impact-intensive travel and supporting policies that default to removing the worst options. Regarding infophilia, the practical approach is to request defaults and rights instead of more labels: local right-to-repair, low-data defaults in public services and straightforward binary warnings where appropriate. The aim is to employ collective pressure to influence regulations, not solely to shop differently. When the consumer demand narrative prevails, political consumerism is better understood as complementary: thoughtful purchasing combined with civic action via campaigns, workplace organisation and shareholder engagement to instigate supply-side change. Finally, the myth that growth will ultimately lead to leisure encourages a direct pursuit of time affluence, where possible, through negotiated shorter hours and workweeks that facilitate lower-impact routines and civic participation.

Thus, the most common recommendations and distinctive proposals align closely. They make sufficiency actionable through rules, infrastructure, business models and daily routines; they guide innovation alongside planned phase-outs; and they consider time and well-being as vital resources for sustainable living. In doing so, they address the barriers identified in Section 14.3 not separately but as an interconnected set, enabling governmental authority, corporate capacity and civic energy to reinforce each other as parts of a shared endeavour to live well within planetary limits.

14.5 Pathways to sustainability transformation

This section shifts its focus from outlining what policymakers, businesses and citizens should do to promote sustainable consumption towards identifying new myths for future efforts and explaining how to debunk them. This is because new or resurging narratives continually emerge in public debate, potentially hindering progress towards this transition by reducing political will, delaying regulatory measures and weakening public support if left unchallenged. To help readers recognise further myths, we drew on a stakeholder workshop described in the introduction, involving representatives from Swedish policy, business, the public sector, civil society and academia, where participants discussed myths related to sustainable consumption they encountered in their work and daily lives. From this, three influential claims emerged. They have not been addressed in this book but continue to affect understanding and decision-making in various contexts. These could be explored in future research.

'You are what you own'. This myth connects dignity, adulthood and success with accumulating possessions. Ownership is presented as proof of competence and care and as the legitimate way to gain recognition and security. The story is partly true: owning a home or durable goods can indeed provide control, stability and pride in caring for something across generations. However, when ownership becomes a social ideal, it encourages accumulation for its own sake and limits the idea of freedom to just acquiring more and more. Alternatives like access, sharing or repairing are seen as lesser or second-best, while policies focusing on use instead of possession are viewed as diminishing status. Seen as a myth rather than a fact, this story can be challenged. Why should recognition and dignity depend on accumulation, rather than on stewardship, borrowing, repairing or collective ownership? Broadening the range of valued identities, such as from owner to steward, borrower, repairer or commoner, allows recognition and security to be disconnected from material growth. This makes sufficiency-based changes more practical and legitimate.

'Globalisation is inevitable and always cheaper'. This myth depicts long-distance sourcing of goods as both unavoidable and cost-effective. It gains support from a partial truth: producing at larger scales and across borders can lower prices for consumers. However, it overlooks hidden costs transferred to others – environmental damage from shipping and aviation, resource depletion in producing regions, exploitative labour conditions and supply chain fragility revealed during crises like the COVID-19 pandemic or the war in Ukraine. By presenting globalisation as inevitable and a bargain, the myth stifles debate: regional or local provisioning is often dismissed as unrealistic or protectionist, even when it could improve resilience, reduce emissions and promote fair work. Recognising this as a myth rather than a natural law, however, invites scrutiny. It raises important questions: What qualifies as a cost? Whose costs are factored into the price of a product, and whose are left out? Where might proximity add value through more reliable delivery, easier repairs, shorter supply chains or lower material consumption? Addressing these questions allows sustainability to focus not only on economic efficiency but also on resilience, fairness and ecological stability.

'Sustainable consumption is often seen as an urban-elite project'. This misconception implies that calls for sufficiency and reduced consumption mainly come from urban middle classes and are imposed on those with fewer resources. It is based on real concerns about affordability and access: healthier food, energy-efficient housing or public transport are often more expensive or less available outside major cities, making sustainability seem like a privilege rather than a shared goal. At the same time, this misconception is reinforced by culture-war signals that divide 'city elites' from 'ordinary people'. Sufficiency is portrayed as status policing by outsiders, meaning telling rural communities to drive less, eat less meat or give up traditional habits, while those with higher incomes continue to consume more. Its initial impact, therefore, depends on existing inequalities: who is asked to bear the costs of change first (through higher prices, taxes, or limited options), who benefits later (through cleaner air, healthier food, or savings on energy) and whose voices are included in decision-making. Any real transformation must address these issues directly: by ensuring fair distribution of costs and benefits, involving trusted local institutions alongside national governments in implementing changes, and delivering short-term improvements in comfort, security and time across all regions, not just in city centres.

To debunk these myths, one could use the analytical sequence employed throughout this volume: definition, origins, consequences, dispelling and implications. An alternative is to adopt a more compact 3D model: diagnose, debate and design. In this approach,

'*Diagnose*' includes defining, exploring origins and understanding impacts. It involves clarifying the claim; tracing its emergence and spread through simplification, value alignment, partial truths or powerful coalitions; mapping the channels through which it circulates, such as policy debates, business strategies, media communication or educational materials; and recognising the consequences once it becomes embedded in society.

'*Debate*' involves gathering counter-arguments and alternative perspectives. It includes recognising the values and aspirations that make a myth appealing, while demonstrating that the material ways of pursuing them are not inevitable and can be approached differently. Research on framing and knowledge resistance suggests that reframing concepts in qualitative terms, such as prosperity as security and time, rather than GDP growth, or recognition through contribution rather than material display, reduces identity threats and makes disagreements easier to handle (Klintman, 2021, 2025).

'*Design*' ultimately transforms analysis and counter-arguments into constructive proposals. At this stage, one can offer recommendations, showcase inspiring examples and suggest tangible arrangements such as rules, policies and routines for various actors and stakeholders. While this book focuses on three groups, examining the channels through which myths emerge, are constructed or travel can help identify additional audiences and tailor recommendations to their specific roles in maintaining or challenging myths. For example, media actors may need guidance on reframing stories to avoid reinforcing unsustainable assumptions. Simultaneously, businesses might require support in redesigning product strategies or marketing practices and policymakers could benefit from examples of sufficiency-oriented regulations that balance fairness with effectiveness. In this way, design links the analysis of myths to practical pathways for change.

14.6 Final message

This book demonstrates how myths about sustainable consumption develop, persist and hinder systemic change towards sustainability. The influence of myths lies less in their factual correctness and more in their ability to simplify complexity, resonate with values and become ingrained in routines, strategies and policies. By revealing myths, we can understand how they obstruct institutional reform and broader structural transformation. Throughout the chapters, five barriers emerged. Four – technological optimism, growth dependence, shifting responsibility to individuals and consumption as identity and therapy – were analysed as separate myths but also appeared as overarching constraints that influence multiple consumption sectors. A fifth, short-termism, recurred in several chapters as a structural tendency that hampers long-term change. These barriers also reinforce each other and limit the potential for transformation.

They can be addressed by reframing values in qualitative terms, reducing the obsession with GDP as the main measure, linking everyday actions with institutional reforms so that systemic support aligns with personal efforts, promoting cultural narratives that connect recognition to contribution, care or creativity instead of material wealth, and defining well-being through time, relationships and security rather than consumption. Additionally, embedding long-term goals into policy and planning is crucial. We have also identified myths worth exploring in future research, even though new ones will inevitably emerge. The challenge is to continue diagnosing, debating and designing alternatives so that ways of living well within planetary boundaries can be envisioned and achieved.

References

Barthes, R. (2009). *Mythologies*. Hill and Wang. (Original work published 1957)

Cap, S., de Koning, A., Tukker, A., & Scherer, L. (2024). (In)Sufficiency of industrial decarbonisation to reduce household carbon footprints to 1.5°C-compatible levels. *Sustainable Production and Consumption*, *45*, 216–227.

Hirth, S., Kreinin, H., Fuchs, D., Blossey, N., Mamut, P., Philipp, J., Radovan, I., Consortium, T. E. 5°Lifestyles, Antal, O., Belousa, I., Bösch, M., Brizga, J., Bronstering, G., Dumitru, A., Langner, S., Laksevics, K., Leutermann, C., Klosterberg, C., Kramer, N., . . . Zsemberovszky, L. (2023). Barriers and enablers of 1.5° lifestyles: Shallow and deep structural factors shaping the potential for sustainable consumption. *Frontiers in Sustainability*, *4*. https://doi.org/10.3389/frsus.2023.1014662

Jackson, T. (2011). *Prosperity without growth: Economics for a finite planet* (Reprinted). Earthscan.

Kahneman, D. (2011). *Thinking, fast and slow*. Farrar, Straus and Giroux.

Klintman, M. (2021). *Knowledge resistance: How we avoid insight from others*. Manchester University Press.

Klintman, M. (2025). Framing: The social art of influence. In *Framing*. Manchester University Press. https://www.manchesterhive.com/display/9781526170422/9781526170422.xml

Koch, M., & Mont, O. (2016). *Sustainability and the political economy of welfare* (Vol. 2016). Routledge.

Mamut, P. (2023). *Sufficiency – An emerging discourse?* Nomos Verlagsgesellschaft mbH & Co. KG. https://doi.org/10.5771/9783748942627

Maniates, M. F. (2001). Individualization: Plant a tree, buy a bike, save the world? *Global Environmental Politics*, *1*(3), Article 3. https://doi.org/10.1162/152638001316881395

Meyer, J. W., & Rowan, B. (1977). Institutionalised organisations: Formal structure as myth and ceremony. *American Journal of Sociology*, *83*(2), 340–363.

Mont, O., Heiskanen, E., Power, K., & Kuusi, H. (2013). *Improving Nordic policy-making by dispelling myths on sustainable consumption*. Nordic Council of Ministers. http://www.diva-portal.org/smash/get/diva2:702825/FULLTEXT01.pdf

Norgaard, K. M. (2011). *Living in denial: Climate change, emotions, and everyday life*. MIT Press.

Shove, E., Pantzar, M., & Watson, M. (2012). *The dynamics of social practice: Everyday life and how it changes*. Sage.

Thaler, R. H., & Sunstein, C. R. (2008). *Nudge: Improving decisions about health, wealth, and happiness*. Yale University Press.

INDEX

For Product Safety Concerns and Information please contact our EU representative GPSR@taylorandfrancis.com Taylor & Francis Verlag GmbH, Kaufingerstraße 24, 80331 München, Germany